THE EVERYTHING® LOW-FAT HIGH-FLAVOR COOKBOOK

The Everything Series:

THE EVERYTHING®

LOW-FAT HIGH-FLAVOR COOKBOOK

**From appetizers to desserts, 300 deliciously easy
recipes that you won't believe are low-fat!**

Lisa Shaw

Adams Media Corporation
HOLBROOK, MASSACHUSETTS

An Everything® Series Book.
The Everything® Series is a registered trademark of Adams Media Corporation.

Published by
Adams Media Corporation
260 Center Street, Holbrook, MA 02343

ISBN: 1-55850-802-3

Printed in the United States of America.

J I H G F E D C B

Library of Congress Cataloging-in-Publication Data
Shaw, Lisa Angowski Rogak.
The everything low-fat, high-flavor cookbook / Lisa Shaw. — 1st ed.
p.   cm.
ISBN 1-55850-802-3
1. Low-fat diet—Recipes. I. Title.
RM237.7. S486   1998
641.5'638—dc21   97-39333
CIP

This publication is designed to provide accurate and authoritative information with regard to the subject matter covered. It is sold with the understanding that the publisher is not engaged in rendering legal, accounting, or other professional advice. If legal advice or other expert assistance is required, the services of a competent professional person should be sought.
—From a *Declaration of Principles* jointly adopted by a Committee of the American Bar Association and a Committee of Publishers and Associations

Illustrations by Barry Littmann

This book is available at quantity discounts for bulk purchases.
For information, call 1-800-872-5627 (in Massachusetts, call 781-767-8100).

Visit our home page at http://www.adamsmedia.com

Contents

398 Recipes

DELICIOUS, EASY, LOW-FAT RECIPES

Introduction

Okay, you've finally decided that it's time—time to start looking after your health, time to start eating healthier foods that are lower in fat. In other words, it's time to start thinking about *you*. So you've picked up *The Everything® Low-Fat, High-Flavor Cookbook* to jumpstart your plans and to give you some new ideas. Congratulations!

No matter how strong your resolve, if you're like most people, there's a tiny part of you that is saying, sure, you want to eat healthier foods and probably lose some weight in the process, and all this is very well and good. But what it still comes down to is that you're taking these steps because they are good for you, and not because you'll enjoy it.

I'm telling you to stop thinking that way right now. Eating a low-fat diet is not the same thing as going on a low-calorie diet where carrot sticks and hard-cooked eggs—and no enjoyment—is the order of the day. On the contrary, eating a low-fat diet is a wonderful adventure where, once the sensation of "missing" your usual dose of greasy fries and burgers wears off—and it will, sooner than you think—you'll discover that you're able to experience the variety of tastes, textures, and temperatures that eating freshly prepared low-fat food delivers—an experience that is never possible with a diet of fat-laden foods.

For instance, you'll discover the true sweetness and crispy crunch of a red bell pepper, the nuttiness and tang of a spoonful of brown rice that's been sprinkled with scallions and freshly ground black pepper, or the salty bite that comes with a forkful of fresh fish that's been simply prepared with lemon and spices and perhaps a touch of fruity olive oil. If these same foods were buried under ladlefuls of fatty salad dressing, gobs of butter, or a deep-fried coating, you would be missing these taste sensations.

In fact, following a low-fat diet is easier than you think. As with anything new, old habits initially die hard, but a recent study suggests that with time, you may learn to like and even prefer— gasp!—dishes that contain little or no fat.

A study conducted at Philadelphia's Monell Chemical Senses Center involved 18 men and women who ate low-fat diets. Some were extremely low in fat, while others were just moderately low in fat. After six months on the diets, the researchers found that the people who were following the diet lowest in fat actually came to prefer low-fat foods to fatty foods.

Like many people, I grew up eating the typical American diet, high in fat and sodium, while avoiding anything green and fresh whenever possible. Today, unfortunately, many children follow the same pattern, which is especially disheartening given all the information we now know about how an excess of fat in the diet can affect health, both in the short-term and decades down the road. If you are a member of today's

average American family, where everyone is running around from work to home to appointments to chores, you need to cut corners on time. One easy way is by opting for takeout and restaurant dishes that tend to be high in fat.

The good news about the recipes in *The Everything® Low-Fat, High-Flavor Cookbook* is that the majority of them take less than 15 minutes to assemble. During the time the dish is cooking, you can get other things done or just relax and put your feet up. Plus, once you find a number of dishes that turn out to be your favorites, you can double or even triple the recipes and place the extras in the freezer for future meals.

It's a good idea to use each recipe as a guideline, not as gospel. For instance, I love garlic and have used it liberally in the recipes where I think the dish would be enhanced by "the stinking rose." I know that not everyone feels the same way, however. So, you can cut way down on the use of garlic—or any other spice or seasoning—in the recipes here, or even eliminate it completely. If you're a fan of rosemary or tarragon, or any other herb or spice, then by all means go ahead and use it.

At the same time, you shouldn't transform yourself into such a virtuous creature that you never indulge in a rich dessert. Humans are so single-minded that frequently we get off on one track—in this case, the low-fat track—and we refuse to allow anything to divert us from our goal. Then, suddenly, a craving for a piece of chocolate—or anything else considered to be a "bad" food—derails us. After that first bite of heaven, all hell breaks loose, and we figure that since we've fallen

off the wagon, we might as well go all the way. Days or weeks later, after eating so much "bad" food that we're actually sick of it, we return to our roots and get started on the "right track" again.

The good thing about following a low-fat diet and not a low-calorie diet is that these extremes can easily be tempered. If you eat a low-fat salad for lunch, you can allow yourself a bit of a rich dessert and be satisfied. Experiment with the point at which you feel satisfied and learn to recognize when you've crossed over the line. Keep these parameters in mind for the next time and consciously stop short of that line. It may make you feel a bit anxious at the time you're doing it, but I guarantee you'll forget all about it an hour later.

Indeed, if you completely forego the kinds of foods you have come to view as forbidden, the world can sometimes seem like a much harsher place, no matter what your circumstances are or where you live. A sense of balance—eating a low-fat diet but remembering to occasionally treat yourself—will go a long way toward helping you to feel better about your life.

As you leaf through this book, you may wonder how to choose a particular dish for a meal you're planning for friends and family, or for one you're just throwing together in minutes. My opinion? The best way to select a recipe from the 300 in the pages that follow is to use your own gut instinct. What catches your eye? What are you in the mood for at this moment? Of course, the time of year will also influence your choices: In the summer, you probably won't want to heat up your kitchen by preparing a long-cooking oven dish.

And remember that you don't always have to follow your mother's advice. Don't feel as though it's absolutely necessary to make sure that the entrée you choose "matches" the vegetable and the salad. Wine connoisseurs agree that it's okay to serve white wine with beef and red wine with fish, so you have my permission to mix and match as you see fit. If you cook with love and spirit, it's a good bet that no matter what you serve—a creamy dessert to follow a rich entrée, or a light dessert that follows a salad—that people will clean their plates.

Why Low Fat?

In the 1960s and 1970s, weight-conscious men and women were concerned with the calorie content of the food they were eating. Diet doctors-turned-book-writers at the time suggested that eating a combination of high-fat foods with high-protein foods—in addition to drinking a gallon of water to wash it all down—but almost no carbohydrates, was enough to cause pounds to melt away effortlessly. And melt away they did...at least for a few weeks. After a steady diet of fatty meat and a gallon of water, people were too nauseated to eat much more, and therefore started to eat as little as possible, making it easy to drop 20 pounds or more over the course of a month.

The decade of the 1980s saw the entry of high-carbohydrate diets, mainly to coincide with the running boom and marathoners' need to load up on as much pasta and bread they could choke down before hitting the race circuit. Again, people who followed this high-carb program lost weight for awhile.

For most of the 1990s, low-fat eating has been extolled as a sane way of life, and perhaps the first diet program in years that didn't promise that you'd lose seven to ten pounds during the first couple of weeks. At first people balked at the idea of a low-fat diet. But as the truth about decades of unrealistic crash diets began to sink in, the low-fat lifestyle started to make a lot of sense. For one, it didn't ask that you give up anything, just eat everything in moderation. Plus, if you follow a low-fat lifestyle, it means that you are able to eat lots of food, since many low-fat foods, like whole-grain breads, fruits, and vegetables, have bulk, therefore fewer calories per spoonful, slice, or serving.

What Is Low Fat?

Opinion is greatly divided among the experts in this country who regularly dish out statistics and prescriptions to tell Americans how they can live healthier lives. The U.S. Department of Agriculture, for one, thinks that Americans should not get more than 30 percent of our daily allotment of calories from fat. Most nutritionists think that this figure is way too high.

The ultra-low-fat proponents, like the famous Pritikin Diet that was popular in the early 1980s, believe that 5 percent is the number to strive for. One thing about this goal, however: since most food contains at least some fat—including most vegetables, cereals, and even fish—getting 5 percent of our daily calories from fat means cutting out at

least some of these foods that we already think of as low-fat. Fat is what provides us with satiety and that feeling of fullness after a meal; without at least 10 percent fat, well, you may be eating pounds of vegetables and fruits every day, but it's doubtful that you'll ever feel really full.

Fat is a nutrient that contains nine calories per gram. Carbohydrates and protein contain only 4 calories per gram. You can then use this information to calculate the percentage of fat calories that a particular food contains, once you know the number of fat grams. For instance, say that the ingredient panel for a frozen chicken dinner says that the chicken contains 4 grams of fat per ounce. Sounds okay, until you figure that a serving equals 3 ounces and contains 270 calories in all. (A tablespoon of vegetable oil, even though the label will scream that it contains *no cholesterol*, is still not a heart-healthy food, since it contains anywhere from 11 to 13 grams of fat.) There are a total of twelve grams of fat per serving, which translates to 108 calories that are pure fat, which means that the chicken is 40 percent fat, which in no way translates to a low-fat food. By the way, the USDA estimates that most Americans who follow the conventional meat-and-potatoes diet consume a diet that gets 40 percent of its calories from fat.

Low-Fat Health Benefits You Didn't Expect

Everyone knows that following a low-fat diet can help you to reduce the chances of getting heart disease and some types of cancer. Here are a few other unexpected benefits:

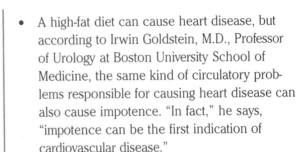

- A high-fat diet can cause heart disease, but according to Irwin Goldstein, M.D., Professor of Urology at Boston University School of Medicine, the same kind of circulatory problems responsible for causing heart disease can also cause impotence. "In fact," he says, "impotence can be the first indication of cardiovascular disease."

- A diet that's high in fat generally increases your chances of developing atherosclerosis, a disease where fatty deposits known as plaque build up on the inside of the walls of your blood vessels, which narrows arteries and restricts the flow of blood. When plaque forms in the arteries that carry blood to the spine, the supply of oxygen and nutrients to the spine is decreased, sometimes significantly. This can result in disk degeneration, which causes chronic back pain.

- A recent two-year study at Baylor College of Medicine in Houston discovered that when patients with skin cancer ate a low-fat diet with 20 percent of calories from fat, they developed 70 percent fewer precancerous lesions than those patients who stuck to their regular high-fat diet with an average of 40 percent of calories from fat.

How These Recipes Were Selected

In a world where high-fat everything reigns, sometimes it's difficult to find tasty low-fat recipes. Indeed, it took some time to scout out recipes that were truly low in fat and still tasted delicious.

Many of the recipes were modified from the original high-fat version. Others were created by combining low-fat foods that would work well together and still be enticing enough to make a hungry diner choose the dish without knowing it was deliberately low in fat.

Use these recipes as a springboard for your own culinary imagination. If an item of produce is out of season, substitute another fruit or vegetable that you and your family enjoy. And use some of the suggestions in the introduction to further reduce the fat content of the recipes. Sometimes this is as easy as just adding more of a food that is naturally low in fat, so that the fat—and calorie—content of the entire recipe is reduced. For instance, in a chicken and vegetable stir-fry, cut the amount of meat you use by one-third, while doubling the amount of vegetables, which is really how people in most Asian countries prepare stir-fried dishes. Then cut the amount of oil by one-half and substitute an equal amount of low-fat chicken broth.

Once you become familiar with the ingredients and cooking methods that a low-fat recipe entails, you can then experiment with reducing the fat in your own high-fat recipes.

In the meantime, keep these tips in mind when you're cooking at home or eating out to make sure that a low-fat diet will turn into a habit that is easy to follow—and delicious enough to keep you following it.

Low-Fat Questions and Answers

Q: Does red meat include pork and ham? What's the leanest red meat available?

A: According to the National Cattlemen's Beef Association, the category of red meat includes beef, pork, lamb, and veal.

The National Institutes of Health reports that a lean cut of meat is one that has less than 10 grams of fat and 4.5 grams or less of saturated fat in a cooked, 3-ounce serving. The eye of the round and top round are the leanest cuts of beef. Veal shoulder, ground veal, cutlets, or sirloin are low in fat. Pork tenderloin, sirloin, and top loin are low in fat.

Meats, Seafood, and Poultry

- Choose the leanest cuts and remove as much fat as possible before cooking.
- Broil, bake, or grill instead of frying.
- Poach poultry or fish in seasoned broth, or broth diluted with wine.

Vegetables

- Steam vegetables rather than stir-fry them.
- Use vegetable oils rather than butter and sour cream for cooking and flavoring.
- Substitute low-fat versions of sour cream and yogurt for full-fat versions.

Milk and Cheese

- Substitute low-fat milk for heavy cream and evaporated skim milk for whole milk.
- Use low-fat cheese in pasta salads and other recipes.
- Use Parmesan cheese frugally.

Sauces

- Mix flour with low-fat milk, evaporated skim milk, or broth.
- Increase the broth and reduce the oil in recipes.
- Use cornstarch, dissolved in liquid, to thicken stir-fry sauces quickly.
- Purée part-skim ricotta cheese or low-fat sour cream to enrich a cream sauce.

Easy Low-Fat Cooking Tips

- Pancakes are lighter and fluffier when you substitute club soda for milk in the batter.
- Don't throw out those overripe bananas! When bananas become overripe, place them in the freezer, peel and all. Then when you are ready to bake, take out what you need, thaw, peel, and mash. Once frozen, bananas are easy to mash into a fine pulp for your favorite recipe.
- For high rising, rounded tops on muffins like you see in the bakeries, preheat your oven to 500°F. As soon as you put the muffins into the oven, decrease the temperature to whatever the recipe indicates. Remember to decrease the baking time. This may take a bit of watching and practice, but the results will be worth it. The increased temperature causes the muffins to rise quickly, giving them that nice dome-shaped top.
- To make lighter, fluffier mashed potatoes, add a pinch or two of baking powder to the potatoes before whipping.
- When greasing and flouring cake pans for baking chocolate cakes, use cocoa powder instead of flour. The cake will have a rich dark color. This is especially great for bundt cakes and cakes that don't need frosting.
- To make perfect hard-cooked eggs, poke a hole, using a needle, in the rounder end of each egg. Bring a saucepan of water to a boil, then remove from the heat. Add the eggs and return the pan with boiling water to boil gently for 9 to

10 minutes. Pour out the water and shake the eggs in the pan to crack them. Drop the eggs into a bowl of water and ice. Remove the shell under water for easier peeling, then place the peeled egg back in the water. This will prevent green-tinged egg yolks and a sulfur smell.

- Use good nonstick baking pans. They will help reduce the amount of oil needed in cooking.
- Coat your baking pans with flour or cornmeal to prevent sticking. You won't have the added fat and calories of shortening or oil.
- In recipes calling for multiple eggs, replace some of the whole eggs called for with 2 egg whites. Each egg replaced with 2 egg whites will save 5 grams of fat. It's usually a good idea to keep at least 1 or 2 whole eggs to maintain the correct taste and consistency. For example, replace 3 whole eggs with 1 whole egg and 4 egg whites. You'll save 10 grams of fat.
- When baking a cake, bake at 325°F for a moist cake every time.
- To remove salt from overly salty gravies and sauces, add a peeled potato to the sauce and cook; discard when finished.
- For easier removal of muffins and cupcakes, spray the paper liners with nonstick cooking spray.
- Drain all crispy fried foods on the inside of brown-paper grocery bags. They will help the food retain more crispiness and eliminate more fat than by draining on paper towels, which tend to make the food soggy.
- Cut a small X in the bottom of each Brussels sprout for even cooking.

- To remove the core from iceberg lettuce, whack the head of lettuce, core side down, on the countertop.
- The most efficient way to remove fat from soups, stews, and gravies is to refrigerate the dish. When the fat congeals, it will rise to the top and you can spoon if off easily. Alternatively, place thin strips of paper towels on the top of the dish while it is still hot. They will soak up grease.
- You can reduce the amount of fat in baked products by one-fourth to one-third. For example, if a cookie, quick bread, or muffin recipe calls for 1 cup oil, use $2/3$ cup instead. (Do not use this method for yeast breads and pie crusts.)
- Crumble dried herbs in your hands before using to release their oils and flavor.
- Peel broccoli stems instead of discarding them. Slice on the diagonal for stir-fries or soups.
- To remove salt from overly salty sauces, add a dash (no more or the flavor of the dish will be dramatically changed) of vinegar to the sauce. This works particularly well for tomato-based sauces.
- When measuring flour, stir it first to loosen and aerate it. Carefully spoon the flour into a measuring cup, never scoop. To level, use the flat side of a knife.
- When measuring liquids, use a measuring cup specifically for liquids. When measuring dry ingredients, use a measuring cup specifically for dry ingredients.

- To restore crystallized honey, microwave just to add a bit of warmth to melt the crystals, then stir.
- Store flour in the freezer to avoid bugs.
- Never store onions with potatoes. Onions give off gasses that make the potatoes turn bad quickly.
- Don't store carrots in the same refrigerator bin as apples. The carrots will become bitter.
- Soak harsh-smelling fish in milk for 30 to 40 minutes to freshen it.
- When buying sun-dried tomatoes packed in oil, drain them and rinse thoroughly. Use the reddest tomatoes. Avoid the dark brown ones.
- Avocados and tomatoes ripen more quickly when placed in brown paper bags and put into a cupboard.
- Place a piece of white bread in with hardened brown sugar to soften it.

- Make sure your pan is hot before adding oil when frying. You'll use less oil and you'll also have no problem with food sticking.
- Use low-fat salad dressings to marinate meat, poultry, and fish before baking, broiling, or grilling.
- To remove the garlic smell from your hands, wash with soap and cold water, then, before drying, run them along your stainless-steel faucet (if you have one).
- Never marinate meat or poultry in metal containers. The acids in the marinade may pit the container and ruin the flavor of the marinade.
- Store unpopped popcorn in your freezer to retain freshness.
- A low-calorie solution for high-fat frying of corn tortillas is to place them in the oven, directly on the rack. Bake at 350°F, to desired crispness. The tortillas will automatically fold over into taco-shell form with just a little positioning help.

Low-Fat Substitutions

Original ingredient	Substitution	Use for
¾ cup heavy cream	2 egg whites	Mousse
1 cup heavy cream	¾ cup nonfat yogurt + ¼ cup nonfat milk	Baked goods
1 cup whole milk	1 cup buttermilk	Baked goods
8 ounces cream cheese	8 ounces part-skim ricotta cheese	Cheesecakes
4 ounces sour cream	4 ounces plain low-fat yogurt	Baked goods
3 whole eggs	3 egg whites + 1 egg yolk	Cakes, custards

Cooking Method Substitutions

- Bake instead of deep-fry.
- Grill or broil instead of pan-fry.
- Broil instead of pan-fry to brown meats, fish, and poultry.
- Broth-soften instead of fry. Use broth instead of fat, which is required in many Mexican dishes such as refried beans.
- Griddle-roasting or toasting is a standard Mexican cooking method that intensifies flavors in foods. Tortillas are dry-toasted on a griddle; many people grease the griddle with a bit of oil first, which is unnecessary.
- As a substitute for sautéing or poaching, fresh vegetables with a high moisture content, such as tomatoes, can be placed on a griddle over high heat and turned often until surfaces are charred.

United States Department of Agriculture (USDA) Nutritional Guidelines

Bread, cereal, rice and pasta: 6 to 11 servings each day.

One serving equals 1 slice bread, ½ bagel, ½ English muffin, 1 ounce ready-to-eat cereal, ½ cup cooked rice or pasta, 1 pancake.

Vegetables: 3 to 5 servings each day.

One serving equals 1 cup raw leafy vegetables; ½ cup vegetables, cooked or chopped raw; ½ cup compact salads; ¼ cup vegetable juice.

Fruit: 2 to 4 servings each day.

One serving equals 1 medium apple, banana, orange, kiwi fruit, pear, or peach; ½ cup canned, chopped fresh, or cooked fruit; ¼ cup dried fruit; ¼ cup fruit juice.

Milk, yogurt, and cheese: 2 or 3 servings each day.

Avoid high-fat products; instead use nonfat or low-fat (1%) milk, nonfat yogurt, and part-skim, low-fat, or nonfat cheeses.

One serving equals 1 cup milk or yogurt, 1½ ounces natural cheese.

Meat, poultry, seafood, dried beans, eggs, and nuts: 2 or 3 servings each day.

One serving equals 2 or 3 ounces cooked lean meat, poultry (no skin), or fish; ½ cup cooked dried beans; 4 to 6 tablespoons peanut butter; 2 to 3 eggs (limit to no more than 4 per week).

Fats, oil, and sweets: Use sparingly.

How to Achieve 30 Percent or Less Fat in Your Diet

The American Heart Association recommends that you get no more than 30 percent of your total calories from fat. This applies to all the food you eat in a day or week.

The following is based on a 2,000-calorie-a-day eating plan: Multiply the total calories by 0.30 (30 percent) to get the allowable calories from fat. Then divide the calories from fat by 9 (1 gram of

fat = 9 calories) to get the allowable grams of fat per day. Therefore, 2,000 calories per day x 0.30 = 600 calories from fat, and 600 ÷ 9 = 67 grams of fat. So no more than 67 grams of fat per day.

This is meant to be a guideline for your overall eating. If you go slightly over the 30-percent line once in a while, be easy on yourself: pull back on the next meal.

To figure out the percentage of calories of fat for an individual recipe, first multiply the grams of fat by 9, which will give you the total number of calories from fat. Then divide that number by the number of calories in the recipe to get the percentage.

Always look at the number of grams of fat in a food item or recipe, as well as the percentage of calories from fat. A given recipe might list 45 percent of calories from fat. But on closer look, it may list only 7 grams of fat and 145 calories. When the calories are low, chances are the percentage will be misleadingly high.

Modifying Recipes to Reduce Fat

- To compensate for removing fat, increase the use of extracts, spices, and condiments such as mustard, vinegar, garlic, lemon juice, and fresh ginger.
- Use an equal amount of evaporated skim milk in soups or sauces that call for cream or half-and-half.
- If you reduce the amount of oil, replace the liquid with an equal amount of milk, water, broth, or fruit juice.

- Sprinkle nuts and cheese on top of food rather than mix them throughout.
- Replace up to half the fat in muffins and baked goods with applesauce or puréed fruit.
- Cook onions used for seasoning in water, broth, or wine.
- Substitute water for up to one-third of the oil called for in salad dressings.
- For baked goods calling for buttermilk, substitute nonfat yogurt to provide added moistness.
- Use no more than 1 to 2 tablespoons of oil or butter per 1 cup flour in muffins and quick breads.

Reducing Fat in Baked Goods

Ingredients high in fat, such as margarine, butter, shortening, oil, heavy cream, cream cheese, sour cream, and chocolate add flavor to recipes but also add calories and grams of fat to our diet. In addition to enhancing flavor, fat makes pastry flaky, cakes moist and tender, and cookies crisp. Decreasing fat in a baked item can create a drier, coarser, denser texture and reduce overall flavor. If you would like to try reducing the fat in baked recipes, here are some suggestions:

- Reduce the amount of margarine, butter, shortening, or oil in a recipe by one-fourth to one-third.
- Substitute nonfat milk for low-fat milk (2%) or whole milk.
- Substitute low-fat versions of yogurt, sour cream, and cream cheese in place of the

regular products. Although nonfat counterparts are readily available, they are not always as successful in baked recipes.

- Use evaporated skim milk instead of heavy cream in dessert sauces.
- Substitute or add flavorings and/or seasonings to replace the flavor lost from fat. For example, add chocolate and rum flavoring to a cocoa sauce for more intense flavor.
- Serve low-fat baked items such as muffins and coffeecakes warm from the oven. The texture change is not as noticeable when they're eaten warm.

Replacing Fats and Oils

- In place of $1/2$ cup oil, margarine, or butter in baking, use $1/2$ cup applesauce or $1/4$ cup applesauce and $1/4$ cup buttermilk.
- In place of $1/2$ cup oil for marinades and salad dressings, use $1/2$ cup broth or unsweetened pineapple juice.
- In place of 2 tablespoons oil for sautéing, use 2 tablespoons broth, unsweetened pineapple juice, or dry wine.

How to Cook Lean Meat

- Trim off all visible fat from meat before cooking. This significantly reduces the total fat and cholesterol in the cooked portion.
- Choose such lean cooking techniques as broiling, grilling, pan broiling, poaching, or roasting.

- Remember to roast and broil meats on a rack so fat drips away during cooking.
- Discard drippings instead of making them into gravy.
- Limit additional fats or, better yet, refrain from using them in meat recipes.
- Use nonstick cooking spray instead of oil for browning.
- Use low-fat ingredients whenever possible.
- For juicier results, cook lean meats to no more than medium doneness. Lean meats that are cooked until well done may taste less flavorful and may be dry and tough. Not overcooking is especially important for beef cuts graded prime.

Lower Fat, Lighter Muffins and Breads

Sometimes, low-fat cooking and baking methods can change the texture from what we're used to in their high-fat cousins. Here are some suggestions that will help make the low-fat versions indistinguishable from the high-fat varieties.

- Rubbery or tough textured:
  Ordinarily fat is used to coat flour particles so that the gluten will not develop during mixing. By eliminating the fat, you will eliminate this. To solve this problem, add a small amount of grated apple to the batter. This will add moistness and compensate for the tough texture, or add some fat back into the recipe (you may have taken out too much). You may also add chopped dried fruits and nuts to the

batter to add another texture to the baked product.

- Not enough body:

  Using a fat-free liquid substitute, such as nonfat milk, fruit juice, or water, which is much less viscous than oil can cause this problem. Use buttermilk as the liquid in the batter, or add a small amount of grated apple.

- Wet texture:

  Different kinds of flours absorb different amounts of moisture from doughs and batters. All-purpose flour absorbs less water than whole-wheat flour. Use whole-wheat flour to replace up to half of the all-purpose flour, or add a few tablespoons of wheat germ or oat bran.

  Substituting 2 egg whites for each whole egg increases the moisture in baking products. Decrease baking temperature and increase baking time, or use an oven thermometer to check your oven. You may also stir an extra tablespoon of flour or cornstarch into the batter to absorb excess moisture.

Reducing the Fat in Salad Dressings

- If you are replacing oil with a liquid that is thinner than oil, whisk 1 to 2 teaspoons arrowroot into the dressing. Bring to a gentle boil, and cook and stir for 2 minutes. You may also replace the oil with a fat-free or reduced-fat substance that has body, such as buttermilk, yogurt, or sour cream.

Low-Fat Eating Out

- Ask your waiter to suggest lower-fat appetizers, entrées, and desserts.
- Start with soups such as onion (without the cheese and buttery toast), Manhattan clam chowder, or broth with rice or noodles. It's a low fat way to help your stomach fill up.
- Always order your salad dressing on the side. Light is best, but if all you can get is regular, mix it half and half with vinegar or lemon juice.
- If you do order a creamy dressing, dip your fork in the dressing, then spear some salad. You'll get the taste with far less fat.
- Order a baked potato instead of French fries. Limit the sour cream to 1 tablespoon, the butter to 1 pat.
- In Chinese, Thai, Indian, Mexican, or Japanese restaurants, order extra steamed rice. Take it home with half the entrée or share it with a friend.
- Eat plenty of unbuttered bread before and during your meal. Eat plain Italian bread instead of oil-soaked garlic bread.
- In general, order vegetarian, seafood, or poultry entrées instead of beef or pork.
- In Italian restaurants, order entrées largely made of pasta. Keep to tomato sauce rather than cream sauces.
- If main dishes are notoriously large, order two appetizers and request one be served as the main course.
- Ask for lower-fat substitutes such as fresh fruit or vegetables instead of high-fat French fries.

- In theaters, ask for air-popped popcorn. Ask if they pop their corn in canola or other lower-saturated-fat oils.
- For dessert, have sorbet, sherbet, or fat-free or low-fat frozen yogurt.
- Many fast-food chains now display nutritional information about their food. Focus on those items lower in fat.
- Watch out for sauces and condiments. Scrape off the tartar sauce on a fish sandwich and eliminate two-thirds the fat. Eliminate the syrup and butter on breakfast pancakes and eliminate two-thirds the fat. Order a Burger King burger without mayo and eliminate 15 grams of fat.
- Use low-fat dressings on your salads. At the salad bar, avoid pasta salads and potato salad. The mayonnaise can add as much fat as a hamburger.
- French fries usually carry the highest fat of any item on the menu. Think about a salad with low-fat dressing as a side dish instead.
- Watch out for desserts. A Danish or cookie can have as much fat and as many calories as a single hamburger.

Low-Fat Eating at Home

- Make extensive use of your microwave. Just about everything can be cooked without fats or oils while keeping all their vitamins and minerals.
- A modern pressure cooker is great for reducing cooking time without adding any fat.
- Avoid frying or sautéing anything. Instead, grill, bake, poach, broil, or steam.

- Replace your pots and pans with nonstick cookware. It makes cooking with little or no oil much easier.
- Use nonstick cooking spray instead of greasing pans for cooking and baking.
- Season your sauté pans by heating them on high until they smoke, then rub the inside with salt. It helps keep oil from being absorbed by the metal, so you use less when cooking.
- Use butter sprinkles to top vegetables, pasta, rice, or potatoes to get a buttery flavor without the fat.
- Switch from whole milk to 1% low-fat or nonfat. Note that 2% low-fat milk still contains 5 grams of fat in an 8-ounce glass.
- Use margarine instead of butter; it contains no cholesterol and you can find lower-fat margarines and spreads.
- Try using no butter or margarine. Good bread tastes good without it, or think about a pure-fruit spread.
- For sauces and gravies that call for sour cream or heavy cream, substitute plain low-fat yogurt. Add a little cornstarch to keep it from separating.
- Use nonfat milk or 1% low-fat milk when making cream sauces and gravies. Add a little flour for thickness.
- Break up flavored fat-free rice cakes for salads to take the place of fat-filled croutons.
- Chopped chestnuts and water chestnuts are great low-fat replacements for regular nuts in salads.

- Substitute wine, lemon juice, or vegetable broth for cooking instead of oils or butter. There's no fat and they add flavor to your recipe.
- When cooking stews, soups, and chili, let the pot cool down. The fat will float to the top and you can skim it off. Then reheat right before serving.
- Keep your meat portions limited to 3 ounces. That's about the size of a deck of playing cards. It will provide plenty of protein and nutrition and cut down considerably the high-fat content of a larger serving.
- Avoid croissants, which are high in butter and fat, in favor of bagels or muffins.
- If meat is essential, consider ham. It usually has less saturated fat than most cuts of beef.
- Don't skip breakfast! It can be a great low-fat meal packed with nutrition and will help keep you from eating fatty foods in the middle of the day.
- Light or dark corn syrup can fill in for some fat in desserts. Substitute 1 tablespoon syrup per 2 tablespoons of fat removed. You'll save 28 grams of fat and 200 calories.
- Read your food labels! Keep a majority of your food choices to those containing 20 percent of calories or less from fat.
- Be careful in the snack section of the market. Pretzels are great because they have little or no fat. Watch out for potato chips and microwave popcorn. Watch labels on "new wave" snacks like carrot chips, pita, and bagel chips. They can have up to 9 grams of fat in a 1-ounce serving.
- Buy bag popcorn over microwave. Hot air popped, it's totally fat free. But watch the fatty butter! Spray on soy, teriyaki, or other nonfat flavors. Use butter buds and nonfat Parmesan cheese for added flavor.
- If you're buying meat, choose select over choice or prime. Choose chicken and turkey over beef or pork.
- Avoid processed meats like salami, sausage, and hot dogs. They're generally very high in fat. Look for healthier turkey franks or vegetarian versions.
- Buy small or medium rather than large eggs. They have less fat and cholesterol.
- If a recipe calls for nuts, try walnuts. They're among the lowest in saturated fat.
- Substitute capers for olives. Using 1 tablespoon of capers in place of 1/4 cup olives saves 4 grams of fat and 30 calories.
- Exercise! Anything is better than nothing for burning the fat out of your diet. Walk, bike, stretch—they're all great for your heart, mind, and body!

Secrets to Healthy Food Shopping

- Never shop on an empty stomach.
- Select canned fruits and tuna packed in water, not in syrup or oil.
- Check labels for the words *hydrogenated* or *partially hydrogenated*. The earlier they appear in the ingredient list, the higher the amount of unhealthy trans fatty acids a food contains.
- Buy skinless turkey or chicken breasts.

- If selecting frozen dinners, choose those that are not only low in fat, but also low in sodium and cholesterol.
- Try calcium-fortified orange juice if you're not consuming enough dairy products.
- Opt for whole-grain breads, rolls, and cereals.
- Stock up in the bread, pasta, rice, and bean aisles of the market. They all have lots of protein, fiber, and nutrition with low fat levels.
- Stock up big on fruits and vegetables. Except for a few, they contain little fat and plenty of nutrition.
- Consider cantaloupe. For just 95 calories, half a melon provides more than a day's supply of vitamin C and beta carotene.
- Don't be fooled by yogurt-covered raisins or nuts. The coating is usually made of sugar and partially hydrogenated oil.
- Go for these low-fat goodies: pretzels, gingersnaps, graham crackers, and angel food cake.
- Plan your meals before heading to the store. Make a shopping list to reduce impulse purchases and to save money and time.
- Consider using store brands; they're usually less expensive than name brands and the quality is generally comparable.
- Choose a variety of fish, chicken, turkey, and veal. And when selecting beef, pork, or lamb, look for leaner cuts.
- Buy fresh fruits and vegetables and lean meats whenever possible. Canned soups, frozen dinners, and processed meats may be difficult to fit into a healthy diet.

Olestra and Other Fat Substitutes

Americans' growing preference for reduced-fat diets has food manufacturers cooking up new substances to replace most, if not all, of the fat in a food. Some of these fat substitutes, with trade names such as Olestra, Simplesse, and Avicel, already are on the market and being used in a variety of foods, including cheese, chips, frozen desserts, and candy. Others remain in development.

The idea behind all these substitutes is to reduce a food's fat and calories while maintaining the texture provided by fat. They often fall short, however. While most contain fewer calories than fat, they don't withstand the cooking temperatures that natural fats do.

Olestra appears to be an exception. Because Olestra is formed by chemical combination of sucrose (sugar) with fatty acids, it has properties similar to those of a naturally occurring fat. But, unlike the natural products, this synthetic substitute provides no calories or saturated fat because it is undigestible: it passes through the digestive tract but is not absorbed into the body.

As promising as that sounds, Olestra and similar fat substitutes that may come along in the future raise new concerns: What effect can they have on the gastrointestinal system if they are not absorbed? Can they affect absorption of fat-soluble vitamins? Can they interfere with absorption of other nutrients or with drugs? What particular effects might they have in people

with conditions that affect nutrition, such as intestinal disease?

Unlike other food additives, which make up only a minute amount of the diet, fat substitutes, such as Olestra, have the potential to make up a substantial portion of the diet because they replace fat, a major dietary component. This raises another concern: how best to determine if there are possible toxic effects from such fat substitutes. The usual method for studying toxicity of food additives—giving upward of 100 times the likely human intake of the substance to laboratory animals—is impractical for fat substitutes like Olestra. It is not possible to feed laboratory animals the large amount of fat substitutes that would be required to conduct a traditional toxicology test as is done with other food additives to determine safety.

Replacing Fat in the Diet

Replacing fat in the diet is not as easy as it may sound. Contrary to public perception, natural fats actually have many useful roles in the diet. They are one of the nutrient categories essential for proper growth and development and maintenance of good health. They carry the fat-soluble vitamins A, D, E, and K and aid in their absorption in the intestine. They are the only source of linoleic acid, an essential fatty acid. And they are an especially important source of calories for people who are underweight and for infants and toddlers, who have the highest energy needs per kilogram of body weight of any age group.

Fat also plays important roles in food preparation and consumption. It gives taste, consistency, stability, and palatability to foods.

On the other hand, too much fat in the diet can be harmful. Fat is calorie-dense: It contains 9 calories per gram, compared to 4 calories per gram for protein and carbohydrates. So eating a lot of fat can result in excess calorie intake, which in turn can perhaps lead to undesirable weight gain.

Fat intake also is linked to several chronic diseases. There is some evidence of a link between high intakes of fat and a possible increased risk of certain cancers, such as breast, colon, and prostate cancers. There also is a link between high intakes of saturated fat and cholesterol and an increased risk of coronary heart disease.

The Dietary Guidelines for Americans recommend that fat intake be limited to 30 percent or less of calories and saturated fat to less than 10 percent.

Many Americans are trying to reduce their fat intake. According to a survey by the Calorie Control Council, an association of low-calorie and diet food manufacturers, nearly two-thirds of the adult U.S. population consume low- or reduced-fat or reduced-calorie foods and beverages, and two-thirds also believe there is a need for food ingredients that replace fat.

Manufacturers are responding by adding more and more reduced-fat foods to their product lines. These products often contain fat substitutes already approved by FDA.

Lifestyle Tips for Low-Fat Eating

- Drink at least 64 ounces (8 cups) of water each day. Don't eat dinner until you've finished drinking your daily water requirement.
- Pick one place at home and one at work where you will do all your eating. Be sure you are seated. Don't eat anywhere but in that spot. No counter eating, couch eating, car eating, or the like.
- Keep healthful foods like fruit or vegetables handy. Eat only if you are hungry.
- Keep a diary of what you eat and your feelings, far away from the kitchen. Document everything that you eat before you eat it. Describe how you feel healthwise as you progress. Describe how you feel when you cheat yourself.
- Soups are a great meal. They are filling, tasty, and healthful.
- If you are going to a restaurant, decide ahead of time what you will be eating. Then stick to it.
- Set up a schedule for when you will eat your food and snacks.
- Keep all food in the kitchen or pantry, not in any other places.
- Never starve yourself, especially before going out to eat (or you will binge). Never skip meals. You must have some kind of regular nourishment or your body's starvation defenses will kick in, lower your metabolism, and store fat.

- Don't think that just because you are eating low-fat, low-calorie foods that you can eat all that you want. The calories still add up and must be burned off regardless of what kind of food you eat. Balance is key.
- Give away or throw away leftover food.
- Have the rest of your family make their own snacks.
- Don't put extra food in bowls on the kitchen table. Keep it in the refrigerator or put it away in a cupboard.
- If you get the urge to eat when not truly hungry, go do something (go for a walk or do a small chore). Try to accomplish some small thing instead of going backward on your diet. Try jogging in place for a few minutes when you think you might go sneak a snack. It will give you time to think about what you're doing.
- If a certain food store or restaurant drives you crazy with desire when you drive by, change your route.
- Try to do at least 30 minutes of low-impact, moderate exercise (walking) at least three times per week. Start off easy and gradually increase over time.
- The best exercise is walking. Plain and simple walking. You should walk briskly but not to the point where you are short of breath. You should be able to carry on a conversation.
- Whatever exercise you do to lose weight, be sure it is aerobic. This means that you do not run short of breath. When you run short of breath and have to breath deeply (anaerobic

exercise), your body will burn sugar and not as much fat.

- You should keep track of your measurements (inches) as well as pounds. Write them down every week. Inches will come off even though weight is not coming off, or is coming off slowly. This is due to muscle buildup in your body. Muscle is heavier than fat.
- Wherever you work, walk along the longest route possible to get from wherever you are to wherever you're going. (But don't be late!)
- Keep your exercise bike or equipment in plain sight. This acts as a constant reminder of the effort you have invested, so you don't eat the wrong foods and waste those efforts.
- Always warm up with some stretching before exercising. This will make your body burn more fat when you actually do start exercising, and will help prevent accidental muscle damage.
- Play with your kids! It is hard enough for us to find time to be with them with all the pressures of life. Play some kind of game requiring physical movement. They will love you for it, and your overall health will benefit.
- Take the stairs instead of the elevator.
- When parking your car at a store, park it as far away from the store as possible. (This will also reduce dents in your car doors from careless people.)
- If you sit a lot at your job or at home, you probably have a flabby stomach. In order to tighten your abdominal muscles, stand or sit

with a tall posture, and hold your stomach in as much as possible. Here is the best exercise you can do during the day to tighten those muscles: When you exhale, pull your stomach in, pushing the air out. Pull your stomach in tightly and a little quickly, then let it out naturally while you breath air back into the lungs. Pulling the stomach in tightly acts to push the air out of your lungs as you build those abdominal muscles.

- Eat less and you won't have to exercise as much!
- Eat very slowly and enjoy the flavors.
- Vary your caloric intake so that your body doesn't go into a starvation-prevention mode. If you keep calories low everyday, your body will adjust to that amount as if it were all it needed to maintain your weight, and you'll stop losing weight.
- Don't go more than about five hours during the day without eating. That causes you to eat more at mealtime. Eat healthful, low-fat snacks in between meals if you are going to go more than five hours without a meal.
- Don't deprive yourself! If you really enjoy eating a certain food, plan for it. Make it a reward for doing extra situps or for spending more time on cardiovascular exercise. This helps to avoid bingeing.
- Imagine yourself as thin and healthy, and keep that image in mind and recall it once a day, most likely in the morning.
- Right after eating a meal, especially dinner, go straight to the bathroom to brush, floss,

and gargle with mouthwash so that your mouth is feeling nice and clean. This makes it less appealing to eat more, especially before bedtime.

- If you get hungry you should chew gum. Some people just like to chew things. Chew gum while preparing meals or making lunch for the next day, to prevent you from nibbling food while it is right in front of you.
- If you eat your meals away from the TV and other distracting places, you will enjoy your meal more and you will take a little longer o eat it. Also, drink at least two glasses of water or one glass of milk during your meal; you'll feel fuller and less likely to go back for seconds.
- Never eat after 7:00 P.M. The body's metabolism slows down immensely while it is sleeping.
- Try to work out as much as possible, but at your own pace, and reward yourself, but not with a snack. Instead, put a certain amount of money in a jar every time you work out. The more you work out, the more money you save. Then go on a shopping spree, and buy yourself a new wardrobe for your new thin, trim body.
- Eat to live. Don't live to eat!
- The most important thing to consider before going on a diet is the reason you are doing so. Never diet because you think it will make people like you. Diet because you want to look and feel good for yourself. Otherwise, you may be disappointed.

Your Low-Fat Choices

Choose a diet low in saturated fat

Fats contain both saturated and unsaturated (monounsaturated and polyunsaturated) fatty acids. Saturated fat raises blood cholesterol more than other forms of fat. Reducing saturated fat to less than 10 percent of calories will help you lower your blood cholesterol level. The fats from meat, milk, and milk products are the main sources of saturated fats in most diets. Many bakery products are also sources of saturated fats.

Vegetable oils supply smaller amounts of saturated fat.

Choose a diet low in monounsaturated and polyunsaturated fat

Olive and canola oils are particularly high in monounsaturated fats; most other vegetable oils, nuts, and high-fat fish are good sources of polyunsaturated fats. Both kinds of unsaturated fats reduce blood cholesterol when they replace saturated fats in the diet. The fats in most fish are low in saturated fatty acids and contain a certain type of polyunsaturated fatty acid (omega-3) that is under study because of a possible association with a decreased risk for heart disease in certain people. Remember that fat in the diet should be consumed at a moderate level—that is, no more than 30 percent of calories. Mono- and polyunsaturated fat sources should replace saturated fats within this limit.

Partially hydrogenated vegetable oils, such as those used in many margarines and shortenings, contain a particular form of unsaturated fat known as trans-fatty acids that may raise blood cholesterol levels, although not as much as saturated fat.

Choose a diet low in cholesterol

The body makes the cholesterol it requires. In addition, cholesterol is obtained from food. Dietary cholesterol comes from animal sources such as egg yolks, meat (especially organ meats such as liver), poultry, fish, and higher-fat milk products. Many of these foods are also high in saturated fats. Choosing foods with less cholesterol and saturated fat will help lower your blood cholesterol levels. You can keep your cholesterol intake at this level or lower by eating more grain products, vegetables, and fruits, and by limiting intake of high cholesterol foods.

Choosing for children

The advice in the previous sections does not apply to infants and toddlers below the age of two years. After that age, children should gradually adopt a diet that, by about five years of age, contains no more than 30 percent of calories from fat. As they begin to consume fewer calories from fat, children should replace these calories by eating more grain products, fruits, vegetables, and low-fat milk products or other calcium-rich foods, and beans, lean meat, poultry, fish, or other protein-rich foods.

Facts About Fat

- In the United States, food can be labeled "fat free" and listed as having 0 grams of fat if the actual fat content is less than 0.5 grams. This is how foods can have oil or high-fat items listed in their ingredients yet claim to have 0 grams of fat.

- All oils are 100 percent fat. This includes olive oil, sesame oil, chili oil, fish oil, avocado oil, walnut oil, canola oil, safflower oil, and every other oil. Oils and fats have 9 calories per gram. Of course, oils vary widely in the proportion of saturated, polyunsaturated, and monounsaturated fats they contain.

- Vegetables that are high in fat include olives (96 percent of the calories come from fat), avocados (86 percent), sunflower seeds (75 percent), coconut (61 percent), coconut milk (93 percent) and, surprisingly, tofu (50 percent).

- We need some fat in our diet for our bodies to function properly. It would be unhealthy to eliminate all fat. Even with a non-junk-food diet composed of a healthy variety of foods as recommended by the FDA, it is virtually impossible to eliminate all fat. Almost all foods have fat. A diet consisting only of beans, fruits, vegetables, and grains with no added oils or high-fat ingredients will derive up to 10 percent of its calories from fat.

- We need fat for two main reasons: to help absorb fat-soluble vitamins (such as vitamin A)

and to supply two types of essential fatty acids (EFAs) that our bodies need but cannot produce. A diet with at least 10 grams of fat per day will result in normal vitamin absorption (some recommend at least 5 grams per meal, or 15 grams per day). Experts disagree on how much EFA we need, but it is generally a very small amount.

- No Recommended Dietary Allowances (RDA) for either essential fatty acid have been established, primarily because essential fatty acid deficiency has been observed exclusively in patients with medical problems affecting fat intake or absorption. However, the human requirement for linoleic acid has been estimated to be approximately 1 percent to 2 percent of the total energy intake (2.7 percent for infants). This level is generally more than met in varied diets since fats from vegetables are particularly rich sources of linoleic acid. It

has been proposed that omega-3 fatty acids should be equal to 10 percent to 25 percent of the linoleic acid intake (or 0.1 to 0.5 percent of total energy intake), particularly during pregnancy, lactation, and infancy.

- As long as you eat a varied non-junk-food diet, you will most likely get all the EFAs you need. But, if you would like to consume more, the number one best vegetarian source of both EFAs is flaxseeds. However, whole flaxseeds are not usually digested well by the body and linoleic acid is very unstable and goes rancid quickly. You should either use cold-pressed flaxseed oil that is no more than three months old or freshly ground flaxseeds. You may eat them raw or use them as an egg replacement in baked goods. Some people like to add ground flaxseed to their breakfast cereal or to make a vinaigrette with flaxseed oil and add it to salad.

THE EVERYTHING LOW-FAT HIGH-FLAVOR COOKBOOK

Appetizers

CHAPTER ONE

Amount Per Chapter
16 Recipes

	% Daily Value
Easy to Prepare	**100%**
Low Fat / High Flavor	**100%**
Simple to Understand	**100%**

DELICIOUS, EASY, LOW-FAT RECIPES

W e've all gotten used to serving salad before the main course, but somehow offering an appetizer before the entrée is too often reserved only for special occasions.

It doesn't have to be this way. In fact, most of the appetizers that follow can be prepared in just 10 or 15 minutes—something you can do while the rest of the meal is cooking.

Appetizers are a great way to put the unexpected into a meal, whether it's on a gray day in the dead of winter or in the middle of a too-hectic work week. And if you find cooking to be relaxing, fixing a tasty appetizer is the perfect antidote to a busy day.

Chilied Bean Dip

Yield: 2 cups

> 1 can (16 ounces) kidney beans, drained
>   and rinsed
> 2 jalapeño peppers, finely chopped
> 1 tablespoon red wine vinegar
> 1 teaspoon chili powder
> 1/4 teaspoon ground cumin
> 1 tablespoon minced onion
> 1 tablespoon minced fresh parsley

Place the beans, jalapeño peppers, vinegar, chili powder, and cumin in a food processor. Process until smooth. Transfer the mixture to a bowl. Stir in the onion and parsley and serve.

Nutritional Analysis

Calories	43.59 Kcal.	Protein	3.05 gm.
Fat	0.37 gm.	Carbohydrate	7.09 gm.
Sodium	74.19 mg.	Cholesterol	0.00 mg.
Saturated Fat	0.02 gm.		

Stuffed Celery Stalks

Serves: 12

> 12 long celery stalks with leaves attached
> 6 ounces nonfat cream cheese, at room
>   temperature
> 1/2 cup nonfat cottage cheese
> 1/4 onion, cut up (optional)
> 2 tablespoons nonfat milk (if needed)
> 12 large pimiento-stuffed green olives, cut into
>   1/4-inch-thick slices
> several shakes of paprika

Set the celery stalks on a cutting board, hollow side up. In small blender or food processor, combine the cream cheese, cottage cheese, and the onion, if using. Process at high speed for 4 minutes until smooth. If the mixture is very thick, add the milk, a few drops at a time, to thin to spreading consistency.

Using a knife, spread the mixture in the hollows of the celery stalks, dividing it evenly among the stalks. Push olive slices into the spread

along the entire length of each stalk. Wrap in plastic wrap and chill well. Just before serving, unwrap and sprinkle with paprika.

Nutritional Analysis

Calories	31.02 Kcal.	Protein	3.60 gm.
Fat	0.54 gm.	Carbohydrate	3.03 gm.
Sodium	234.03 mg.	Cholesterol	2.37 mg.
Saturated Fat	0.06 gm.		

Fruit Smoothie

Serves: 4

1 can (8 ounces) fruit cocktail, chilled
1 cup 1% milk
1/4 cup regular nonfat dry milk powder
1/2 teaspoon vanilla extract
2 dashes of ground cinnamon, plus extra for garnish (optional)
1/2 cup ice cubes

In a blender container, combine the undrained fruit cocktail, milk, milk powder, vanilla, and cinnamon. Blend until smooth. Add the ice cubes and blend again until smooth. Pour into glasses and sprinkle with additional cinnamon, if desired. Serve immediately.

Nutritional Analysis

Calories	68.64 Kcal.	Protein	3.75 gm.
Fat	0.67 gm.	Carbohydrate	11.95 gm.
Sodium	56.14 mg.	Cholesterol	3.20 mg.
Saturated Fat	0.41 gm.		

Baked Mushrooms with Spinach and Cheese

Serves: 6

1 tablespoon butter
24 medium-sized white mushrooms, quartered
1 1/2 cups drained lightly cooked spinach
1/2 cup Basic Low-Fat White Sauce (Chapter 2)
1/4 cup shredded low-fat cheddar cheese
1/4 cup shredded low-fat mozzarella cheese
salt and pepper to taste

Preheat oven to 350°F.

In a skillet over medium-high heat, melt the butter until it foams. Add the mushrooms and sauté until tender and lightly browned, 4 to 6 minutes. Set aside.

Line the bottom of a small baking dish with the spinach. Arrange the mushrooms evenly on top. Pour the white sauce evenly over the mushrooms, then sprinkle with the cheddar and mozzarella cheeses, salt, and pepper.

Bake until the cheeses are hot and bubbly, 20 to 25 minutes.

Nutritional Analysis

Calories	73.87 Kcal.	Protein	6.84 gm.
Fat	2.37 gm.	Carbohydrate	8.10 gm.
Sodium	169.68 mg.	Cholesterol	6.58 mg.
Saturated Fat	1.26 gm.		

Yogurt Dip

Yield: 1½ cups

1 cup (8 ounces) nonfat plain yogurt
½ cup shredded cucumber
⅓ teaspoon dried dill, crumbled

Combine all the ingredients in a bowl and mix well. Serve with vegetables for dipping.

Nutritional Analysis

Calories	6.72 Kcal.	Protein	0.65 gm.
Fat	0.02 gm.	Carbohydrate	0.94 gm.
Sodium	8.69 mg.	Cholesterol	0.22 mg.
Saturated Fat	0.01 gm.		

Cheese Coins

Yield: 24 coins

¼ cup buttery light, reduced-fat margarine, at room temperature
2 cups shredded low-fat cheddar cheese
½ teaspoon dry mustard
½ teaspoon seasoned salt
2 teaspoons minced canned green chile peppers
2 teaspoons minced pimiento
½ teaspoon Worcestershire sauce
1¼ cups all-purpose flour

Preheat oven to 350°F.

In a bowl, using a mixer, beat together the margarine, cheese, mustard, seasoned salt, green chiles, pimiento, and Worcestershire sauce until

blended. Add the flour, beating it in until a stiff dough forms. Shape into small balls (about ½ inch in diameter), and place well-spaced on ungreased baking sheets. Press each ball lightly with the tines of a fork.

Bake until lightly browned, about 15 minutes. Remove from the oven and serve piping hot or let cool and serve warm or at room temperature. Store in an airtight container at room temperature for up to 2 weeks.

Nutritional Analysis

Calories	47.43 Kcal.	Protein	4.00 gm.
Fat	1.07 gm.	Carbohydrate	5.66 gm.
Sodium	108.10 mg.	Cholesterol	1.00 mg.
Saturated Fat	0.25 gm.		

Stuffed Mushrooms Parmesan

Serves: 12

12 large mushrooms
1 tablespoon buttery light, reduced-fat margarine
1 medium onion, minced
¼ cup minced green bell pepper
1 clove garlic, minced
½ cup cracker crumbs
1½ tablespoons grated Parmesan cheese
1 tablespoon minced fresh parsley
¼ teaspoon dried oregano, crumbled
seasoned salt and pepper to taste
⅓ cup reduced-sodium, fat-free chicken broth

Preheat oven to 325°F.

Rinse the mushrooms briefly or wipe clean with damp paper towels. Trim off the stem ends, then remove the stems and finely chop; reserve.

Melt the margarine in a skillet over medium heat. Add the onion, bell pepper, garlic, and chopped mushroom stems. Cook for about 10 minutes, or until all the vegetables are tender but not browned. Add the crumbs, cheese, parsley, and oregano and season with seasoned salt and pepper. Mix well. Stir in the chicken broth until well mixed. Remove from the heat.

Spoon the filling into the mushroom caps, rounding the tops. Place the caps in a shallow baking dish and add water to the dish to a depth of about ¼ inch. Bake, uncovered, until the mushrooms are tender and the filling is heated through, about 25 minutes. Serve hot.

Nutritional Analysis

Calories	34.32 Kcal.	Protein	1.41 gm.
Fat	1.17 gm.	Carbohydrate	5.00 gm.
Sodium	71.47 mg.	Cholesterol	0.49 mg.
Saturated Fat	0.30 gm.		

Buttermilk Quickbread

Serves: 20

1¼ cups whole-wheat flour
¾ cup all-purpose flour
½ teaspoon baking powder
½ teaspoon salt
1 tablespoon corn oil
1 cup buttermilk

Preheat oven to 425°F. Spray a nonstick baking sheet with nonstick cooking spray.

In a bowl, stir together the flours, baking powder, and salt. In another, smaller bowl, stir together the oil and buttermilk. Add the buttermilk mixture to the flour mixture. Mix well to form a stiff dough. Turn out onto a floured board and knead until smooth. Shape into a flat, round loaf on the prepared baking sheet.

Bake 40 to 45 minutes. Cool on a rack for 15 minutes before slicing.

Nutritional Analysis

Calories	55.23 Kcal.	Protein	1.94 gm.
Fat	1.01 gm.	Carbohydrate	9.91 gm.
Sodium	83.35 mg.	Cholesterol	0.49 mg.
Saturated Fat	0.16 gm.		

Tomato Bruschetta

Serves: 4

8 slices French bread
2 garlic cloves, halved
1 teaspoon olive oil
2 tablespoons minced onion
1 tomato, diced
pinch of dried oregano, crumbled
pinch of pepper
2 teaspoons grated Parmesan cheese (optional)

Toast the bread on both sides. Rub one side of each piece of toast with the cut side of the cloves. Keep hot.

(continued)

Heat the oil in a nonstick skillet over medium-high heat. Add the onion and cook, stirring, until tender, about 10 minutes. Remove from the heat and stir in the tomato, oregano, and pepper.

Spoon the tomato mixture over garlic-rubbed side of the toast, dividing evenly. Serve immediately. Alternatively, sprinkle with the Parmesan and slip under a preheated broiler for 1 minute to brown slightly, then serve.

Nutritional Analysis

Calories	157.68 Kcal.	Protein	4.80 gm.
Fat	2.72 gm.	Carbohydrate	28.32 gm.
Sodium	307.67 mg.	Cholesterol	0.00 mg.
Saturated Fat	0.48 gm.		

Cold Sesame Noodles

Serves: 6

10 cloves garlic, minced
2-inch piece fresh ginger, peeled and minced
3 tablespoons water
1/3 cup tahini (sesame-seed paste)
3 tablespoons soy sauce
1/4 cup cold strong brewed tea
2 tablespoons Asian sesame oil
1 tablespoon white wine vinegar
1 tablespoon sugar
1/2 teaspoon five-spice powder
chili oil to taste
6 scallions, minced
1 pound thin wheat noodles

Purée the garlic, ginger, and water together in a food processor. In a medium bowl, stir together the tahini, soy sauce, tea, sesame oil, vinegar, sugar, five-spice powder, and chili oil. Add the garlic-ginger mixture and the scallions and stir well.

Cook the noodles in boiling water until al dente. Drain, rinse under cold water, and drain again. Transfer to a large bowl.

Add the noodles to the sauce mixture, toss well to coat, and serve.

Nutritional Analysis

Calories	427.12 Kcal.	Protein	13.00 gm.
Fat	12.89 gm.	Carbohydrate	65.47 gm.
Sodium	539.10 mg.	Cholesterol	0.00 mg.
Saturated Fat	1.80 gm.		

Creamy Garlic–Red Pepper Dip

Yield: 2/3 cup

1 jar (7 ounces) roasted red peppers, drained
1 tablespoon balsamic vinegar
1/3 cup low-fat cottage cheese
2 cloves garlic, minced
salt and pepper to taste

Combine the roasted peppers and vinegar in a food processor. Purée until smooth. Add the cottage cheese, garlic, salt, and pepper and process until smooth. Serve with vegetable crudite and/or pita triangles.

Nutritional Analysis

Calories	5.75 Kcal.	Protein	0.03 gm.
Fat	0.00 gm.	Carbohydrate	1.63 gm.
Sodium	25.96 mg.	Cholesterol	0.00 mg.
Saturated Fat	0.00 gm.		

Black Bean Dip

Yield: 2 cups

2 cans (15 ounces each), black beans, drained
2 jalapeño peppers, seeded, if desired, and
  chopped
2 cloves garlic, chopped
1 large tomato, chopped
2 tablespoons minced fresh coriander
1/2 teaspoon salt
1/2 teaspoon freshly ground pepper

Combine the beans, jalapeños, and garlic in a food processor. Purée until smooth.

Transfer to a bowl and add the tomato and cilantro. Mix well and serve with vegetable crudite and/or pita bread triangles.

Nutritional Analysis

Calories	22.65 Kcal.	Protein	1.50 gm.
Fat	0.22 gm.	Carbohydrate	3.95 gm.
Sodium	118.70 mg.	Cholesterol	0.00 mg.
Saturated Fat	0.00 gm.		

Herbed Clam Dip

Yield: 1 cup

1 cup low-fat cottage cheese
1 can (10 ounces) minced clams
1/3 cup chopped fresh parsley
3 tablespoons plain low-fat yogurt
1 tablespoon dried basil
l tablespoon minced onion
1 tablespoon lemon juice
dash of Tabasco sauce

Process the cottage cheese in a food processor until smooth, then transfer to a bowl. Drain the clams, reserving 1 tablespoon of the liquid, and add the clams and the 1 tablespoon liquid to the cottage cheese. Then add the parsley, yogurt, basil, onion, lemon juice, and Tabasco. Mix well. Cover and chill for at least 1 hour before serving.

Nutritional Analysis

Calories	27.00 Kcal.	Protein	4.29 gm.
Fat	0.36 gm.	Carbohydrate	1.39 gm.
Sodium	72.40 mg.	Cholesterol	6.88 mg.
Saturated Fat	0.12 gm.		

Cajun Chicken Fingers

Serves: 8

2 cloves garlic, minced
1/4 cup dried bread crumbs
1 tablespoon grated Parmesan cheese
1 tablespoon minced fresh parsley
1/2 teaspoon paprika

1/2 teaspoon dried oregano, crumbled
black pepper to taste
1/2 pound boneless, skinless chicken breasts, cut into long, narrow strips
1/4 cup low-fat milk

Preheat oven to 425°F. Spray a baking sheet with nonstick baking spray.

In a shallow dish, mix together the garlic, bread crumbs, Parmesan cheese, parsley, paprika, oregano, and pepper. Dip the chicken strips in the milk, then roll in the crumb mixture and arrange on the prepared baking sheet.

Bake for 5 minutes; turn and bake for 5 more minutes, or until the chicken is done. Serve hot.

Nutritional Analysis

Calories	53.41 Kcal.	Protein	7.55 gm.
Fat	0.92 gm.	Carbohydrate	3.22 gm.
Sodium	63.32 mg.	Cholesterol	17.24 mg.
Saturated Fat	0.29 gm.		

Candy Corn

Yield: 4 cups

2 tablespoons packed brown sugar
1 tablespoon butter
1 tablespoon corn syrup
4 cups popped corn

Preheat oven to 275°F.

Mix together the sugar, butter, and corn syrup in a small saucepan. Place over low heat and stir until the butter melts. Remove from the heat. Place the popcorn in a large plastic bag. Pour the

sugar-butter mixture over the popcorn and shake to mix well. Spread on a baking sheet and bake, stirring every 5 minutes, or until piping hot and the coating is set, about 20 minutes. Serve cooled to room temperature.

Nutritional Analysis

Calories	96.26 Kcal.	Protein	0.99 gm.
Fat	3.20 gm.	Carbohydrate	16.83 gm.
Sodium	38.47 mg.	Cholesterol	7.76 mg.
Saturated Fat	1.82 gm.		

Low-Fat Tortilla Chips

Yield: 2 cups chips

6 flour tortillas, each 8 inches in diameter
1 teaspoon ground cumin
2 teaspoons garlic powder
$1/2$ teaspoon salt

Preheat oven to 350°F.
Spray one side of each tortilla with nonstick cooking spray. Mix the cumin, garlic powder, and salt together in a small bowl. Sprinkle over the sprayed side of the tortillas. Cut each tortilla into 6 wedges and arrange on a baking sheet. Bake until crisp, about 10 minutes.

Nutritional Analysis

Calories	187.64 Kcal.	Protein	4.87 gm.
Fat	5.34 gm.	Carbohydrate	30.42 gm.
Sodium	541.67 mg.	Cholesterol	0.00 mg.
Saturated Fat	0.57 gm.		

Popcorn

The advent of air-popped popcorn machines in the '70s and '80s made it possible for Americans to enjoy one of their favorite snacks—popcorn—without all the fat. In the '90s, of course, microwaveable popcorn packets became all the rage, but even the low-fat versions contain lots more fat than the air-popped variety.

Do your family a favor and dig out the air-popped machine. Sprinkle Parmesan cheese, a bit of garlic salt, even a bit of honey on your finished popcorn for a flavor the microwaved popcorn can't match.

THE EVERYTHING LOW-FAT HIGH-FLAVOR COOKBOOK

Sauces and Relishes

CHAPTER TWO

Amount Per Chapter

27 Recipes

	% Daily Value
Easy to Prepare	**100%**
Low Fat / High Flavor	**100%**
Simple to Understand	**100%**

DELICIOUS, EASY, LOW-FAT RECIPES

S auces and relishes are the true spice of low-fat cooking. These low-fat, often low-calorie sauces and relishes offer a burst of flavor that can enhance any meal, whether you serve the Special Occasion Tomato Sauce on a bed of fresh pasta topped with freshly grated Parmesan cheese, or a snack such as the zesty Tropical Salsa.

Most of these sauces and relishes can be prepared in advance, which leaves you free to prepare the rest of the meal. Even more inspiring is the fact that, like people, the flavors usually get better with age.

Basic Low-Fat White Sauce

Yield: 1 cup sauce

 2 tablespoons all-purpose flour
 1 tablespoon cornstarch
 1 teaspoon lemon pepper
 1 cup nonfat milk

Place the cornstarch and flour in a small saucepan over medium-low heat and cook until lightly toasted but not browned, stirring constantly. Add the cornstarch, lemon pepper, and milk, stirring constantly. Continue cooking and stirring until thickened, about 10 minutes. Serve over vegetables or use as a base for cheese sauce or country gravy.

Nutritional Analysis

Calories	43.28 Kcal.	Protein	2.48 gm.
Fat	0.14 gm.	Carbohydrate	7.77 gm.
Sodium	137.31 mg.	Cholesterol	1.22 mg.
Saturated Fat	0.07 gm.		

Special Occasion Tomato Sauce

Yield: 2 cups sauce

 1 cup plain low-fat yogurt
 1 cup tomato sauce
 1/4 cup grated Parmesan cheese
 handful of fresh basil leaves, torn

Combine all the ingredients in a saucepan, stir well, and place over low heat. Heat until hot and well blended; do not allow to boil. Toss with hot pasta to serve.

Nutritional Analysis

Calories	39.84 Kcal.	Protein	3.04 gm.
Fat	1.26 gm.	Carbohydrate	4.49 gm.
Sodium	251.12 mg.	Cholesterol	3.67 mg.
Saturated Fat	0.75 gm.		

Chunky Pasta Sauce

Yield: 1 quart sauce

1 onion, coarsely chopped
3 cloves garlic, minced
1/2 pound mushrooms, sliced
1 green bell pepper, cut into 1-inch chunks,
   seeds reserved
1 celery stalk, cut into 1/2-inch-thick slices
1 can (28 ounces) tomatoes, undrained
1 can (6 ounces) tomato paste
1 can (8 ounces) tomato sauce
1/2 cup red wine or water
1 teaspoon brown sugar
1 teaspoon dried oregano, crumbled
2 tablespoons dried basil, crumbled, or
   4 tablespoons chopped fresh basil
2 teaspoons chopped fresh parsley
1/8 teaspoon red pepper flakes (optional)
salt to taste

In a nonstick skillet over low heat, combine the onion and garlic with several tablespoons of water and cook until tender, about 4 minutes.

Add the mushrooms and continue cooking over low heat for about 3 minutes. Add the bell pepper, pepper seeds, and celery and cook until barely tender, about 4 minutes. Add the tomatoes and their juice. In a small bowl, whisk together the tomato paste and sauce and the wine or water and add to the pan along with the sugar, oregano, basil, parsley, red pepper flakes, and salt and cook, stirring occasionally, for an additional 15 minutes to blend the flavors. Toss with hot pasta to serve.

Nutritional Analysis

Calories	41.26 Kcal.	Protein	1.63 gm.
Fat	0.30 gm.	Carbohydrate	8.05 gm.
Sodium	254.54 mg.	Cholesterol	0.00 mg.
Saturated Fat	0.02 gm.		

Low-Fat Country Gravy

Yield: 1 1/2 cups sauce

1 tablespoon Worcestershire sauce
2 tablespoons dried onion soup mix
1/4 teaspoon dried thyme, crumbled
1/4 teaspoon garlic powder
1 cup Low-Fat White Sauce (on opposite page)
nonfat milk, if needed

In a saucepan, combine the Worcestershire sauce, soup mix, thyme, garlic powder, and white sauce. Place over low heat and heat until the soup mix is well dissolved and onions are limp, just a few minutes. If sauce becomes too thick, add a little nonfat milk to thin to desired consistency. Serve hot.

Nutritional Analysis

Calories	43.65 Kcal.	Protein	2.24 gm.
Fat	0.32 gm.	Carbohydrate	7.93 gm.
Sodium	477.37 mg.	Cholesterol	1.01 mg.
Saturated Fat	0.10 gm.		

Low-Fat Cheese Sauce

Yield: 1¼ cups sauce

1 cup Low-Fat White Sauce
¼ cup grated low-fat cheese of choice

Pour the white sauce into a saucepan and heat to serving temperature. Add the cheese and continue heating until the cheese is melted and the sauce is smooth. Serve hot.

Nutritional Analysis

Calories	43.62 Kcal.	Protein	3.98 gm.
Fat	0.11 gm.	Carbohydrate	6.61 gm.
Sodium	151.86 mg.	Cholesterol	1.58 mg.
Saturated Fat	0.06 gm.		

Cranberry Chutney

Yield: 8 cups

1½ cups walnut pieces, toasted
1 pound cranberries
1 cup golden raisins
1 small red onion, sliced
½ cup orange marmalade
½ cup orange juice
2 tablespoons orange zest
⅓ cup white wine vinegar
1 cup granulated sugar
½ cup firmly packed brown sugar
½ teaspoon salt
¼ teaspoon cayenne pepper
½ teaspoon ground ginger
1 cinnamon stick
1 bay leaf

In a pressure cooker, combine all the ingredients. Stir well. Secure the lid in place and bring to medium pressure over high heat. Maintain medium pressure and cook for 5 minutes. Release the pressure according to manufacturer's directions. Remove the lid.

Remove the cinnamon stick and bay leaf and discard. Stir the chutney well, then ladle into sterilized jars. Cover tightly and store in the refrigerator for up to 4 weeks.

Nutritional Analysis

Calories	27.54 Kcal.	Protein	0.25 gm.
Fat	0.87 gm.	Carbohydrate	5.02 gm.
Sodium	10.47 mg.	Cholesterol	0.00 mg.
Saturated Fat	0.07 gm.		

California Salsa

Yield: About 2 cups

2 cups peeled and chopped tomatoes
1 celery stalk, cut up
1 onion, cut up
1 green bell pepper, cut up
1½ teaspoons salt
1 tablespoon cider vinegar
1 tablespoon sugar
1 green chile pepper, seeded, if desired, and chopped

In a food processor, combine all the ingredients and process until well blended. If a finer texture is desired, pass the ingredients through a food mill using a fine blade. Transfer to a bowl, cover tightly, and chill overnight before serving.

Nutritional Analysis

Calories	6.94 Kcal.	Protein	0.17 gm.
Fat	0.03 gm.	Carbohydrate	1.60 gm.
Sodium	111.31 mg.	Cholesterol	0.00 mg.
Saturated Fat	0.00 gm.		

Nectarine Chutney

Yield: About 2 cups

> 3 nectarines, peeled, pitted, and cut into
> $^1/_2$-inch chunks
> 1 onion, coarsely chopped
> $^1/_2$ cup firmly packed brown sugar
> $^1/_2$ cup golden raisins
> $^1/_4$ cup cider vinegar
> $^1/_2$ teaspoon chili powder
> $^1/_2$ teaspoon ground allspice
> $^1/_2$ cup almonds, toasted and chopped

In a 2-quart microwave-safe container, combine all the ingredients except the almonds. Microwave on high for 25 to 30 minutes, stirring every 5 minutes, or until the mixture is very thick and the fruit and onion are tender. Let cool, cover, and refrigerate until well chilled. Stir in the almonds before serving. Serve on sandwiches or as a relish with poultry, lamb, or pork.

Nutritional Analysis

Calories	40.43 Kcal.	Protein	0.64 gm.
Fat	1.12 gm.	Carbohydrate	7.65 gm.
Sodium	2.40 mg.	Cholesterol	0.00 mg.
Saturated Fat	0.10 gm.		

Chile Pepper Primer

Do you know your poblano from your jalapeño? Here's how to tell the difference:

Jalapeño: The jalapeño is short, fat, and dark green. It's the most popular fresh chile pepper sold in supermarkets and can be eaten raw or cooked. It is very hot.

Poblano: Like the jalapeño, the poblano is dark green, but shaped like a cone and milder in flavor. The flavor intensifies when the pepper is roasted.

Anaheim: Also known as a New Mexico chile, the Anaheim ranges from 3 to 6 inches in length. It is a lighter green than either the jalapeño or poblano, and it is also the chile with the least bite.

Persimmon Jam

Yield: 3 cups

8 ripe persimmons
1/4 cup lemon juice
1 package (1 3/4 ounces) powdered pectin
6 cups sugar

Cut off the stem ends from the persimmons, then force the fruits through a food mill or coarse strainer. Measure 4 cups pulp into a deep saucepan. Add the lemon juice and pectin and mix well.

Place over high heat and heat to boiling, stirring constantly. Add the sugar and mix well. Bring to a full rolling boil, stirring constantly. Boil without stirring for 4 minutes. Remove from the heat and alternately stir and skim for 5 minutes to cool slightly.

Spoon into hot, sterilized jars and seal with sterilized lids. Let cool and check for seal. If the seal is good, store in a cool, dark place for up to one year. If the seal is not good, store in the refrigerator for up to one month.

Nutritional Analysis

Calories	105.65 Kcal.	Protein	0.03 gm.
Fat	0.01 gm.	Carbohydrate	27.37 gm.
Sodium	2.61 mg.	Cholesterol	0.00 mg.
Saturated Fat	0.00 gm.		

Raspberry and Plum Butter

Yield: 2 pints

2 pounds plums, pitted and quartered
10 ounces frozen raspberries, thawed and
*   liquid reserved*
1 cup water
2 1/2 cups sugar
2 tablespoons lemon juice

Combine the plums, the thawed raspberries and their liquid, and the water in a heavy saucepan. Place over high heat and bring to a boil. Reduce the heat to low and cook, stirring occasionally, for 5 minutes, or until the fruit is very tender. Remove from the heat and purée in a blender. Return the purée to the saucepan and add the sugar and lemon juice. Cook over low heat, stirring occasionally, until the sugar is dissolved. Raise the heat to medium and cook, stirring constantly, for 5 minutes, or until the butter is thick and glossy. The butter is ready when it sheets from a spoon. Alternatively, drop a spoonful on a plate; if no rim of liquid forms around the edge of the butter, it's ready. Ladle into hot, sterilized jars and seal with sterilized lids. Let cool and check for seal. If the seal is good, store in a cool, dark place for up to 6 months. If the seal is not good, store in the refrigerator for up to 2 weeks. Serve with bread, fruit, or over ice cream.

Nutritional Analysis

Calories	40.08 Kcal.	Protein	0.14 gm.
Fat	0.12 gm.	Carbohydrate	10.18 gm.
Sodium	0.16 mg.	Cholesterol	0.00 mg.
Saturated Fat	0.00 gm.		

Southwestern Apricot Salsa

Yield: About 2 cups

1 can (16 ounces) apricots in light syrup,
   drained, rinsed, and cut into chunks
2 tablespoons chopped red onion
1½ teaspoons olive oil
1 tablespoon chopped fresh coriander
1½ teaspoons lime juice
½ teaspoon white vinegar
½ teaspoon minced jalapeño pepper
¼ teaspoon grated lime zest
¼ teaspoon ground cumin
salt and white pepper to taste

Combine all the ingredients in a bowl and stir gently. Cover and refrigerate until ready to serve.

Nutritional Analysis

Calories	44.77 Kcal.	Protein	0.35 gm.
Fat	0.87 gm.	Carbohydrate	9.67 gm.
Sodium	2.81 mg.	Cholesterol	0.00 mg.
Saturated Fat	0.11 gm.		

Tangy Peach Salsa

Yield: 2 cups

4 fresh peaches, pitted and chopped
½ cup orange marmalade
½ cup thinly sliced scallions
2 tablespoons cider vinegar
1 teaspoon peeled and grated fresh ginger

In a bowl, combine all the ingredients. Cover and refrigerate until ready to serve. Serve as a sauce for lamb, pork, or fish.

Nutritional Analysis

Calories	20.01 Kcal.	Protein	0.14 gm.
Fat	0.01 gm.	Carbohydrate	5.28 gm.
Sodium	3.05 mg.	Cholesterol	0.00 mg.
Saturated Fat	0.00 gm.		

Fresh Peach Salsa

Yield: 2 cups

2 fresh peaches, pitted and diced
2 fresh plums, pitted and diced
⅓ cup raisins
¼ cup diced red onion
1 tablespoon lemon juice
1 tablespoon chopped fresh mint

In a bowl, combine all the ingredients and stir gently to mix. Cover and refrigerate until ready to serve, preferably 1 day in advance. Serve spooned onto warm flour tortilla quarters.

Nutritional Analysis

Calories	43.82 Kcal.	Protein	0.64 gm.
Fat	0.14 gm.	Carbohydrate	11.13 gm.
Sodium	1.84 mg.	Cholesterol	0.00 mg.
Saturated Fat	0.00 gm.		

Asian Pear, Quince, and Apple Sauce
Yield: About 5 cups

1 cup sugar
2 cups water
1 cinnamon stick

(continued)

*2 quinces, peeled, cored, and cut into
2-inch chunks*
*2 Asian pears, peeled, cored, and cut into
2-inch chunks*
*2 pippin apples, peeled, cored, and cut into
2-inch chunks*

In a large, heavy saucepan over medium heat, combine the sugar, water, and cinnamon stick and cook, stirring often, until the sugar is dissolved. Add the quinces and bring to a low simmer. Cover and cook, stirring occasionally, until fruit is tender, about 40 minutes.

Add the pears and apples and continue cooking for about 30 minutes, stirring occasionally, or until the apples have softened. Remove and discard the cinnamon stick. If you prefer a puréed, saucelike consistency, purée the sauce in the pot with an immersion blender to achieve the desired consistency. Serve warm, at room temperature, or chilled. If storing, spoon into containers, cover, and refrigerate for up to 1 week.

Nutritional Analysis

Calories	56.49 Kcal.	Protein	0.10 gm.
Fat	0.05 gm.	Carbohydrate	14.61 gm.
Sodium	0.47 mg.	Cholesterol	0.00 mg.
Saturated Fat	0.00 gm.		

Smoky Salsa

Yield: 2 cups

5 plum tomatoes, halved
1 small red onion, thickly sliced

3 scallions
*1/3 bunch fresh coriander, tough stem ends
removed*
1 clove garlic
1 teaspoon chopped canned chipotle pepper
1 teaspoon cider vinegar
1 teaspoon salt
*1/4 cup reduced-sodium, fat-free chicken broth,
or more as needed*

Prepare a fire in a charcoal grill. In a grill basket, grill the tomatoes, red onion slices, and scallions over medium-hot coals until partially charred, turning occasionally. The red onions will take the longest. Transfer to a plate. Grill the coriander for about 30 seconds, just until it wilts and gives off a slight smoky scent.

With the motor running, add the garlic to a food processor and purée. Add the grilled vegetables and all the remaining ingredients and process until all the vegetables are puréed. Taste and adjust for seasonings. For a thinner consistency, add more broth. Cover and refrigerate until ready to serve or for up to 1 week.

Serve with chips or as a condiment for grilled chicken or meat.

Nutritional Analysis

Calories	14.07 Kcal.	Protein	0.66 gm.
Fat	0.10 gm.	Carbohydrate	3.05 gm.
Sodium	318.83 mg.	Cholesterol	0.00 mg.
Saturated Fat	0.01 gm.		

Mock Sour Cream

Yield: 2 cups

1 cup nonfat milk, or more as needed
³/₄ cup low-fat cottage cheese, or more as needed
2 to 4 teaspoons white wine vinegar

Pour the 1 cup milk and ³/₄ cup cottage cheese into a blender. Blend on medium speed until smooth. Add more cottage cheese or milk to bring the mixture to the consistency of sour cream. Stir in the vinegar to taste to give the mix a "tang."

Nutritional Analysis

Calories	26.22 Kcal.	Protein	3.66 gm.
Fat	0.26 gm.	Carbohydrate	2.11 gm.
Sodium	101.94 mg.	Cholesterol	1.45 mg.
Saturated Fat	0.16 gm.		

Marinara Sauce

Yield: About 1 quart

1 can (28 ounces) plum tomatoes, drained
4 large cloves garlic, minced
1 can (6 ounces) tomato paste
2 teaspoons oregano, dried
black pepper to taste
¹/₄ cup minced fresh basil

Place the tomatoes in a food processor and blend until smooth. Spray pan with nonstick cooking spray and place over low heat, add the garlic and sauté briefly. Add the puréed tomatoes, tomato paste, oregano, and pepper. Bring to a boil, then reduce the heat to low and simmer, uncovered, to blend the flavors and thicken slightly, about 10 minutes. Remove from the heat and stir in basil. Toss with pasta to serve.

Nutritional Analysis

Calories	21.69 Kcal.	Protein	0.97 gm.
Fat	0.27 gm.	Carbohydrate	4.62 gm.
Sodium	165.08 mg.	Cholesterol	0.00 mg.
Saturated Fat	0.02 gm.		

Barbecue Sauce

Yield: 1 cup sauce

¹/₃ cup cider vinegar
¹/₂ cup water
1 tablespoon Dijon mustard
2 tablespoons firmly packed brown sugar
¹/₂ teaspoon black pepper
¹/₄ cup lemon juice
1 large onion, finely minced
¹/₄ cup Worcestershire sauce
¹/₃ cup ketchup

In a saucepan, mix together all ingredients except the ketchup. Bring to a boil, then reduce the heat to low and simmer for 20 minutes. Remove from the heat and stir in the ketchup.

For barbecued chicken, place a layer of skinless chicken breasts in a baking pan. Spoon the sauce over the chicken, cover the pan with a piece of foil, and bake in a 325°F oven for 1 hour, or until done.

(continued)

Nutritional Analysis

Calories	93.36 Kcal.	Protein	1.78 gm.
Fat	0.20 gm.	Carbohydrate	22.28 gm.
Sodium	497.69 mg.	Cholesterol	0.00 mg.
Saturated Fat	0.01 gm.		

Dijon Mustard Sauce

Yield: ⅓ cup

2 tablespoons plain nonfat yogurt
2 tablespoons 1% cottage cheese
2 tablespoons low-fat mayonnaise
½ teaspoon Dijon mustard
¼ teaspoon soy sauce

For a smooth sauce, combine all the ingredients in a blender and process until smooth. Otherwise, stir together the ingredients thoroughly and serve.

Nutritional Analysis

Calories	44.73 Kcal.	Protein	2.59 gm.
Fat	1.15 gm.	Carbohydrate	5.52 gm.
Sodium	280.16 mg.	Cholesterol	0.84 mg.
Saturated Fat	0.11 gm.		

Tomato-Lime Salsa

Yield: 2 cups

2 large tomatoes, finely chopped
1 clove garlic, minced
2 teaspoons finely chopped fresh coriander
1 red onion, finely chopped

1 jalapeño pepper, seeded, if desired, and
*   finely chopped*
juice of 1 lime
salt and pepper to taste

In a bowl, stir together the tomatoes, garlic, coriander, onion, and jalapeño pepper. Add the lime juice, salt, and pepper. Mix well, cover, and chill before serving. Serve with low-fat tortilla chips or as a topping on cold chicken or salad.

Nutritional Analysis

Calories	22.62 Kcal.	Protein	0.88 gm.
Fat	0.20 gm.	Carbohydrate	5.13 gm.
Sodium	7.59 mg.	Cholesterol	0.00 mg.
Saturated Fat	0.02 gm.		

Easy Applesauce

Yield: 1½ cups

4 apples, peeled, cored, and diced
⅓ cup unsweetened apple juice

Put the apples and apple juice in a food processor and purée thoroughly.

Nutritional Analysis

Calories	55.05 Kcal.	Protein	0.12 gm.
Fat	0.27 gm.	Carbohydrate	14.25 gm.
Sodium	0.40 mg.	Cholesterol	0.00 mg.
Saturated Fat	0.04 gm.		

Cooked Applesauce

Yield: 1 quart

10 large apples, cored and thinly sliced
1 teaspoon ground cinnamon
1/3 cup apple juice
3 tablespoons lemon juice

Put all the ingredients except the lemon juice into a slow cooker or a heavy saucepan. Cover. If you are using a slow cooker, turn it to the slow setting and leave overnight or longer, until the apples are cooked. If you are cooking on top of the stove, cook over medium-high heat, checking for doneness after 45 minutes. Stir in the lemon juice. Serve hot or at room temperature.

Nutritional Analysis

Calories	67.15 Kcal.	Protein	0.21 gm.
Fat	0.38 gm.	Carbohydrate	17.36 gm.
Sodium	0.77 mg.	Cholesterol	0.00 mg.
Saturated Fat	0.06 gm.		

Tuna Tomato Sauce

Yield: 2½ cups

1 tablespoon olive oil
2 large cloves garlic, minced
1 teaspoon anchovy paste
1 teaspoon red pepper flakes
2 cups tomato purée
1 teaspoon black pepper
1 can (7 ounces) water-packed tuna, drained and flaked
1/3 cup minced fresh parsley

Heat the oil and garlic in a saucepan over medium-high heat for 1 minute. Remove from the heat and add the anchovy paste and pepper flakes. Stir in the tomato purée and black pepper and bring to a boil over high heat. Reduce the heat to low and cook for 20 minutes, stirring occasionally. Stir in the tuna and half of the parsley and cook for another 10 minutes. Toss with pasta to serve. Sprinkle on the remaining parsley.

Nutritional Analysis

Calories	59.55 Kcal.	Protein	6.32 gm.
Fat	1.56 gm.	Carbohydrate	5.63 gm.
Sodium	281.75 mg.	Cholesterol	7.68 mg.
Saturated Fat	0.22 gm.		

Herbed Yogurt Dressing

Yield: 2½ cups

2 cups plain low-fat yogurt
1/2 cup chopped fresh parsley
1/2 cup chopped fresh dill
2 cloves garlic, minced
2 tablespoons lemon juice
1 tablespoons Dijon mustard
salt and pepper to taste

In a small bowl, stir together all the ingredients. Cover and chill before serving. Serve over grilled chicken, beef, or lettuce greens.

(continued)

Nutritional Analysis

Calories	8.16 Kcal.	Protein	0.60 gm.
Fat	0.17 gm.	Carbohydrate	0.92 gm.
Sodium	17.45 mg.	Cholesterol	0.68 mg.
Saturated Fat	0.11 gm.		

Tropical Salsa

Yield: About 3¹/₂ cups

1 cup diced cantaloupe
1 cup diced honeydew
1 can (4¹/₂ ounces) chopped mild green chiles,
drained
6 scallions, minced
¹/₄ cup chopped fresh coriander
2 tablespoons lime juice
¹/₄ teaspoon cayenne pepper

In a bowl, stir together all the ingredients. Chill for at least 1 hour before serving.

Nutritional Analysis

Calories	46.19 Kcal.	Protein	1.27 gm.
Fat	0.24 gm.	Carbohydrate	11.42 gm.
Sodium	207.73 mg.	Cholesterol	0.00 mg.
Saturated Fat	0.00 gm.		

Black Bean and Corn Salsa

Yield: 2¹/₂ cups

kernels from 2 large ears corn
2 jalapeño peppers, seeded, if desired, and
chopped

1 can (19 ounces) black beans, drained and
rinsed
2 large tomatoes, chopped
2 tablespoons lemon juice
salt and pepper to taste

In a bowl, stir together all the ingredients. Chill for at least 1 hour before serving. Serve with chips or use as a condiment for grilled chicken.

Nutritional Analysis

Calories	77.54 Kcal.	Protein	4.26 gm.
Fat	0.88 gm.	Carbohydrate	15.08 gm.
Sodium	175.02 mg.	Cholesterol	0.00 mg.
Saturated Fat	0.07 gm.		

Fannie Flagg Salsa

Yield: 1¹/₂ cups

2 jalapeño peppers, seeded, if desired, minced
6 small green tomatoes, chopped
2 tablespoons chopped fresh coriander
1 teaspoon ground cumin
2 tablespoons red wine vinegar
¹/₄ cup diced red onion

In a bowl, stir together all the ingredients. Chill for at least 1 hour before serving. Serve as a side dish with grilled chicken or fish.

Nutritional Analysis

Calories	15.67 Kcal.	Protein	0.70 gm.
Fat	0.15 gm.	Carbohydrate	3.29 gm.
Sodium	6.57 mg.	Cholesterol	0.00 mg.
Saturated Fat	0.01 gm.		

THE EVERYTHING LOW-FAT HIGH-FLAVOR COOKBOOK

Soups

CHAPTER THREE

Amount Per Chapter

40 Recipes

% Daily Value

Easy to Prepare	**100%**
Low Fat / High Flavor	**100%**
Simple to Understand	**100%**

DELICIOUS, EASY, LOW-FAT RECIPES

I love soups because you can usually throw all the ingredients together into one pot, they don't require a lot of attention while cooking, and they provide sustenance for a full meal, supplemented only by a salad and a loaf of crusty bread.

The soups here range from traditional stick-to-the-ribs dishes suitable for winter fare to no-cooking gems light enough for the stickiest summer days. Many of the recipes are as easy to prepare as opening a few cans of soup. In addition, because you're making it yourself, the soup will be lower in fat and sodium, a claim the big soup manufacturers can't make.

Onion Soup

Serves: 8

2 tablespoons olive oil
6 large onions, thinly sliced
1 clove garlic, minced
1 cup dry red wine
½ cup dry sherry
½ cup Marsala wine
1 tablespoon dried thyme, crumbled
1 tablespoon black pepper
1 tablespoon dried rosemary
4 cups reduced-sodium, fat-free chicken broth
4 cups reduced-sodium, fat-free beef broth
8 slices French bread, each ½ inch thick
½ cup grated Parmesan cheese

Heat the oil in a soup pot over low heat, add the onions and garlic, and sauté until tender and lightly caramelized, about 30 minutes. Add all three wines, bring to a boil, and boil for about 15 minutes. Add the thyme, pepper, rosemary, and the broths, reduce the heat to medium, and simmer for 1 hour.

Preheat the oven to 375°F. Sprinkle 1 teaspoon of cheese on each bread slice. Place the slices on a baking sheet, cheese side up, and bake for 8 minutes.

Preheat the broiler. Ladle the soup into individual ovenproof crocks, and top each serving with a slice of prepared bread. Broil for a minute or two until the bread is lightly browned. Serve at once.

Nutritional Analysis

Calories	219.33 Kcal.	Protein	9.55 gm.
Fat	6.00 gm.	Carbohydrate	32.52 gm.
Sodium	850.43 mg.	Cholesterol	3.95 mg.
Saturated Fat	1.66 gm.		

Summertime Strawberry Soup

Serves: 6

> 3 cups strawberries, stemmed
> 1/2 teaspoon ground cinnamon
> 4 ounces frozen orange juice concentrate
> 1/2 cup water
> 1/4 cup dry red wine
> dash of ground cloves
> 2 tablespoons cornstarch
> 2 tablespoons water
> 1 pint vanilla low-fat frozen yogurt
> 1 pint low-fat plain yogurt

Mix the strawberries, cinnamon, orange juice concentrate, water, wine, and cloves in a saucepan. Bring to a boil, reduce the heat to medium-low, and simmer for 10 minutes.

Mix together the cornstarch and water in a small bowl. Stir 1/3 cup of the strawberry mixture into the cornstarch mixture until smooth and then add to the saucepan. Bring to a boil and boil, stirring, until thick, about 5 minutes. Remove from the heat, let cool for 1 hour or longer, and then add both yogurts. Stir until the frozen yogurt melts. Cover and refrigerate for 1 hour before serving.

Nutritional Analysis

Calories	278.76 Kcal.	Protein	10.51 gm.
Fat	3.74 gm.	Carbohydrate	50.67 gm.
Sodium	142.82 mg.	Cholesterol	11.79 mg.
Saturated Fat	2.14 gm.		

Cioppino

Serves: 6

> 1 1/2 tablespoons olive oil
> 1 large onion, chopped
> 1 large green bell pepper, chopped
> 2 cloves garlic, minced
> 2 cups bottled clam juice
> 1 cup coarsely chopped tomatoes
> 1/2 cup dry white wine
> 2 tablespoons minced fresh parsley
> 1 bay leaf
> salt and pepper to taste
> 4 soft-shelled crabs
> 12 mussels, well scrubbed and debearded
> 12 clams, well scrubbed
> 12 large shrimp, peeled and deveined
> 1 pound cod fillet, cubed

In a nonstick frying pan, add the olive oil, onion, bell pepper, and garlic and sauté for 3 minutes, or until the onion is translucent. Stir in the clam juice, tomatoes, wine, parsley, and bay leaf. Bring to a boil, reduce the heat to medium-low, cover, and simmer for 30 minutes. Add the salt and pepper and remove and discard the bay leaf.

Add the crabs, mussels, clams, shrimp, and fish and stir gently. Bring to a boil, reduce the heat to low, and cook for 5 to 10 minutes, or until the shellfish and fish are cooked. Discard any mussels or clams that remain closed. Serve at once.

(continued)

Nutritional Analysis

Calories	211.18 Kcal.	Protein	30.14 gm.
Fat	6.26 gm.	Carbohydrate	8.02 gm.
Sodium	528.69 mg.	Cholesterol	130.05 mg.
Saturated Fat	1.10 gm.		

Cream of Mushroom Soup

Serves: 4

1 pound button or other mushrooms, sliced or
chopped
1 large onion or 6 shallots, coarsely chopped
1 clove garlic, minced (optional)
1 celery stalk, sliced or chopped
1/4 cup water
4 cups skim milk
1/4 teaspoon ground nutmeg
3 tablespoons Madeira, Marsala, dry white
wine, dry vermouth, or dry sherry
2 tablespoons all-purpose flour
2 tablespoons cornstarch
salt and pepper to taste
1/2 cup chopped fresh parsley or enoki
mushrooms for garnish

Combine the mushrooms, onion (or shallots), garlic, celery, and water in a saucepan over medium heat. Bring to a simmer and cook until soft, about 5 minutes. Add 3 cups of the milk, the nutmeg, and the wine. Reduce the heat to very low, cover, and simmer for 20 minutes.

In a small bowl, combine the remaining 1 cup milk, the flour, and cornstarch and whisk well

until smooth. Add to the soup and stir continuously for at least 4 minutes (to cook the flour), until thick. Add more milk (or broth) to adjust the thickness, if needed. Season with salt and pepper. Ladle into bowls and garnish with the parsley (or enoki mushrooms).

Nutritional Analysis

Calories	175.35 Kcal.	Protein	12.03 gm.
Fat	1.11 gm.	Carbohydrate	30.93 gm.
Sodium	146.74 mg.	Cholesterol	4.90 mg.
Saturated Fat	0.39 gm.		

Light and Lean Chowder

Serves: 8

1 can (14 1/2 ounces) reduced-sodium, fat-free
chicken broth
1 cup small broccoli florets
1 cup sliced mushrooms
1/2 cup chopped onion
1 tablespoon buttery light, reduced-fat
margarine
2 tablespoons all-purpose flour
1/4 teaspoon salt
1/8 teaspoon pepper
1 can (13 1/2 ounces) evaporated skim milk
1 can (8 ounces) corn kernels, drained
1 tablespoon chopped pimiento

In a small saucepan, combine the broth and broccoli and bring to a boil. Reduce the heat to low, cover, and simmer for 5 minutes. Do not drain. Set aside.

In a large saucepan over medium heat, cook the mushrooms and onions in the margarine until tender. Stir in the flour, salt, and pepper. Add the milk all at once. Cook, stirring until bubbly. Cook and stir 1 minute more. Stir in broccoli and broth, corn, and pimiento. Heat through and serve.

Nutritional Analysis

Calories	92.10 Kcal.	Protein	6.26 gm.
Fat	1.84 gm.	Carbohydrate	13.34 gm.
Sodium	321.95 mg.	Cholesterol	2.15 mg.
Saturated Fat	0.32 gm.		

Curried Mushroom Soup

Serves: 4

> 1 cup mixed dried morel and porcini
> mushrooms (1 ounce dried mushrooms)
> 2 cups boiling water
> 1½ cups chopped leek, white part only (2 to
> 3 leeks)
> 2 tablespoons all-purpose flour
> 1 tablespoon curry powder
> 4 cups skim milk
> 1 chicken bouillon cube
> 2 cups chopped fresh portobello mushrooms
> (3 small mushrooms)
> 1 tablespoon dry sherry (optional)
> 1 tablespoon chopped fresh chervil

Combine the dried mushrooms and boiling water in a bowl and set aside to soak for 15 to 30 minutes.

Preheat a saucepan over medium heat for about 1 minute, then spray it twice with nonstick cooking spray. Add the leeks and sauté, stirring constantly until translucent, about 3 minutes. Add the flour and curry powder and stir until the leeks are well coated. Add the milk and bouillon cube. Raise the heat to high and cook just until bubbles begin to form around the edges. Reduce the heat to low and whisk until all ingredients are thoroughly combined. Stir in the fresh mushrooms and cook for 5 minutes.

Meanwhile, drain the reconstituted mushrooms and squeeze out excess moisture. Chop roughly. Add to the saucepan and cook for 1 minute more. Stir in the sherry, if using. Ladle into bowls and garnish with the chervil. Serve at once.

Nutritional Analysis

Calories	163.02 Kcal.	Protein	11.13 gm.
Fat	1.57 gm.	Carbohydrate	27.81 gm.
Sodium	380.28 mg.	Cholesterol	4.90 mg.
Saturated Fat	0.32 gm.		

Apple-Squash Soup

Serves: 8 to 10

> 1 tablespoon safflower or canola oil
> 1½ cups thinly sliced leeks, white and light
> green parts, or coarsely chopped onions
> 4 cups boiling water
> 3 pounds butternut squash, seeded and cut
> into 1½-inch chunks

(continued)

3 Granny Smith apples, peeled, cored, and
    quartered
1/3 cup old-fashioned rolled oats
2 tablespoons peeled and finely minced fresh
    ginger
1 1/2 tablespoons mild curry powder
1 teaspoon salt, or to taste

Heat the oil in the pressure cooker over
medium-high heat. Add the leeks and cook, stirring frequently, for 1 minute. Add the water (stand
back to avoid splattering oil), squash, apples, oats,
ginger, curry powder, and salt.

Secure the lid in place. Bring to high pressure
over high heat. Adjust the heat to maintain high
pressure and cook for 5 minutes. Turn off the
heat and allow the pressure to come down naturally, or use a quick-release method. Remove the
lid, tilting it away from you to allow any excess
steam to escape. If the squash is not fork-tender,
replace (but do not lock) the lid, and cook for a
few more minutes in the residual heat.

Purée the soup in two or three batches in a
blender (preferred) or food processor. Return to
the cooker and reheat to serving temperature.

Nutritional Analysis

Calories	121.21 Kcal.	Protein	2.21 gm.
Fat	2.13 gm.	Carbohydrate	26.44 gm.
Sodium	268.26 mg.	Cholesterol	0.00 mg.
Saturated Fat	0.20 gm.		

Luscious Corn Chowder

Serves: 8

3 slices bacon
1/2 cup minced onions
1/2 teaspoon minced garlic
1/2 cup minced green bell pepper
2 cups corn kernels
2 cups water
2 cups 1% milk
1 medium potato, cut into 1-inch cubes
1/2 cup chopped fresh parsley
pepper to taste
2 dashes of Tabasco sauce

In a skillet, fry the bacon until crisp. Using
tongs, transfer to paper towels to drain. Pour off
all but 1 tablespoon of the drippings from the
skillet and add the onions, garlic, and green
pepper to the bacon drippings and sauté over
medium heat until wilted.

Transfer the sautéed onion mixture to a
saucepan and add all the remaining ingredients
except the bacon. Bring to a boil, reduce the heat
to low, cover, and simmer until the potato is
tender, about 20 minutes. Ladle into bowls and
sprinkle with the bacon.

Nutritional Analysis

Calories	107.74 Kcal.	Protein	4.64 gm.
Fat	3.57 gm.	Carbohydrate	15.63 gm.
Sodium	85.96 mg.	Cholesterol	5.60 mg.
Saturated Fat	1.27 gm.		

Italian Bean Soup

Serves: 8

1 tablespoon olive oil
1/2 cup chopped onions
1 clove garlic, minced
3 cups mixed dried beans picked over and
    soaked overnight in water to cover
2 quarts reduced-sodium, fat-free beef broth
1 teaspoon dried oregano, crumbled
1 1/4 cups crushed tomatoes
2/3 cup julienned carrots
1/2 cup julienned celery
1 2/3 cups loosely packed torn spinach
1/2 cup cooked small pasta shells
salt to taste
1/2 cup grated romano cheese

In a saucepan, heat the oil over medium heat. Add the onion and garlic and sauté for about 5 minutes, or until translucent. Drain the beans and add to the saucepan along with the broth and oregano. Bring to a simmer, cover, and cook until the beans are tender, about 40 minutes.

Add the tomatoes, carrots, and celery. Simmer for 15 minutes. Stir in the spinach and pasta; adjust the seasoning with salt. Simmer for 5 minutes, or until heated through, then sprinkle with cheese and serve.

Nutritional Analysis

Calories	332.69 Kcal.	Protein	23.69 gm.
Fat	3.89 gm.	Carbohydrate	53.03 gm.
Sodium	727.21 mg.	Cholesterol	5.20 mg.
Saturated Fat	1.25 gm.		

Cooking Beans

Place dried beans in a vessel with two to three times as much water as beans. Remove and discard any beans or any debris that floats. Soak overnight and bring to boil. Reduce heat and simmer until beans are tender.

If you have failed to soak the beans overnight, cover them with cold water, bring to a boil, and simmer for 2 minutes. Remove from the heat and let stand tightly covered for 1 hour before continuing with the recipe. Do not overcook the beans to the point of mushiness. One test for doneness is to scoop up a few cooked beans in a spoon and blow on them. If the skins burst, they are cooked.

Black Bean Soup

Serves: 8

1¹/₂ cups dried black beans, picked over and soaked overnight in water to cover
¹/₄ cup olive oil
1 large onion, chopped
1 large bunch fresh coriander, stemmed and chopped
8 cloves garlic, minced
2¹/₂ teaspoons ground cumin
2 teaspoons ground coriander
¹/₂ teaspoon dried oregano, crumbled
1¹/₂ tablespoons chili powder
1¹/₂ teaspoons crushed dried red chiles
1 can (28 ounces) tomato purée
1 teaspoon black pepper
3 cups reduced-sodium, fat-free chicken broth
¹/₄ cup brandy or dry sherry
¹/₄ cup grated Parmesan cheese for garnish
chopped fresh coriander for garnish

Drain the beans and place in a large pot. Add water to cover, bring to a boil, reduce the heat to low, cover, and simmer for 2¹/₂ to 3 hours, or until the beans are very tender.

In a large skillet, heat the oil over medium-high heat. Add the onion, fresh coriander, garlic, cumin, ground coriander, oregano, chili powder, and crushed chiles until the onion is tender. Stir in the tomatoes, black pepper, and chicken broth. Cook for 5 minutes over medium heat, then set aside.

Drain the beans and let cool for 10 minutes. Purée in a blender or food processor. Return to the pot, add the contents of the skillet, and stir well. Place over medium heat and cook until heated through. Add additional broth if the soup is too thick. Stir in the brandy or sherry. Ladle the soup into bowls. Garnish with the Parmesan cheese and fresh coriander and serve.

Nutritional Analysis

Calories	285.29 Kcal.	Protein	12.67 gm.
Fat	8.62 gm.	Carbohydrate	37.80 gm.
Sodium	673.72 mg.	Cholesterol	1.97 mg.
Saturated Fat	1.53 gm.		

Broccoli-Leek Soup

Serves: 8

2 tablespoons olive oil
2 medium leeks, white parts only, finely chopped
1 pound red potatoes, peeled and finely chopped
1¹/₂ pounds broccoli florets and stalks, cut into 1-inch pieces
5 cups reduced-sodium, fat-free chicken broth
salt and white pepper to taste

Parmesan Topping:
¹/₂ cup plain nonfat yogurt
¹/₄ cup grated Parmesan cheese
pinch of white pepper

2 tablespoons snipped fresh chives for garnish

In a large soup pot heat the olive oil over medium heat. Add the leeks and sauté, until softened, 3 to 5 minutes. Add the potatoes and broccoli and sauté, stirring frequently, for 2 minutes. Add the broth and bring to a simmer. Cover partially and simmer until the vegetables are tender when pierced with a knife, 15 to 20 minutes.

Purée the soup in the pot with an immersion blender or in a food processor. Add salt and pepper and taste for seasoning. Reheat, if necessary, to serving temperature.

To make the Parmesan topping, combine the yogurt, cheese, and pepper in a small bowl and whisk until combined.

Ladle the soup into bowls and spoon the Parmesan topping on top, dividing it evenly. Garnish with the chives. Serve immediately.

Nutritional Analysis

Calories	141.37 Kcal.	Protein	7.66 gm.
Fat	4.60 gm.	Carbohydrate	18.88 gm.
Sodium	585.49 mg.	Cholesterol	2.25 mg.
Saturated Fat	0.99 gm.		

Cauliflower Soup

Serves: 8

2 tablespoons olive oil
2 small white onions, thinly sliced
3 small leeks, white parts only, chopped
2 shallots, chopped
2 quarts plus 1 cup reduced-sodium, fat-free
    chicken broth

2 large cauliflowers, cut into florets
about 1 cup plain low-fat yogurt
salt and white pepper to taste
16 asparagus tips

In a medium sauté pan, heat the olive oil over medium heat. Add the onions, leeks, and shallots and sauté, stirring often, until tender, 3 to 4 minutes; do not let them brown.

In a large saucepan, combine the sautéed vegetables, the 2 quarts chicken broth, and the cauliflower florets. Bring to a boil over high heat, reduce the heat to low, and simmer, uncovered, until the cauliflower florets are tender, about 30 minutes.

Working in batches, purée the cauliflower mixture until smooth. Strain through a sieve into a clean saucepan and add the yogurt in small amounts, stirring it in until the desired consistency is achieved.

Season the soup with salt and white pepper.

In a small saucepan, heat the 1 cup chicken broth until it simmers. Add the asparagus tips and cook until just tender, 3 to 5 minutes; do not overcook. Drain the asparagus.

Ladle the soup into bowls, and float 2 asparagus tips on each serving.

Nutritional Analysis

Calories	119.98 Kcal.	Protein	7.88 gm.
Fat	4.08 gm.	Carbohydrate	14.07 gm.
Sodium	674.21 mg.	Cholesterol	1.70 mg.
Saturated Fat	0.76 gm.		

Chili Bean Soup

Serves: 6

1 pound dried pink beans, picked over and
    soaked overnight in cold water to cover
6 to 8 cups water
1 teaspoon garlic salt
1 teaspoon onion salt
$1/4$ teaspoon dried thyme
$1/4$ teaspoon dried marjoram
$1^1/4$ cups reduced-sodium, fat-free beef or
    chicken broth
1 can (16 ounces) chopped tomatoes
1 packet McCormick's chili seasoning mix
1 cup hot water

Drain the beans and place in a large pot. Add the water, garlic and onion salts, thyme, and marjoram. Bring to a boil, reduce the heat to low, cover, and simmer until tender, $2^1/2$ to 3 hours. Don't let the beans boil dry; add hot water as needed.

Spoon out 3 cups of the cooked beans to use another day in another way. Using a potato masher, mash the remaining beans with their liquid. Add the broth, tomatoes, chili mix, and the 1 cup hot water. Stir well and heat for at least 10 minutes to blend the flavors. Ladle into soup bowls and serve.

Nutritional Analysis

Calories	298.11 Kcal.	Protein	17.84 gm.
Fat	1.35 gm.	Carbohydrate	55.36 gm.
Sodium	904.57 mg.	Cholesterol	0.00 mg.
Saturated Fat	0.24 gm.		

Pumpkin Cheese Soup

Serves: 8

1 large pumpkin, about 5–6 pounds
2 teaspoons butter, melted
1 large onion, chopped
2 large carrots, shredded
2 celery stalks, chopped
$4^1/2$ cups reduced-sodium vegetable broth
1 clove garlic, minced
$1/2$ teaspoon salt
$1/2$ teaspoon pepper
$1/2$ teaspoon nutmeg
$3/4$ cup plus 2 tablespoons 1% milk
1 cup low-fat cheddar cheese, grated
6 tablespoons dry white wine
$1/3$ cup minced fresh parsley

Preheat oven to 350°F. Butter a baking sheet.

To prepare the pumpkin, cut off the top and scoop out the seeds. Brush the inside with the melted butter. Replace the top and place the pumpkin on the baking sheet. Bake until tender when pierced with a fork, about 45 minutes. The pumpkin should be a bit droopy but still hold it shape well.

Meanwhile, melt the butter in a big saucepan. Add the onion, carrots, and celery and sauté until soft, about 10 minutes. Add the broth, garlic, salt, pepper, and nutmeg. Cover and simmer for 20 minutes. Remove from the heat and let cool slightly.

Working in 2 or 3 batches, purée the vegetable mixture in a blender or food processor.

Pour back into the saucepan and stir in the milk. Reheat gently. Add the cheese and wine and heat until the cheese melts, stirring frequently to avoid scorching.

Place the hot pumpkin on a serving platter and ladle in the soup. Sprinkle with the parsley.

To serve, ladle out soup at the table, scooping a little bit of pumpkin into each serving. The pumpkin then makes a great centerpiece for your table, while allowing people to have second helpings. After the soup is all gone, the pumpkin can be peeled, cut up, rinsed, and used in pumpkin pie. It may need more baking to become soft enough to purée for the pie filling.

Nutritional Analysis

Calories	122.45 Kcal.	Protein	8.31 gm.
Fat	3.80 gm.	Carbohydrate	13.48 gm.
Sodium	458.45 mg.	Cholesterol	11.62 mg.
Saturated Fat	2.29 gm.		

Hearty Bean Soup

Serves: 4

> 2 tablespoons buttery light, reduced-fat margarine
> 1/2 cup chopped celery
> 1/4 cup diced onions
> 2 tablespoons all-purpose flour
> 1 cup water
> 2/3 cup 1% low-fat milk
> 2 cans (16 ounces) white beans, drained
> 1 can (16 ounces) whole kernel corn with liquid

> 1 can (8 ounces) crushed tomatoes
> 3/4 cup low-fat shredded jack cheese
> 1/4 teaspoon salt
> 1/8 teaspoon pepper
> dash of Tabasco sauce
> sourdough bread for serving

In a saucepan, melt the margarine over medium heat. Add the celery and onion and sauté until onion is translucent, about 10 minutes. Stir in the flour until well blended. Slowly pour in the water and milk while stirring constantly, then cook, stirring, for 5 minutes, or until thickened and smooth. Add the beans, corn (with liquid), tomatoes, and cheese. Heat through, stirring often, but do not boil. Season to taste with salt, pepper, and Tabasco sauce. Serve with wedges of sourdough bread.

Nutritional Analysis

Calories	328.79 Kcal.	Protein	18.27 gm.
Fat	9.64 gm.	Carbohydrate	46.36 gm.
Sodium	1130.38 mg.	Cholesterol	16.63 mg.
Saturated Fat	4.18 gm.		

Cuban Black Bean Soup

Serves: 6

> 1 pound dried black beans, picked over and soaked overnight in water to cover
> 1 tablespoon butter
> 1 cup chopped onion
> 4 cups water
> 1 beef bouillon cube

(continued)

Blanching Vegetables

One way to make sure that vegetables are well cooked before you add them to a soup and to ensure that they don't turn soggy during cooking is to blanch them ahead of time. In a saucepan, bring about 4 cups of water to a boil. Add the vegetables, cook for 3 minutes, then remove and immediately rinse under cold water. This last step prevents the vegetables from absorbing excess liquid, in essence forming a seal on the skin.

2 bay leaves
$\frac{1}{2}$ teaspoon dried thyme, crumbled
$\frac{1}{2}$ teaspoon dried oregano, crumbled
$\frac{1}{2}$ teaspoon salt
1 red bell pepper, chopped
1 green bell pepper, chopped
4 cups hot cooked white rice

Drain the beans. In a large pot, melt the butter over medium heat. Add the onion and sauté for 5 minutes, or until onion is translucent. Add the drained beans, water, bouillon cube, bay leaves, thyme, oregano, salt, and red bell pepper. Bring to a boil, reduce the heat to low, cover, and simmer until the beans are tender, 1 to 1$\frac{1}{2}$ hours.

Remove 1 cup of the beans and mash in a bowl with a potato masher or fork. Return the mashed beans to the pot and mix well to thicken. Remove and discard the bay leaves. Add the green pepper and the rum (if using) to the beans. Cover and simmer for 15 minutes to blend the flavors. To serve, ladle the beans over the rice in shallow bowls.

Nutritional Analysis

Calories	431.43 Kcal.	Protein	19.83 gm.
Fat	3.40 gm.	Carbohydrate	81.22 gm.
Sodium	362.77 mg.	Cholesterol	5.19 mg.
Saturated Fat	1.55 gm.		

Tortilla Soup

Serves: 6

1 tablespoon vegetable or olive oil
1 small onion, chopped
4 or 5 green chile peppers, roasted, peeled, seeded, and chopped
2 cloves garlic, crushed
1 cup peeled and chopped tomatoes
1 can (14.5 ounces) reduced-sodium, fat-free beef broth
1 can (14.5 ounces) reduced-sodium, fat-free chicken broth
1$^1/_2$ cups water
1$^1/_2$ cups tomato juice
1 teaspoon ground cumin
1 teaspoon chili powder
1 teaspoon salt
$^1/_8$ teaspoon pepper
2 teaspoons Worcestershire sauce
1 tablespoon bottled steak sauce
3 corn tortillas, cut in $^1/_2$-inch-wide strips
$^1/_4$ cup shredded fat-free or low-fat cheddar cheese

In a large saucepan, heat the oil over medium heat. Add the onion, chiles, and garlic and cook until soft, about 5 minutes. Add the tomatoes, both broths, water, tomato juice, cumin, chili powder, salt, pepper, and Worcestershire and steak sauces. Bring to a boil, reduce the heat to low, cover, and simmer for 1 hour.

Add the tortillas and cheese, stir well, and simmer for 10 minutes longer. Ladle into soup bowls and serve.

Nutritional Analysis

Calories	110.38 Kcal.	Protein	5.97 gm.
Fat	2.92 gm.	Carbohydrate	16.81 gm.
Sodium	1082.45 mg.	Cholesterol	0.49 mg.
Saturated Fat	0.33 gm.		

Split Pea Soup

Serves: 6

2 tablespoons olive oil
1 medium onion, minced
2 carrots, diced
2 celery stalks, diced
2 cloves garlic, minced
$^1/_2$ teaspoon dried thyme, crumbled
1 teaspoon pepper
1 teaspoon Worcestershire sauce
$^1/_2$ teaspoon Tabasco sauce
2 cups (1 pound) dried green split peas, picked over and soaked overnight in 2 quarts cold water
2 bay leaves
2 whole cloves
2 pounds ham hocks
1 pound russet potatoes, peeled and diced
salt and pepper

In a soup pot, heat the oil over medium heat. Add the onion, carrots, celery, garlic, thyme, pepper, and Worcestershire and Tabasco sauces and sauté for 5 minutes, or until the vegetables soften. Add the split peas along with their soaking

(continued)

liquid, the bay leaves, cloves, ham hocks, and potatoes and bring to a boil. Skim off any foam that appears on the surface. Reduce the heat to low and simmer gently for 2 hours, or until the peas are tender.

Remove the ham hocks and, when cool enough to handle, remove the meat and cut into small cubes. Add to the pot and heat through, then ladle soup into bowls and serve.

Nutritional Analysis

Calories	456.77 Kcal.	Protein	27.56 gm.
Fat	10.04 gm.	Carbohydrate	66.04 gm.
Sodium	992.01 mg.	Cholesterol	21.56 mg.
Saturated Fat	2.00 gm.		

Autumn Soup

Serves: 6

4 cups reduced-sodium, fat-free chicken broth
1 cup chopped onion
2 slices bread, cut into cubes
2 tart apples, cored and coarsely chopped
1 butternut squash, about 1 pound, halved
    lengthwise and seeded
1 teaspoon salt
1 teaspoon diced marjoram
1 teaspoon diced rosemary
1 teaspoon pepper
2 eggs
1/2 cup buttermilk

Combine the broth, onion, bread cubes, apples, squash, salt, marjoram, rosemary, and

pepper in a large, heavy saucepan. Bring to a boil, reduce the heat to low, and simmer, covered, for 45 minutes. Remove from the heat.

Remove the squash halves and let cool slightly. Scoop out the squash flesh from the skins and return it to the saucepan; discard the skin.

Working in batches, purée the soup in a blender. Return the purée to the pan. In a small bowl, beat together the eggs and buttermilk. Stir a little of the hot soup into the egg mixture, and then add it to the soup. Reheat gently for 5 minutes to blend the flavors; do not boil. Ladle into bowls and serve.

Nutritional Analysis

Calories	132.86 Kcal.	Protein	6.48 gm.
Fat	2.43 gm.	Carbohydrate	22.42 gm.
Sodium	853.44 mg.	Cholesterol	71.72 mg.
Saturated Fat	0.72 gm.		

Corn Chowder

Serves: 8

4 cups baking potatoes, peeled and cut into
    large chunks
1 large onion, coarsely chopped
1 green bell pepper, chopped
2 cups corn kernels
1 cup low-fat evaporated milk

In a large soup pot, combine the potatoes, onion, and bell pepper. Add just enough water to cover the vegetables, bring to a boil, reduce the heat to low, and simmer for 10 minutes.

Add the corn and simmer for another 10 minutes, or until the potatoes are tender. Stir in the evaporated milk, bring back to a boil, and ladle into bowls to serve.

Nutritional Analysis

Calories	130.61 Kcal.	Protein	5.18 gm.
Fat	1.06 gm.	Carbohydrate	26.83 gm.
Sodium	46.38 mg.	Cholesterol	5.00 mg.
Saturated Fat	0.08 gm.		

Tuna Chowder

Serves: 8

> 2 tablespoons buttery light, reduced-fat
>   margarine
> 3 celery stalks, chopped
> 1 large onion, chopped
> 1 large baking potato, cut into $1/2$-inch dice
> 3 tablespoons all-purpose flour
> 3 cups 1% milk
> 2 cans ($6^1/2$ ounces each) water-packed tuna,
>   drained and flaked
> 1 cup grated non-fat cheddar cheese
> 1 teaspoon dried thyme, crumbled
> 1 teaspoon dried dill, crumbled
> salt and pepper to taste
> $1/4$ cup chopped fresh parsley

In a large, heavy pot, melt the margarine over medium-high heat. Add the celery, onion, and potato and sauté until the potato is tender. Add the flour and milk and blend thoroughly. Cook, stirring, until the mixture thickens, about 5

minutes. Add the tuna, cheese, thyme, and dill. Mix well and season with salt and pepper. Heat over medium-low heat for 5 to 10 minutes. Ladle into bowls and garnish with parsley, then serve.

Nutritional Analysis

Calories	173.28 Kcal.	Protein	21.55 gm.
Fat	2.78 gm.	Carbohydrate	15.57 gm.
Sodium	327.50 mg.	Cholesterol	22.38 mg.
Saturated Fat	1.03 gm.		

Grandma's Cabbage Soup

Serves: 8

> 1 tablespoon butter
> 1 tablespoon vegetable oil
> 2 cups chopped celery
> 2 cups chopped carrots
> 2 onions, coarsely chopped
> 2 cups chopped green cabbage
> 2 quarts reduced-sodium, fat-free chicken broth
> 1 pound red new potatoes, diced
> $1/2$ teaspoon dried marjoram, crumbled
> 1 teaspoon dried dill, crumbled
> salt and pepper to taste

In a large pot, melt the butter with the oil over medium heat. Add the celery, carrots, and onions and sauté until tender, about 15 minutes. When the vegetables are tender, add the cabbage and cook for 5 more minutes. Add the broth, bring to a boil, reduce the heat to low, and simmer, uncovered, for 15 minutes. Add the potatoes and herbs and cook for another 15 minutes. *(continued)*

Working in 3 batches, purée the soup in a food processor or blender and return to the pot. Cook for another 10 minutes to blend the flavors. Season with salt and pepper, then ladle into bowls to serve.

Nutritional Analysis

Calories	125.98 Kcal.	Protein	5.31 gm.
Fat	3.41 gm.	Carbohydrate	18.74 gm.
Sodium	620.67 mg.	Cholesterol	3.88 mg.
Saturated Fat	1.12 gm.		

Cream of Carrot Soup

Serves: 6

1 tablespoon olive oil
1 pound carrots
1 large onion, chopped
1/2 cup chopped celery
2 cups peeled and diced potato
1 clove garlic, minced
1 teaspoon sugar
4 whole cloves
pepper to taste
4 cups reduced-sodium, fat-free chicken broth

In a saucepan, heat the oil over medium heat. Add the carrots, onion, celery, potato, garlic, and sugar and sauté until onion is translucent, about 3 minutes. Reduce the heat to low, cover, and cook for 10 minutes. Uncover, add the cloves, pepper, and broth, and bring to a boil. Reduce the heat to low and cook, covered, until vegetables are tender, 15 to 30 minutes.

Remove and discard the cloves, then let the soup cool slightly. Working in batches, purée the soup in a food processor or blender until smooth. Return to a clean saucepan, reheat to serving temperature, and ladle into bowls to serve.

Nutritional Analysis

Calories	121.45 Kcal.	Protein	4.33 gm.
Fat	2.51 gm.	Carbohydrate	21.15 gm.
Sodium	413.67 mg.	Cholesterol	0.00 mg.
Saturated Fat	0.34 gm.		

Winter Potato and Vegetable Soup

Serves: 8

1 tablespoon butter
1 clove garlic, minced
1 large onion, chopped
6 cups reduced-sodium, fat-free chicken broth
3 medium russet potatoes, peeled and diced
2 medium carrots, sliced
2 medium celery stalks, minced
1 zucchini, sliced
1 teaspoon dried dill
1 bunch fresh parsley, minced
salt and pepper to taste
2 tablespoons cornstarch mixed with 2
   tablespoons cold water

In a sauté pan, melt the butter over medium heat. Add the garlic and onion and sauté for 4 minutes, or until the onion is soft. Add the broth, potatoes, carrots, celery, and zucchini and bring to

a boil. Reduce the heat to low and cook, covered, until the potatoes are tender, about 20 minutes.

Add the dill, parsley, salt, pepper, and corn-starch-water mixture, stir well, and continue to cook for about 15 minutes, or until the soup is slightly thickened. Ladle into bowls to serve.

Nutritional Analysis

Calories	103.07 Kcal.	Protein	4.28 gm.
Fat	1.64 gm.	Carbohydrate	17.79 gm.
Sodium	458.36 mg.	Cholesterol	3.88 mg.
Saturated Fat	0.89 gm.		

Zesty Gazpacho

Serves: 4

1 large cucumber, peeled and cut in half
2 large tomatoes, peeled and chopped
1 green bell pepper, chopped
1 medium onion, halved
3 cups tomato juice
1/4 cup red wine vinegar
1 tablespoon olive oil
1 teaspoon Tabasco sauce
1/2 teaspoon salt
1 teaspoon pepper
4 cloves garlic, minced

Place half the cucumber, 1 tomato, half the bell pepper, half the onion, and 1 cup of the tomato juice in a food processor and process until blended. Chop the remaining cucumber, tomato, bell pepper, and onion and place in a

(continued)

Reduced-Sodium Soy Sauce

It's always a good idea to choose the reduced-sodium soy sauce at the supermarket. But did you know it's easy to make your own soy sauce with less salt than the bottled variety, and cheaper, too?

Take a bottle of regular soy sauce and pour into a measuring cup. Add an equal amount of water, stir well, and you've made low-salt (relatively speaking) soy sauce. Pour into bottles and store in a cool cupboard.

large bowl. Stir in the purée and add the remaining tomato juice along with the vinegar, oil, Tabasco, salt, pepper, and garlic. Cover and chill for at least 2 hours before serving.

Nutritional Analysis

Calories	121.39 Kcal.	Protein	3.57 gm.
Fat	3.99 gm.	Carbohydrate	21.44 gm.
Sodium	973.53 mg.	Cholesterol	0.00 mg.
Saturated Fat	0.52 gm.		

Rich Potato Soup

Serves: 8

1 tablespoon butter
1 cup sliced leeks
1½ pounds red potatoes, peeled and sliced
3 cups reduced-sodium, fat-free chicken broth
Dash of ground nutmeg
2½ cups 1% milk
salt and pepper to taste

In a saucepan, melt the butter over medium heat. Add the leeks and sauté for 5 to 10 minutes, or until tender. Add the potatoes, broth, and nutmeg and bring to a boil. Reduce the heat to low and simmer, covered, for 30 minutes, or until the potatoes are very tender.

Let cool slightly. Working in batches, purée in a food processor or blender until smooth. Pour into a bowl and stir in the milk, salt, and pepper. Cover and chill well before serving.

Nutritional Analysis

Calories	120.27 Kcal.	Protein	5.29 gm.
Fat	2.40 gm.	Carbohydrate	19.22 gm.
Sodium	271.71 mg.	Cholesterol	6.93 mg.
Saturated Fat	1.39 gm.		

Lentil Soup

Serves: 10

2 tablespoons olive oil
3 large onions, chopped
3 carrots, grated
1 teaspoon dried marjoram, crumbled
1 teaspoon dried thyme, crumbled
1 can (28 ounces) tomatoes with their juice, coarsely chopped
2 quarts reduced-sodium, fat-free chicken broth
1½ cups dried brown lentils
salt and pepper to taste
½ cup dry white wine
¼ cup chopped fresh parsley
¼ cup grated Parmesan cheese

In a large saucepan, heat the oil over medium heat. Add the onions, carrots, marjoram, and thyme and sauté until onion is translucent, about 5 minutes. Add the tomatoes, broth, and lentils and bring to a boil. Reduce the heat to low, cover, and cook until the lentils are tender, about 1 hour. Add the salt, pepper, wine, and parsley and mix well. Ladle into bowls and sprinkle with the cheese.

Nutritional Analysis

Calories	202.39 Kcal.	Protein	13.09 gm.
Fat	3.91 gm.	Carbohydrate	28.28 gm.
Sodium	629.39 mg.	Cholesterol	1.58 mg.
Saturated Fat	0.83 gm.		

Turkey Chowder

Serves: 10

  2 tablespoons butter
  1 large onion, thinly sliced
  1 green bell pepper, chopped
  2 cups reduced-sodium, fat-free chicken broth
  3 medium carrots, sliced
  3 medium baking potatoes, peeled and diced
  2 celery stalks, thinly sliced
  1 teaspoon salt
  3 cups cooked, diced turkey
  1 can (17 ounces) corn kernels, drained
  1/2 teaspoon dried thyme, crumbled
  pepper to taste
  3 cups low-fat milk
  1/4 cup finely chopped fresh parsley

In a large skillet, melt the butter over medium heat. Add the onion and bell pepper and sauté for 10 minutes, or until onion is translucent. Stir in the broth and carrots and bring to a boil. Reduce the heat to low, cover, and cook for 5 minutes. Add the potatoes, celery, and salt. Cover and simmer until the potatoes and carrots are tender, about 10 minutes.

Add the turkey, corn, thyme, pepper, and milk. Heat through. Ladle into bowls, sprinkle with the parsley, and serve.

Nutritional Analysis

Calories	203.23 Kcal.	Protein	17.62 gm.
Fat	5.46 gm.	Carbohydrate	21.50 gm.
Sodium	524.72 mg.	Cholesterol	41.46 mg.
Saturated Fat	2.60 gm.		

Hearty Corn Chowder

Serves: 8

  4 cups cut-up potatoes (large chunks)
  1 large onion, chopped
  1 green bell pepper, chopped
  2 cups frozen corn kernels
  1 cup low-fat evaporated milk

In a saucepan, combine the potatoes, onion, and bell pepper with water to cover. Bring to a boil, reduce the heat to low, and simmer for 10 minutes. Add the corn and cook until vegetables are tender, about 10 more minutes. Stir in the milk and bring to serving temperature, stirring well. Ladle into bowls and serve.

Nutritional Analysis

Calories	133.58 Kcal.	Protein	5.18 gm.
Fat	0.92 gm.	Carbohydrate	28.03 gm.
Sodium	41.76 mg.	Cholesterol	5.00 mg.
Saturated Fat	0.06 gm.		

Chilled Cucumber-Mint Soup

Serves: 4

> 1 cucumber, halved, peeled, and seeded
> 1/4 cup chopped scallions
> 1/4 cup chopped fresh mint
> 2 cups low-fat milk
> 1 cup plain low-fat yogurt
> salt and pepper to taste

Purée the cucumber, scallions, and mint in a food processor or blender. Add the milk and yogurt and process until smooth. Transfer to a large bowl and stir in the yogurt. Season with salt and pepper. Cover and chill for 1 to 2 hours before serving.

Nutritional Analysis

Calories	99.12 Kcal.	Protein	7.59 gm.
Fat	2.26 gm.	Carbohydrate	12.49 gm.
Sodium	106.68 mg.	Cholesterol	8.28 mg.
Saturated Fat	1.37 gm.		

Using Lamb in Soup

Lamb is stronger in flavor than either beef or chicken, so it is a good choice to use in soups, as a little goes a long way. Nearly any cut of lamb will work well; shank or shoulder, for example, is less costly than most other cuts and provide plenty of good flavor. Just be sure to add the lamb early in the cooking, as it tastes best when tender, which comes from long, slow simmering.

Red Bean and Rice Soup

Serves: 6

> 1 tablespoon olive oil
> 1 onion, minced
> 4 celery stalks, chopped
> 2 cloves garlic, minced
> 2 tablespoons all-purpose flour
> 2 cups water
> 2 cups reduced-sodium, fat-free chicken broth
> 1 cup chopped tomatoes

¹/₂ cup white rice
1 tablespoon chili powder
¹/₂ teaspoon salt
1 can (19 ounces) kidney beans, drained
1 tablespoon lemon juice

In a large skillet, heat the oil over medium heat. Add the onion, celery, and garlic and cook for 5 minutes. Stir in the flour and cook for 1 minute. Add the water, broth, tomatoes, rice, chili powder, and salt. Bring to a boil, reduce the heat to low, cover, and cook until rice is tender, about 20 minutes.

Add the beans and lemon juice and heat through. Ladle into bowls to serve.

Nutritional Analysis

Calories	181.27 Kcal.	Protein	7.97 gm.
Fat	3.23 gm.	Carbohydrate	30.34 gm.
Sodium	532.55 mg.	Cholesterol	0.00 mg.
Saturated Fat	0.37 gm.		

Hearty Scotch Broth

Serves: 8

2 cups chopped cooked lamb, all visible fat removed
2 quarts water
1 bay leaf
2 medium onions, chopped
2 celery stalks, diced
4 medium potatoes, peeled and diced
¹/₃ cup pearl barley
2 cups chopped cabbage

3 carrots, grated
¹/₃ cup chopped fresh parsley
salt and pepper to taste

Put the lamb, water, bay leaf, and onions in a large pot. Bring to a boil, reduce the heat to low, cover, and simmer until onions are translucent and lamb is tender, about 45 minutes. Stir in the celery, potatoes, and barley and cook, covered, for 15 minutes. Add the cabbage and carrots and continue to cook until the vegetables are tender, about 15 minutes.

Discard the bay leaf and add the parsley, salt, and pepper. Ladle into bowls to serve.

Nutritional Analysis

Calories	182.23 Kcal.	Protein	12.24 gm.
Fat	3.59 gm.	Carbohydrate	25.81 gm.
Sodium	51.85 mg.	Cholesterol	30.47 mg.
Saturated Fat	1.30 gm.		

Summertime Potato Soup

Serves: 6

1 can (10³/₄ ounces) condensed cream of potato soup
1¹/₄ cups reduced-sodium, fat-free chicken broth
low-fat milk, as needed to fill the soup can
1 small onion, cut into chunks
2 scallions, minced

Place the cream of potato soup, chicken broth, and 1 soup can of milk into a blender or food processor and purée for 10 seconds until blended.

(continued)

Add the onion and purée until smooth. Transfer to a serving bowl, cover, and chill overnight. Ladle into chilled bowls and sprinkle with the scallions.

Nutritional Analysis

Calories	64.81 Kcal.	Protein	3.41 gm.
Fat	1.55 gm.	Carbohydrate	9.24 gm.
Sodium	550.43 mg.	Cholesterol	4.71 mg.
Saturated Fat	0.85 gm.		

Quick Borscht

Serves: 6

1 jar (16 ounces) pickled beets, drained
2 cups buttermilk
1 tablespoon sugar
2 tablespoons lemon juice
1/4 cup snipped fresh chives

Place the beets, buttermilk, sugar, and lemon juice in a blender or food processor. Purée until smooth. Ladle into bowls and top with the chives.

Nutritional Analysis

Calories	91.43 Kcal.	Protein	3.37 gm.
Fat	0.79 gm.	Carbohydrate	18.68 gm.
Sodium	286.54 mg.	Cholesterol	3.26 mg.
Saturated Fat	0.44 gm.		

Sweet Potato–Ginger Soup

Serves: 6

1 tablespoon olive oil
1 onion, chopped
2 tablespoons peeled and minced fresh ginger
1 butternut squash, about 1 1/2 pounds, peeled, seeded, and diced
4 large sweet potatoes, about 1 1/2 pounds total, peeled and diced
1 large russet potato, peeled and diced
2 quarts reduced-sodium, fat-free chicken broth
1/4 teaspoon salt
1/2 cup plain low-fat yogurt

Heat the oil over medium heat in a soup pot for 30 seconds. Add the onion and sauté until translucent, about 5 minutes. Add the ginger and cook for about 1 minute. Add the squash, sweet potatoes, russet potato, and broth. Bring to a boil, reduce the heat to low, cover, and cook until the vegetables are tender, about 30 minutes.

Let cool slightly, then, working in 1-cup batches, purée in a food processor or blender until smooth. Pour into a clean saucepan, stir in the yogurt, and reheat gently. Ladle into bowls and serve.

Nutritional Analysis

Calories	220.14 Kcal.	Protein	8.28 gm.
Fat	2.98 gm.	Carbohydrate	41.15 gm.
Sodium	779.73 mg.	Cholesterol	1.13 mg.
Saturated Fat	0.53 gm.		

Creamy Vegetable Soup

Serves: 6

2 cups water
3 cups broccoli florets
1 large carrot, diced
1 onion, chopped
1 cup coarsely chopped cauliflower
salt and pepper to taste
1/4 teaspoon dry mustard
1 cup 1% milk
3/4 cup shredded low-fat cheddar cheese
1/2 cup diced yellow summer squash

Bring the water to a boil in a saucepan. Add 2 cups of the broccoli, half of the carrot, and the onion and return to a boil. Reduce the heat to low, cover, and cook until the vegetables are tender, about 15 minutes.

Let cool slightly, then transfer to a food processor and purée until smooth. Return the broccoli purée to the saucepan. Add the remaining broccoli and carrot, the cauliflower, salt, pepper, mustard, and milk. Bring to a boil, reduce the heat to low, and cook, covered, until the vegetables are tender, about 10 minutes. Add cheese and squash, stir well, and cook, stirring, until the cheese melts and the squash is tender, about 5 minutes more. Ladle into bowls to serve.

Nutritional Analysis

Calories	83.87 Kcal.	Protein	9.45 gm.
Fat	0.92 gm.	Carbohydrate	11.58 gm.
Sodium	162.39 mg.	Cholesterol	3.12 mg.
Saturated Fat	0.30 gm.		

Potato and Corn Chowder

Serves: 6

4 russet potatoes, peeled and diced
2 1/2 cups water
1 onion, chopped
3 cloves garlic, minced
1 red bell pepper, diced
1 teaspoon ground cumin
1 teaspoon dried basil, crumbled
1 teaspoon salt
1/2 teaspoon black pepper
1 can (4 ounces) diced green chile peppers
1 package (10 ounces) frozen corn, thawed
2 cups 1% milk

Place the potatoes and 2 cups of the water in a large saucepan. Bring to a boil, reduce the heat to low, cover, and cook for 20 minutes, or until potatoes are tender. Heat 1/2 cup water in a saucepan, add the onion, garlic, and bell pepper, and cook for 5 minutes. Add the cumin, basil, salt, and black pepper and cook until the vegetables are tender, about 5 minutes longer. Meanwhile, mash the potatoes in their cooking water and add the onion mixture along with the chiles, corn, and milk. Stir to blend. Heat gently for 5 more minutes, or until heated through. Ladle into bowls to serve.

Nutritional Analysis

Calories	181.58 Kcal.	Protein	6.81 gm.
Fat	1.55 gm.	Carbohydrate	37.29 gm.
Sodium	555.72 mg.	Cholesterol	3.25 mg.
Saturated Fat	0.58 gm.		

Lime-Chicken Soup

Serves: 6

1/2 pound boneless, skinless chicken breasts
4 cups reduced-sodium, fat-free chicken broth
juice of 2 limes
1 teaspoon dried oregano, crumbled
1 teaspoon dried basil, crumbled
1 jalapeño pepper, minced
1 bay leaf
salt and black pepper to taste
1 tomato, peeled and chopped
1 red onion, chopped
1 tablespoon minced fresh coriander
1/4 pound low-fat Monterey Jack cheese, cubed
2 corn tortillas, cut into strips
4 lime slices
4 fresh coriander sprigs

Place the chicken breasts in a saucepan, add water to cover, bring to a simmer, and poach for about 10 minutes or until cooked through. Drain and let cool, then shred the meat. Set aside.

Combine the broth, lime juice, oregano, basil, jalapeño, bay leaf, salt, and pepper in a saucepan. Bring to a boil, reduce the heat to low, and simmer for 15 minutes. Add the chicken, tomato, red onion, and minced coriander. Return to a simmer and cook for 5 minutes. Ladle the soup into a large bowl. Add the cheese cubes. Garnish with the tortillas, lime slices, and coriander sprigs.

Nutritional Analysis

Calories	146.10 Kcal.	Protein	16.68 gm.
Fat	4.79 gm.	Carbohydrate	9.39 gm.
Sodium	577.87 mg.	Cholesterol	35.28 mg.
Saturated Fat	2.81 gm.		

Savory Tomato Soup

Serves: 4

1 teaspoon butter
2 tablespoons minced shallots
5 large tomatoes, diced
1 cup reduced-sodium, fat-free chicken broth
1 cup 1% milk
1 teaspoon dried oregano
1 teaspoon dried basil

In a large skillet, melt the butter over medium heat. Add the shallots and sauté for 5 minutes, or until shallots are tender. Add the tomatoes and chicken broth and simmer for 15 minutes.

Let cool slightly. Transfer to a food processor and purée until smooth. Return to the saucepan and add the milk. Reheat gently for 10 minutes to blend the flavors. Add the oregano and basil and ladle into bowls to serve.

Nutritional Analysis

Calories	103.11 Kcal.	Protein	5.38 gm.
Fat	2.56 gm.	Carbohydrate	17.37 gm.
Sodium	206.88 mg.	Cholesterol	5.03 mg.
Saturated Fat	1.13 gm.		

Onion and Garlic Soup

Serves: 6

  3 onions, sliced
  3 large shallots, minced
  1 head garlic, cloves separated and peeled
  1 tablespoon olive oil
  4 cups reduced-sodium, fat-free chicken broth
  1 teaspoon thyme, dried, crumbled
  salt and pepper to taste

Combine the onions, shallots, garlic, and oil in a large skillet. Place over very low heat and sauté for 15 minutes, or until the onions are golden. Pour in 1 cup of the chicken broth. Stir, loosening the caramelized bits stuck to the skillet bottom. Transfer to a saucepan and add the thyme and the remaining 3 cups of broth. Bring to a boil, reduce the heat to low, cover, and simmer until onion is tender, about 30 minutes. Season with salt and pepper.

Nutritional Analysis

Calories	78.10 Kcal.	Protein	3.61 gm.
Fat	2.42 gm.	Carbohydrate	10.90 gm.
Sodium	378.81 mg.	Cholesterol	0.00 mg.
Saturated Fat	0.32 gm.		

Reduced-Fat Broth

Although meat and chicken broths are relatively low fat already, you may want to go a step further and make them virtually fat free. First, place a lamb shank, beef bone, or chicken carcass in a large soup pot with enough water to cover. Add 1 bay leaf and 1 onion, chopped. Bring to a boil, lower the heat to low, and simmer, uncovered, for 1 hour. Remove the bone or carcass and strain the broth through a sieve into a clean container. Cover and place in the refrigerator overnight. The next day, skim off the fat that has solidified on top. Store in the refrigerator for up to two weeks.

Salads

CHAPTER FOUR

Amount Per Chapter
47 Recipes

% Daily Value

Easy to Prepare	**100%**
Low Fat / High Flavor	**100%**
Simple to Understand	**100%**

DELICIOUS, EASY, LOW-FAT RECIPES

I love salads, not only in hot weather but any time of year. They're easy to fix, usually requiring little preparation besides chopping and stirring for a couple of minutes, and they satisfy my urge for crunchy foods, a craving that commonly comes over me at least once a day.

In addition, most of the following recipes call for only a single bowl for assembly, which reduces stress by producing a minimum of dirty dishes to wash. This is an admirable goal to strive for no matter what the season.

Summertime Potato Salad
Serves: 8

Dressing:
1 cup plain low-fat yogurt
1 teaspoon ground cumin
1 teaspoon ground coriander
1 teaspoon pepper

2 pounds medium potatoes, peeled, boiled until tender, and cut into chunks
1 large onion, thinly sliced into rings
2 tablespoons minced fresh basil
dash of paprika

Whisk together all the dressing ingredients in a serving bowl. Add the potatoes and toss them gently to coat thoroughly. Place the onion rings on top and sprinkle the salad with basil and paprika. Cover and refrigerate for at least 30 minutes.

Nutritional Analysis

Calories	97.98 Kcal.	Protein	3.65 gm.
Fat	0.60 gm.	Carbohydrate	20.08 gm.
Sodium	26.45 mg.	Cholesterol	1.70 mg.
Saturated Fat	0.30 gm.		

Seafood Pasta Salad
Serves: 4

½ pound dry tricolored spiral pasta, cooked and chilled
1 cup cooked and peeled shrimp
1 green bell pepper, diced
¼ cup sliced carrots
½ cup sliced zucchini
⅓ cup Worcestershire sauce
⅓ cup low-fat mayonnaise
salt and pepper to taste

In a bowl, combine the pasta, shrimp, bell pepper, carrots, and zucchini, mixing gently. Add the Worcestershire sauce, mayonnaise, salt, and pepper and toss lightly to combine. Cover and refrigerate for at least 30 minutes before serving.

Nutritional Analysis

Calories	306.36 Kcal.	Protein	16.25 gm.
Fat	2.34 gm.	Carbohydrate	54.07 gm.
Sodium	509.63 mg.	Cholesterol	69.10 mg.
Saturated Fat	0.18 gm.		

Chinese Coleslaw

Serves: 6

4 cups shredded Chinese cabbage
1 can (8¹/₄ ounces) crushed pineapple, drained
1 can (8 ounces) water chestnuts, drained and
*   sliced*
1 cup chopped fresh parsley
¹/₄ cup sliced scallions
¹/₄ cup low-fat mayonnaise
1 tablespoon mustard
1 teaspoon peeled and grated fresh ginger

In a bowl, combine the cabbage, pineapple, water chestnuts, parsley, and scallions. Toss to mix. Cover and chill. In a small bowl, whisk together the mayonnaise, mustard, and ginger. Cover and chill. To serve, spoon the mayonnaise dressing over the cabbage mixture and toss to coat thoroughly.

Nutritional Analysis

Calories	66.43 Kcal.	Protein	1.42 gm.
Fat	0.93 gm.	Carbohydrate	14.41 gm.
Sodium	138.02 mg.	Cholesterol	0.00 mg.
Saturated Fat	0.04 gm.		

Crispy Caesar Salad

Serves: 4

1 large head romaine lettuce, chilled
nonstick olive oil–flavored cooking spray
2 large cloves garlic, minced
¹/₂ teaspoon anchovy paste

1 teaspoon Worcestershire sauce
¹/₄ cup lemon juice
grated Parmesan cheese (optional)
coarsely ground pepper

Place the romaine leaves in a serving bowl and spray lightly with the olive oil spray. In a small bowl, whisk together the garlic, anchovy paste, Worcestershire sauce, and lemon juice until blended. Pour the dressing on the romaine and toss well. Sprinkle with pepper (or cheese) and serve.

Nutritional Analysis

Calories	26.02 Kcal.	Protein	2.21 gm.
Fat	0.45 gm.	Carbohydrate	4.04 gm.
Sodium	39.30 mg.	Cholesterol	0.27 mg.
Saturated Fat	0.04 gm.		

Apricot-Coriander Salad

Serves: 6

2 cups bean sprouts
boiling water as needed
1 can (17 ounces) apricot halves in syrup
3 tablespoons white wine vinegar
1 teaspoon peanut oil
2 tablespoons soy sauce
1¹/₂ teaspoons ground ginger
4 cups shredded lettuce
¹/₄ cup minced fresh coriander
2 scallions, sliced on the diagonal
1 can (8 ounces) water chestnuts, drained
*   and sliced*

(continued)

Place the bean sprouts in a colander or large sieve. Pour boiling water over them; drain and cool. Drain the apricots, reserving 2 tablespoons syrup. Cut the apricots into strips and set aside.

In a jar with screw-top lid, combine the syrup, vinegar, oil, soy sauce, and ginger. Cover and shake well. Place the lettuce into a bowl or onto a platter. Top with the coriander, scallions, bean sprouts, and water chestnuts. Place the apricot strips over the salad. Shake the dressing again and pour over the salad. Toss well and serve.

Nutritional Analysis

Calories	139.97 Kcal.	Protein	3.98 gm.
Fat	1.48 gm.	Carbohydrate	31.28 gm.
Sodium	532.83 mg.	Cholesterol	0.00 mg.
Saturated Fat	0.24 gm.		

Hearts of Palm Salad

Serves: 4

Salad:
4 hearts of palm, quartered
4 Belgian endives, cut on the diagonal into $1/2$-
    inch pieces
2 bunches watercress, chopped
4 large tomatoes, sliced
1 tablespoon snipped fresh chives

Chutney Vinaigrette:
juice of 1 lemon
$1/4$ teaspoon curry powder
1 teaspoon red wine vinegar
$1/2$ teaspoon dry mustard

$1/2$ teaspoon salt
$1/4$ teaspoon white pepper
1 tablespoons virgin olive oil
$1/2$ cup mango chutney

On a large serving platter, arrange the hearts of palm, Belgian endives, watercress, and tomato slices in an attractive way. Cover and chill.

To make the chutney vinaigrette, combine the lemon juice, curry powder, vinegar, mustard, salt, and white pepper in a small bowl. Mix well. Add the olive oil and whisk until fully incorporated. Stir in the chutney. Chill the dressing in the refrigerator for at least an hour.

Spoon the vinaigrette over the salad. Sprinkle on the chives and serve.

Nutritional Analysis

Calories	232.33 Kcal.	Protein	5.83 gm.
Fat	4.45 gm.	Carbohydrate	44.18 gm.
Sodium	987.50 mg.	Cholesterol	0.00 mg.
Saturated Fat	0.64 gm.		

Black and White Bean Salad

Serves: 6

2 cups cooked small white beans
2 cups cooked black beans
$3/4$ cup frozen corn kernels, thawed
1 tomato, diced
$1/2$ cup diced red onions
2 tablespoons minced fresh coriander
1 tablespoon minced fresh mint
$1/2$ teaspoon salt

1/8 teaspoon cayenne pepper
3 tablespoons lime juice
1 tablespoon vegetable oil
2 tablespoons reduced-sodium,
*   fat-free chicken broth*

In a medium bowl, mix together all ingredients. Serve chilled or at room temperature. The salad may be refrigerated for up to 2 days before serving.

Nutritional Analysis

Calories	210.74 Kcal.	Protein	11.51 gm.
Fat	3.18 gm.	Carbohydrate	36.03 gm.
Sodium	211.93 mg.	Cholesterol	0.00 mg.
Saturated Fat	0.49 gm.		

Black Bean and Rice Salad

Serves: 8

1 1/4 cups reduced-sodium, fat-free chicken broth
1/4 cup water
1 cup long-grain white rice
1 can (15 ounces) black beans, drained and
*   rinsed*
1 red bell pepper, chopped
1/2 green bell pepper, chopped
1/2 medium-sized red onion, chopped

Dressing:

1 tablespoon olive oil
3 tablespoons orange juice
1 tablespoon red wine vinegar
2 teaspoons fresh coriander leaves

1 1/2 teaspoons ground cumin
1 teaspoon garlic salt
1/2 teaspoon chili powder

In a 2-quart saucepan, bring the chicken broth and water to a boil. Add the rice, cover, reduce the heat to low, and simmer for 20 minutes, or until all the liquid has been absorbed. Uncover, fluff with a fork, and turn into a large salad bowl.

Add the beans, red and green bell peppers, and onion and stir gently to combine.

In a small bowl, combine all the dressing ingredients and beat with a fork until well combined.

Pour the dressing over the rice mixture and stir gently. Cover and refrigerate for at least 4 hours before serving.

Nutritional Analysis

Calories	155.35 Kcal.	Protein	5.34 gm.
Fat	2.35 gm.	Carbohydrate	28.22 gm.
Sodium	436.42 mg.	Cholesterol	0.00 mg.
Saturated Fat	0.26 gm.		

California Black Bean Salad

Serves: 8

1 can (15 ounces) black beans, drained and
*   rinsed*
1 can (12 ounces) corn kernels, drained
1 tomato, chopped
1/2 cup chopped red onion
1/2 cup chopped green bell pepper
2 cloves garlic, minced

(continued)

3/4 cup low-fat Italian dressing
2 teaspoons minced fresh parsley
3/4 teaspoon tabasco sauce
1/2 teaspoon pepper
1/2 teaspoon garlic powder
1/2 teaspoon chili powder

In a bowl, mix together all the ingredients. Cover and chill for 30 minutes before serving.

Nutritional Analysis

Calories	135.85 Kcal.	Protein	4.02 gm.
Fat	0.77 gm.	Carbohydrate	16.39 gm.
Sodium	415.70 mg.	Cholesterol	0.00 mg.
Saturated Fat	0.04 gm.		

Fruity Brown Rice Salad

Serves: 6

1 can (16 ounces) fruit cocktail
1 cup cooked brown rice, chilled
1 tomato, diced
1 cup sliced celery
1/2 cup sliced scallions
2 tablespoons red wine vinegar
1 tablespoon vegetable oil
1 tablespoon Dijon mustard
1/2 teaspoon dried tarragon, crumbled
1/8 teaspoon garlic powder

Drain the fruit cocktail, reserving 1/4 cup of the liquid; save the remaining juice for another use. In a bowl, toss together the rice, fruit cocktail, tomato, celery, and scallions. Combine the 1/4 cup

Fruit Salad Days

Fruit salads can easily be enhanced or even turned into a main meal with a few judicious additions. Choose your favorites: a little shredded coconut, a handful of walnuts, a drizzle of honey, a scattering of raisins. Just a sprinkle or handful will do, so as not to overpower the delicate fruit and also to keep the fat content low.

reserved liquid, the vinegar, oil, mustard, tarragon, and garlic powder. Stir into the rice mixture. Cover and chill for at least an hour before serving.

Nutritional Analysis

Calories	104.82 Kcal.	Protein	1.67 gm.
Fat	2.65 gm.	Carbohydrate	18.97 gm.
Sodium	85.30 mg.	Cholesterol	0.00 mg.
Saturated Fat	0.34 gm.		

Chili Pepper Potato Salad

Serves: 10

2 pounds potatoes, peeled and chopped
   (about 6 medium)
1 cup low-fat mayonnaise
1 tablespoon vinegar
1 tablespoon mustard
1 teaspoon salt
1/4 teaspoon pepper
2 celery stalks, chopped
1 medium onion, chopped
1 can (4 ounces) chopped green chile peppers,
   drained
1 avocado, pitted, peeled, and chopped
2 tomatoes, chopped

Place the potatoes in a saucepan with water to cover, bring to a boil and cool for about 20 minutes, or until tender. Drain and let cool slightly.

In a large glass or plastic bowl, mix together the mayonnaise, vinegar, mustard, salt, and pepper. Add the potatoes, celery, and onion; toss

well. Stir in the chiles. Cover and refrigerate for at least 4 hours. Just before serving, stir in the avocado and tomatoes.

Nutritional Analysis

Calories	143.36 Kcal.	Protein	2.41 gm.
Fat	4.90 gm.	Carbohydrate	23.90 gm.
Sodium	561.61 mg.	Cholesterol	0.00 mg.
Saturated Fat	0.53 gm.		

Sunshine Bean Salad with Golden Gate Dressing

Serves: 8

Golden Gate Dressing:
1/3 cup sugar
1/2 teaspoon dry mustard
1 teaspoon salt
2 tablespoons all-purpose flour
1 egg
1/2 cup white wine vinegar
1/2 cup water
1 tablespoon butter

1 can (16 ounces) garbanzo beans, drained
1 can (8 ounces) corn kernels, drained
1 cup diced celery
1/2 cup chopped onion
2 tablespoons diced pimiento
1/4 cup diced green bell peppers

To make the dressing, in a small bowl, stir together the sugar, mustard, salt, and flour. In another small bowl, beat the egg with a fork.

(continued)

Beat in the dry mixture. In a small saucepan, heat together the vinegar, water, and butter over low heat until mixture simmers. Remove from the heat and gradually add the egg mixture, stirring vigorously. Return to the heat and cook, stirring constantly, until smooth and thick, 2 or 3 minutes. Chill. You should have about 1³/₄ cups. Leftover dressing is fine for potato, cabbage, tuna, or other salads and will keep in refrigerator for up to one week.

In a large glass bowl, combine the beans, corn, celery, onion, pimiento, and green pepper. Moisten to taste with the dressing. Chill before serving.

Nutritional Analysis

Calories	125.46 Kcal.	Protein	3.79 gm.
Fat	3.19 gm.	Carbohydrate	21.27 gm.
Sodium	431.56 mg.	Cholesterol	30.44 mg.
Saturated Fat	1.14 gm.		

Fruity Chicken Salad

Serves: 8

2¹/₂ cups shredded cooked chicken
1¹/₂ cups peeled melon chunks
1¹/₂ cups peeled cucumber chunks
1¹/₂ cups seedless green grapes
¹/₂ cup low-fat mayonnaise
2 tablespoons plain nonfat yogurt
1¹/₂ teaspoons cider vinegar
¹/₈ teaspoon salt
¹/₈ teaspoon pepper

¹/₃ cup chopped fresh coriander
2 tablespoons lime juice

In a medium bowl, combine the chicken, melon, cucumber, and grapes. In a larger bowl, whisk together the remaining ingredients to make a dressing. Add the chicken-fruit mixture to the dressing and toss to mix. Cover and chill for at least an hour before serving.

Nutritional Analysis

Calories	146.71 Kcal.	Protein	13.46 gm.
Fat	4.50 gm.	Carbohydrate	13.27 gm.
Sodium	222.60 mg.	Cholesterol	39.00 mg.
Saturated Fat	0.94 gm.		

Chicken Pasta Salad

Serves: 6

1 head broccoli, chopped
¹/₄ teaspoon salt
3 cups diced cooked chicken
¹/₂ pound pasta shells, cooked and drained
2 large tomatoes, cubed
¹/₂ cup coarsely chopped red onion
¹/₂ teaspoon pepper
1 cup low-calorie Italian dressing

Steam the broccoli over boiling water for about 5 minutes. Drain, place in a large bowl, and sprinkle with the salt. Chill by rinsing in cold water. Add the chicken, pasta, tomatoes, and onion and sprinkle with the pepper. Pour the

dressing over the salad and mix gently but thoroughly. Cover and chill before serving.

Nutritional Analysis

Calories	374.67 Kcal.	Protein	28.01 gm.
Fat	11.60 gm.	Carbohydrate	39.41 gm.
Sodium	612.48 mg.	Cholesterol	62.30 mg.
Saturated Fat	2.22 gm.		

Avocado-Citrus Salad

Serves: 6

3 corn tortillas, each 6 inches in diameter
4 oranges
4 grapefruits
2 tablespoons honey
2 tablespoons raspberry vinegar
1 avocado, pitted, peeled, and sliced
6 fresh mint sprigs

Preheat oven to 275°F.

Slice corn tortillas into very narrow strips. Spread out on a baking sheet and bake until lightly brown, about 15 minutes. Set aside to cool.

Grate enough zest from the oranges to yield about 4 tablespoons. Set aside. Using a sharp knife, peel the oranges and grapefruits, removing all the bitter white membrane, then free the sections from the membranes by cutting along either side of each section. Remove any seeds and set the sections aside.

In a large bowl, mix together the honey, vinegar, and the orange and grapefruit sections,

tossing to coat evenly. Add the orange zest and the tortilla strips and toss gently to distribute evenly. Transfer to individual plates. Top each serving with the avocado slices and a mint sprig.

Nutritional Analysis

Calories	205.76 Kcal.	Protein	3.16 gm.
Fat	5.81 gm.	Carbohydrate	39.82 gm.
Sodium	23.97 mg.	Cholesterol	0.00 mg.
Saturated Fat	0.89 gm.		

Curried Bean and Rice Salad

Serves: 6

1 tablespoon butter or buttery light, reduced-fat margarine
1 teaspoon curry powder
3/4 cup reduced-sodium, fat-free chicken broth
1/3 cup long-grain rice
1/4 cup chopped celery
2 tablespoons chopped scallions
2 tablespoons chopped green bell peppers
1 tablespoon lime juice
1 can (16 ounces) kidney beans, drained
1/4 cup plain nonfat yogurt
2 tablespoons toasted slivered blanched almonds
1/4 teaspoon salt
dash of pepper
1 large tomato, cut into wedges
1 fresh parsley sprig

(continued)

In a small saucepan, melt the butter (or margarine) over medium-high heat. Add the curry powder and sauté for several seconds. Stir in the chicken broth and bring to a boil. Add the rice, cover, reduce the heat to low, and cook for 20 minutes, or until all the liquid is absorbed and the rice is tender.

Stir in the celery, scallions, bell pepper, and lime juice. Transfer to a bowl, let cool, cover, and chill thoroughly. Stir in the beans, yogurt, almonds, and salt and pepper. Garnish with the tomato and parsley and serve.

Nutritional Analysis

Calories	142.76 Kcal.	Protein	6.55 gm.
Fat	4.03 gm.	Carbohydrate	20.45 gm.
Sodium	295.68 mg.	Cholesterol	5.35 mg.
Saturated Fat	1.38 gm.		

Mixed Greens with Honey and Oranges

Serves: 6

¹/₄ cup water
¹/₄ cup honey
¹/₄ cup white vinegar
2 heads butter lettuce
2 heads radicchio
3 oranges

In a small saucepan, bring the water, honey, and vinegar to a boil; reduce the heat and simmer for 2 minutes. Remove from the heat; let cool.

Arrange the butter lettuce and radicchio on 6 salad plates. Using a sharp knife, peel the oranges, removing all the bitter white membrane, then free the sections from the membranes by cutting along either side of each section. Remove any seeds and divide the orange sections among the salad plates. Drizzle each salad with the cooled dressing and serve.

Nutritional Analysis

Calories	94.63 Kcal.	Protein	1.80 gm.
Fat	0.35 gm.	Carbohydrate	23.80 gm.
Sodium	11.69 mg.	Cholesterol	0.00 mg.
Saturated Fat	0.05 gm.		

Mai Fun Chicken Salad with Hoisin Dressing

Serves: 6

Hoisin Dressing:
3 tablespoons rice vinegar or white wine vinegar
2 tablespoons peanut oil
1 tablespoon hoisin sauce
2 teaspoons sesame seeds
2 teaspoons peeled and minced fresh ginger

napa or savoy cabbage leaves
1 package (8 ounces) mai fun (rice sticks), cooked and chilled
1 cup finely shredded carrots
2 whole chicken breasts, cooked, skinned, boned, and sliced

1/2 *cup sugar snap peas, blanched briefly,*
   drained, and chilled
1 *cucumber, peeled and chopped*

To make the dressing, combine the vinegar, oil, hoisin sauce, sesame seeds, and ginger in a jar with a screw-top lid. Cover and shake well. Chill.

For each serving, line a salad plate with cabbage leaves and arrange a layer of the rice sticks on top. Then arrange the carrots, chicken slices, and sugar snap peas on top. Garnish with cucumber and carrot, as desired. Shake dressing again and pass at the table.

Nutritional Analysis

Calories	293.36 Kcal.	Protein	18.58 gm.
Fat	7.09 gm.	Carbohydrate	37.41 gm.
Sodium	170.15 mg.	Cholesterol	48.73 mg.
Saturated Fat	1.39 gm.		

Manhattan Deli-Style Salad

Serves: 6

1 1/4 *cups pitted black olives, sliced*
1 *cup chopped red or green bell pepper or*
   pimiento
1 *small red onion, thinly sliced into rings*
1/4 *cup grated Parmesan cheese*
1/4 *cup finely chopped fresh parsley*
1 *tablespoon capers*
3/4 *cup low-fat Italian dressing*
1 *package (12 ounces) fusilli, cooked, drained,*
   and cooled

(continued)

Parsley Hints

Lots of fruit and vegetable salads benefit from a couple of sprigs of parsley. The problem is that you need to buy a whole bunch to get those few sprigs. Parsley, however, will stay crisp and fresh for up to a week if you store it standing in a glass of ice water in the refrigerator. Change the water every couple of days, and give some parsley to the dog to freshen his breath.

In a large bowl, combine the olives, bell pepper (or pimiento), onion, cheese, parsley, capers, and dressing. Mix well. Add the pasta and toss to coat evenly. Serve at room temperature or chilled.

Nutritional Analysis

Calories	351.72 Kcal.	Protein	9.34 gm.
Fat	4.94 gm.	Carbohydrate	49.36 gm.
Sodium	621.94 mg.	Cholesterol	2.63 mg.
Saturated Fat	1.15 gm.		

Mariner Bean Salad Plate

Serves: 8

2¹/₂ cups well-drained cooked small white beans

2¹/₂ cups well-drained cooked pink beans

2¹/₂ cups diced, skinned cooked chicken

¹/₂ pound low-fat cheddar cheese, cut into ¹/₂-inch cubes

¹/₄ teaspoon dried basil, crumbled

1 tablespoon sugar

¹/₂ cup low-fat Italian dressing

1 head iceberg lettuce, separated into leaves

1 can (6 ounces) marinated artichoke hearts, drained and halved

1 lemon, cut into wedges

In a bowl, combine the beans and cheese. In a small bowl, stir the basil and sugar into the dressing. Pour over the bean mixture and toss well. Cover and chill for about 1 hour.

Line 8 individual salad plates with the lettuce. Mound about 1 cup of the bean mixture in the center of each plate. Garnish each plate with artichoke hearts and a lemon wedge.

Nutritional Analysis

Calories	394.44 Kcal.	Protein	35.62 gm.
Fat	5.79 gm.	Carbohydrate	44.25 gm.
Sodium	488.30 mg.	Cholesterol	41.93 mg.
Saturated Fat	1.30 gm.		

Peach-Spinach Salad

Serves: 6

1¹/₂ cups spinach, stems removed and leaves torn

1 cup cucumbers, scored and sliced

1 fresh peach, pitted, peeled, and sliced

2 fresh plums, pitted and sliced

¹/₄ cup scallions, sliced

1 cup plain low-fat yogurt

1 tablespoon lemon juice

1 tablespoon water

¹/₄ teaspoon dried dill, crumbled

In a large bowl or on 6 salad plates, combine the spinach, cucumber, peach, plums, and scallions. In a small bowl, whisk together the yogurt, lemon juice, water, and dill until smooth. Toss with salad and serve.

Nutritional Analysis

Calories	52.58 Kcal.	Protein	2.86 gm.
Fat	0.78 gm.	Carbohydrate	9.44 gm.
Sodium	38.54 mg.	Cholesterol	2.26 mg.
Saturated Fat	0.38 gm.		

Summer Peach Pasta Salad

Serves: 3

1 tablespoon olive oil
2 spinach leaves, torn
$1/2$ julienned zucchini
6 ounces penne or rigatoni, cooked and
    drained, chilled
4 peaches, pitted, peeled, and sliced
$1/3$ cup grated Parmesan cheese
$1/4$ cup chopped fresh basil leaves
2 tablespoons white wine vinegar
$1/2$ teaspoon pepper

In a skillet, heat the oil over medium heat. Add the spinach and zucchini and sauté until the spinach is limp, about 5 minutes. In a salad bowl, toss together the pasta, peaches, cheese, basil, vinegar, and pepper, mixing well. Serve chilled.

Nutritional Analysis

Calories	373.02 Kcal.	Protein	12.62 gm.
Fat	8.26 gm.	Carbohydrate	63.59 gm.
Sodium	170.75 mg.	Cholesterol	6.95 mg.
Saturated Fat	2.41 gm.		

Warm Chinese Chicken Salad

Serves: 4

1 cup low-fat Italian dressing
2 teaspoons low-sodium soy sauce
1 teaspoon peeled and minced fresh ginger
2 skinless, boneless whole chicken breasts, split
8 cups torn salad greens
$1/4$ cup chopped fresh coriander (optional)
$1/4$ cup diagonally sliced scallions
5 peaches, peeled
$1/4$ cup sliced almonds, toasted
2 tablespoons sesame seeds, toasted (optional)

In a large lock-top plastic bag, combine the dressing, soy sauce, and ginger. Add the chicken, seal the bag securely, and turn to coat the chicken well. Refrigerate for 30 minutes.

Prepare a fire in a charcoal grill or preheat a broiler.

Arrange greens on 4 salad plates. Sprinkle with the coriander. Top with the scallions. Pit and slice 3 of the peaches and arrange on the lettuce. Remove the chicken from the marinade, reserving the marinade. Grill or broil the chicken, turning once and basting occasionally with the marinade, until browned and cooked through. Set aside; keep warm.

Halve and pit the remaining 2 peaches. Baste with the marinade. Grill or broil, turning once, until browned and tender, about 5 minutes. Slice the chicken breasts and arrange the chicken and grilled peach halves on the lettuce.

(continued)

In a small saucepan, bring the remaining marinade to a boil (this can be done on the grill, if desired). Add the almonds and sesame seeds (if using). Pour over the salads and serve immediately.

Nutritional Analysis

Calories	417.38 Kcal.	Protein	31.28 gm.
Fat	4.93 gm.	Carbohydrate	27.54 gm.
Sodium	679.27 mg.	Cholesterol	68.44 mg.
Saturated Fat	0.71 gm.		

White Bean Salad with Pistachios

Serves: 4

> 1 can (15 ounces) small white beans, drained
>   and rinsed
> 2 cups sliced celery
> 1/2 cup diced red onions
> 1/3 cup shelled pistachio nuts, coarsely chopped
> 1 teaspoon pepper
> 2 tablespoons fresh thyme leaves
> 1 teaspoon dried tarragon, crumbled
> 1/3 cup distilled white vinegar
> 2 tablespoons sugar
> 1 cup mixed greens

In a bowl, combine all the ingredients except the salad greens and toss well. Cover and chill for 1 to 2 hours, to allow the flavors to blend.

Divide the greens among 6 salad plates and spoon the bean mixture on top, dividing it evenly.

Nutritional Analysis

Calories	118.96 Kcal.	Protein	6.11 gm.
Fat	3.78 gm.	Carbohydrate	20.70 gm.
Sodium	284.32 mg.	Cholesterol	0.00 mg.
Saturated Fat	0.44 gm.		

Curried Coleslaw

Serves: 6

> 4 cups shredded cabbage
> 1/2 cup shredded carrot
> 1 medium green bell pepper, cut into slivers
> 1/4 cup cider vinegar
> 1 tablespoon low-fat mayonnaise
> 1/4 cup minced onion
> 2 teaspoons lemon juice
> 1 tablespoon sugar
> 1 teaspoon curry powder
> pepper to taste

Combine the cabbage, carrot, and green pepper in a large bowl. In a small bowl, combine all the remaining ingredients, mixing well. Pour over the cabbage mixture, toss well, and chill it for at least 2 hours. Stir again briefly before serving.

Nutritional Analysis

Calories	36.10 Kcal.	Protein	0.86 gm.
Fat	0.32 gm.	Carbohydrate	8.41 gm.
Sodium	36.02 mg.	Cholesterol	0.00 mg.
Saturated Fat	0.00 gm.		

Fruity Coleslaw

Serves: 6

3 firm pears, peeled, cored, and diced
1 firm tart apple, peeled, cored, and diced
3 tablespoons lemon juice
3 cups shredded cabbage
1/3 cup raisins or dried currants
1 cup plain low-fat yogurt
1 teaspoon grated lemon zest
1 tablespoon honey

Toss the diced pears and apples with 2 tablespoons of the lemon juice. Add the cabbage and raisins (or currants), mixing well. In a small bowl, combine all the remaining ingredients, including the 1 tablespoon lemon juice, and mix well. Add to the cabbage mixture. Toss well and chill for 1 hour before serving.

Nutritional Analysis

Calories	129.82 Kcal.	Protein	3.04 gm.
Fat	1.08 gm.	Carbohydrate	29.99 gm.
Sodium	35.46 mg.	Cholesterol	2.26 mg.
Saturated Fat	0.40 gm.		

Apple Salad

Serves: 4

2 large Red Delicious apples, peeled, cored, and cut into chunks
1 can (6 ounces) crushed pineapple, drained, juice reserved
1/3 cup diced celery

2 tablespoons raisins
1/4 cup plain low-fat yogurt
1 tablespoon low-fat mayonnaise
1/4 teaspoon ground cinnamon

In a large bowl, combine the apples, pineapple, celery, and raisins. In a small bowl, combine all the remaining ingredients, including 2 tablespoons of the reserved juice, and mix well. Add to the fruit mixture and mix gently to coat, then serve.

Nutritional Analysis

Calories	98.11 Kcal.	Protein	1.23 gm.
Fat	0.73 gm.	Carbohydrate	23.61 gm.
Sodium	54.52 mg.	Cholesterol	0.85 mg.
Saturated Fat	0.17 gm.		

Four-Bean Salad

Serves: 8

1 can (19 ounces) garbanzo beans, drained and rinsed
1 can (19 ounces) red kidney beans, drained and rinsed
1 can (19 ounces) black beans, drained and rinsed
1 can (19 ounces) white kidney beans, drained and rinsed
1 large onion, diced
1/2 cup diced celery
1 cup low-fat Italian dressing
salt and pepper to taste
1 tablespoon chopped fresh parsley

(continued)

In a large bowl, combine all the beans. Add the onion and celery. Toss gently with the dressing until the ingredients are thoroughly coated. Season with salt and pepper, and sprinkle with parsley. Cover and refrigerate for 2 hours before serving.

Nutritional Analysis

Calories	284.70 Kcal.	Protein	13.33 gm.
Fat	2.34 gm.	Carbohydrate	35.33 gm.
Sodium	700.41 mg.	Cholesterol	0.00 mg.
Saturated Fat	0.09 gm.		

Waldorf Salad

Serves: 6

> 2 Red Delicious apples, unpeeled, cored and cubed
> 24 red grapes
> 24 green grapes
> 2 oranges, peeled and sectioned
> 1 cup plain nonfat yogurt
> 1 tablespoon honey
> 4 large lettuce leaves
> 2 bananas, peeled and sliced
> 1/4 cup walnuts, chopped

In a bowl, toss together the apples, grapes, and oranges. In a small bowl, stir together the yogurt and honey. Mix into the fruit, tossing to coat evenly.

Place a lettuce leaf on each salad plate and top with the fruit salad, dividing it evenly. Place the bananas around the circumference of the plates, and sprinkle the walnuts over all.

Nutritional Analysis

Calories	190.48 Kcal.	Protein	4.30 gm.
Fat	3.90 gm.	Carbohydrate	38.61 gm.
Sodium	54.59 mg.	Cholesterol	0.75 mg.
Saturated Fat	0.50 gm.		

Busy Day Salad

Serves: 2

> 2 cups lettuce, torn into bite-sized pieces
> 1/4 cup shredded carrots
> 1/4 cup garbanzo beans
> 1 small tomato, sliced
> 1/2 small red onion, sliced
> 4 pitted black olives
> 1/2 cup low-fat dressing of choice

In a large salad bowl, combine the lettuce, carrots, garbanzo beans, tomato, onion, and olives. Toss well. Drizzle with the dressing, toss again, and serve.

Nutritional Analysis

Calories	240.37 Kcal.	Protein	3.61 gm.
Fat	1.71 gm.	Carbohydrate	18.37 gm.
Sodium	573.06 mg.	Cholesterol	0.00 mg.
Saturated Fat	0.19 gm.		

Herbed Pasta Salad

Serves: 4

> 4 cups cooked rotelle pasta
> 1 cup cooked broccoli florets
> 1 cup cooked cauliflower florets
> $1/2$ cup thinly sliced carrots
> 1 red bell pepper, chopped
> 1 jar (4 ounces) marinated artichoke hearts, drained
> $1/2$ cup pitted black olives
> 1 tomato, chopped
> 4 scallions, thinly sliced
> $1/2$ cup low-calorie bottled Italian dressing

In a large bowl, combine the pasta, broccoli, cauliflower, carrots, bell pepper, artichoke hearts, black olives, tomato, and scallions. Toss well. Pour the dressing over the pasta and vegetables and toss to coat thoroughly. Refrigerate for several hours before serving.

Nutritional Analysis

Calories	353.48 Kcal.	Protein	9.62 gm.
Fat	5.23 gm.	Carbohydrate	51.18 gm.
Sodium	566.43 mg.	Cholesterol	0.00 mg.
Saturated Fat	0.68 gm.		

Cooking Pasta for Salad

When preparing a cold pasta salad, you can save time by cooking a batch of pasta in advance. Once cooked, rinse immediately under cold water and drain thoroughly, then pat with paper towels to absorb the excess moisture. Place in a large lock-top plastic bag and store in the refrigerator. The pasta will keep for up to 3 days.

Citrus Rice Salad

Serves: 4

> 1 celery stalk, thinly sliced
> 4 scallions, sliced
> $1/2$ cup drained canned mandarin oranges

(continued)

¹/₂ cup sliced cucumber
¹/₄ cup raisins
2 cups cooked white rice, at room temperature
1 cup plain low-fat yogurt
2 tablespoons orange juice
2 tablespoons honey
¹/₂ teaspoon ground ginger

In a large bowl, combine the celery, scallions, oranges, cucumber, and raisins. Gently stir in the rice. In a small bowl, stir together the yogurt, orange juice, honey, and ginger, mixing well. Pour over the salad and toss gently to coat.

Nutritional Analysis

Calories	269.07 Kcal.	Protein	6.93 gm.
Fat	5.83 gm.	Carbohydrate	49.58 gm.
Sodium	56.05 mg.	Cholesterol	3.40 mg.
Saturated Fat	1.03 gm.		

Tomato and Red Onion Salad

Serves: 6

4 large tomatoes, sliced
1 teaspoon dried basil, crumbled
2 teaspoons olive oil
1 tablespoon red wine vinegar
2 cloves garlic, minced
salt and pepper to taste
1 red onion, sliced

Make a layer with about one-third of the tomato slices in a shallow serving dish. Sprinkle

Buying Fresh Herbs

It used to be that I could only find fresh herbs in the summertime. Today, suppliers have recognized that people all over the country appreciate fresh basil, dill, and other herbs year-round. Some are sold prepackaged, while others are sold loose. Look for them in the produce department of your market.

Before you buy, check for any brown or dry leaves. Sniff the herbs: they should be fully aromatic. If none of the herbs appear fresh, tell your produce manager. A new shipment of herbs may be sitting in the stockroom, ready to be put out.

with about one-fourth of the basil, olive oil, vinegar, garlic, salt, and pepper. Cover with half of the onion slices, and sprinkle with more of the oil, vinegar, and seasonings. Cover with another layer of tomato slices and more of the seasonings. Repeat the layers, using the remaining tomatoes, onions, and seasonings. Chill before serving.

Nutritional Analysis

Calories	59.01 Kcal.	Protein	1.83 gm.
Fat	2.02 gm.	Carbohydrate	10.20 gm.
Sodium	16.88 mg.	Cholesterol	0.00 mg.
Saturated Fat	0.27 gm.		

Mediterranean Lentil and Bean Salad

Serves: 6

3 red bell peppers
1 can (19 ounces) white beans, drained and rinsed
2 cups well-drained cooked lentils
1/2 cup diced celery
1/4 cup chopped fresh basil
1/4 cup chopped fresh parsley
1/3 cup balsamic vinegar
salt and pepper to taste

Preheat a broiler.

Grill the bell peppers under the broiler for 15 minutes, turning once or twice, until the skin is blackened and blistered. Remove from the broiler and, when cool enough to handle, pull away the blackened skin. Then remove the skins and seeds and cut into narrow strips. Combine the peppers, beans, lentils, celery, basil, and parsley in a medium bowl. Add vinegar and mix thoroughly. Season with salt and pepper. Chill for at least one hour before serving.

Nutritional Analysis

Calories	196.59 Kcal.	Protein	12.98 gm.
Fat	0.61 gm.	Carbohydrate	36.44 gm.
Sodium	17.03 mg.	Cholesterol	0.00 mg.
Saturated Fat	0.40 gm.		

Light Chinese Chicken Salad

Serves: 6

2 tablespoons soy sauce
1 tablespoon white wine vinegar
1 tablespoon Asian sesame oil
1 tablespoon peanut oil
1 tablespoon peeled and minced fresh ginger
3 cloves garlic, minced
1/2 teaspoon pepper
1/4 teaspoon dry mustard
1 whole chicken breast, poached, boned, skinned, and diced
3 cups cooked white rice
1 red bell pepper, chopped
1 cup sliced celery
1 cup bean sprouts
1 cup sliced scallions
1/2 pound snow peas

(continued)

In a medium bowl, stir together the soy sauce, vinegar, sesame oil, peanut oil, ginger, garlic, pepper, and mustard. Add the chicken, toss well, and chill for 1 hour.

Add the rice, red pepper, celery, sprouts, scallions, and snow peas to the chicken mixture. Stir gently and serve.

Nutritional Analysis

Calories	230.14 Kcal.	Protein	13.56 gm.
Fat	5.95 gm.	Carbohydrate	30.22 gm.
Sodium	388.20 mg.	Cholesterol	24.36 mg.
Saturated Fat	1.05 gm.		

Daikon Salad

Serves: 4

2 tablespoons rice vinegar
1 tablespoon sake
1 tablespoon soy sauce
1 teaspoon sugar
9 ounces or 10 medium radishes, sliced
1 carrot, sliced

In a bowl, stir together the rice vinegar, sake, soy sauce, and sugar, mixing well. Add the radishes and carrot, and toss well with the dressing. Cover and chill for 2 hours before serving.

Nutritional Analysis

Calories	29.71 Kcal.	Protein	0.79 gm.
Fat	0.37 gm.	Carbohydrate	5.67 gm.
Sodium	279.11 mg.	Cholesterol	0.00 mg.
Saturated Fat	0.01 gm.		

Snow Pea Salad

Serves: 4

1 pound snow peas
1 small red onion, chopped
1/4 cup fresh mint leaves, chopped
1 cup cooked, chilled rice
2 tablespoons raspberry vinegar
1 tablespoon olive oil
salt and pepper to taste
1/4 teaspoon sugar

Steam the snow peas for 3 minutes. Rinse under cold water, drain, and place in the refrigerator for 30 minutes to chill.

Place the peas in a serving bowl. Add the rice, onion, and mint; toss well. In a small bowl, stir together the vinegar, oil, salt, pepper, and sugar. Pour the dressing over the salad and toss again. Chill for 30 minutes before serving.

Nutritional Analysis

Calories	140.62 Kcal.	Protein	4.78 gm.
Fat	3.76 gm.	Carbohydrate	22.38 gm.
Sodium	9.62 mg.	Cholesterol	0.00 mg.
Saturated Fat	0.52 gm.		

Macaroni and Bean Salad

Serves: 4

> 1 cup elbow macaroni
> 1/4 cup grated Parmesan cheese
> 1 can (16 ounces) kidney beans, drained,
>   liquid reserved, and rinsed
> 1 onion, chopped
> 3 celery stalks, minced
> 1 teaspoon curry powder
> 1 tablespoon honey
> 1/3 cup cider vinegar
> 1/2 cup raisins

Cook the macaroni for 8 to 10 minutes, until done. Drain, transfer to a serving bowl and toss with the cheese. Add the beans, onion, and celery. Pour the liquid from the beans into a measuring cup and add enough water to make 1 cup. Put the liquid into a small saucepan. Add the curry powder, honey, vinegar, and raisins and stir well. Bring to a boil, reduce the heat to low, and cook for 5 to 10 minutes, or until the raisins are plump. Pour the dressing over the macaroni mixture and toss well. Chill for 1 hour before serving.

Nutritional Analysis

Calories	307.98 Kcal.	Protein	12.67 gm.
Fat	2.51 gm.	Carbohydrate	61.57 gm.
Sodium	518.63 mg.	Cholesterol	3.95 mg.
Saturated Fat	1.10 gm.		

Garbanzo Beans 101

It's simple to pick up a couple of cans of garbanzo beans at the supermarket, but if you really like garbanzo beans, cook your own.

First, soak 1 pound (about 2 cups) dried garbanzo beans in 4 cups of water overnight. Drain, place in a saucepan, and add water to cover. Bring to a boil, then reduce the heat to low. Cover and cook very gently for at least 2 hours, or until tender.

Tricolor Pepper Salad

Serves: 8

2 red bell peppers, chopped
2 yellow bell peppers, chopped
2 green bell peppers, chopped
2 celery stalks, minced
2 large cucumbers, diced
1 red onion, chopped
2 cups cherry tomatoes, halved
3 tablespoons lime juice
1 tablespoon lemon juice
2 tablespoons white wine vinegar
1 tablespoon olive oil
4 cloves garlic, minced
1/2 teaspoon salt
cayenne pepper to taste
1/4 cup chopped fresh parsley

In a large salad bowl, combine the bell peppers, celery, cucumbers, onion, and tomatoes. In a small bowl, stir together the lime and lemon juices, vinegar, oil, garlic, salt, cayenne, and parsley. Add the dressing to the salad; toss well to combine. Cover and chill for 1 hour, tossing occasionally, before serving.

Nutritional Analysis

Calories	60.08 Kcal.	Protein	1.64 gm.
Fat	1.98 gm.	Carbohydrate	10.43 gm.
Sodium	162.87 mg.	Cholesterol	0.00 mg.
Saturated Fat	0.25 gm.		

Orzo Salad

Serves: 4

2 cups fresh basil leaves, minced
1/2 cup minced fresh parsley
4 cloves garlic, minced
1/2 teaspoon salt
1/4 cup olive oil
1 pound orzo pasta, cooked, drained, and cooled
1 red bell pepper, chopped

In a serving bowl, stir together the basil, parsley, garlic, salt, and oil. Add the orzo and red pepper and mix well. Chill for 1 hour. Toss the salad before serving.

Nutritional Analysis

Calories	563.79 Kcal.	Protein	16.08 gm.
Fat	15.60 gm.	Carbohydrate	89.29 gm.
Sodium	302.95 mg.	Cholesterol	0.00 mg.
Saturated Fat	2.09 gm.		

Carrot, Apple, and Raisin Salad

Serves: 8

1 can (6 ounces) frozen orange juice concentrate, thawed
2 pounds carrots, grated
3 large Granny Smith apples, peeled, cored, and grated
1/2 cup black raisins
1/2 cup golden raisins

Place the orange juice concentrate in a medium serving bowl. Fill the concentrate can with water and add to the bowl, stirring to combine. Add the carrots, apples, and raisins. Toss well and serve.

Nutritional Analysis

Calories	177.11 Kcal.	Protein	2.46 gm.
Fat	0.51 gm.	Carbohydrate	44.21 gm.
Sodium	42.67 mg.	Cholesterol	0.00 mg.
Saturated Fat	0.07 gm.		

Cool Beans Salad

Serves: 4

1 can (15 ounces) white beans, drained and rinsed
1/4 cup cubed cooked lean pork
1 red bell pepper, chopped
2 cloves garlic, chopped
1/2 teaspoon dried sage, crumbled
1/2 tablespoon olive oil
1 tablespoon red wine vinegar

In a medium bowl, combine the beans, pork, bell pepper, garlic, and sage. Add the oil and vinegar and toss well. Chill for 30 minutes before serving.

Nutritional Analysis

Calories	111.33 Kcal.	Protein	8.66 gm.
Fat	3.29 gm.	Carbohydrate	17.79 gm.
Sodium	375.29 mg.	Cholesterol	7.26 mg.
Saturated Fat	0.64 gm.		

Salmon Tortellini Salad

Serves: 4

1 package (8 ounces) frozen or fresh cheese tortellini
4 carrots, thinly sliced
1 zucchini, sliced
1 red bell pepper, cut into narrow strips
2 cans (6 1/2 ounces each) salmon, drained and flaked
1 cup plain low-fat yogurt
1/4 cup grated Parmesan cheese
1/4 cup chopped fresh parsley
1 tablespoon low-fat milk
1 teaspoon dried oregano, crumbled

Cook the tortellini as directed on the package. Drain, rinse under cold water, and drain again. In a medium bowl, gently toss together the pasta, carrots, zucchini, and bell pepper. Add the salmon and mix. In a small bowl, stir together the yogurt, cheese, parsley, milk, and oregano until well mixed. Add to the pasta mixture and toss gently to coat evenly. Cover and refrigerate for several hours before serving.

Nutritional Analysis

Calories	385.64 Kcal.	Protein	30.38 gm.
Fat	10.86 gm.	Carbohydrate	41.90 gm.
Sodium	728.90 mg.	Cholesterol	60.66 mg.
Saturated Fat	4.35 gm.		

Potato and Tuna Salad

Serves: 8

2 pounds red new potatoes, cubed
½ pound green beans
¼ cup cider vinegar
1 tablespoon water
1 tablespoon Dijon mustard
1 tablespoon anchovy paste
2 tablespoons olive oil
2 cloves garlic, minced
pepper to taste
3 celery stalks, minced
1 red bell pepper, chopped
1 medium onion, chopped
¼ cup fresh parsley leaves, coarsely chopped
1 can (6½ ounces) water-packed tuna, drained and flaked

In a saucepan, combine the potatoes with water to cover. Bring to a boil, reduce the heat to medium and simmer until nearly tender, about 10 minutes. Add the green beans to the pan and cook until the potatoes and beans are tender, about 5 minutes; drain well and place in a bowl.

In another bowl, mix together the vinegar, water, mustard, anchovy paste, oil, garlic, and pepper. Add the dressing to the potatoes and beans and toss well. Add celery, bell pepper, onion, parsley, and tuna and toss well.

Nutritional Analysis

Calories	182.27 Kcal.	Protein	9.99 gm.
Fat	3.99 gm.	Carbohydrate	26.77 gm.
Sodium	226.13 mg.	Cholesterol	9.86 mg.
Saturated Fat	0.52 gm.		

Creamy Dill-Parsley Dressing

Yield: About 1 cup

1 cup plain nonfat yogurt
1 teaspoon dried dill, crumbled
½ teaspoon lemon juice
1 teaspoon chopped fresh parsley

In a bowl, mix ingredients well.

Nutritional Analysis

Calories	8.14 Kcal.	Protein	0.82 gm.
Fat	0.02 gm.	Carbohydrate	1.12 gm.
Sodium	10.96 mg.	Cholesterol	0.28 mg.
Saturated Fat	0.02 gm.		

Buttermilk Salad Dressing

Yield: About 1 cup

½ cup buttermilk
½ cup low-fat mayonnaise
3 tablespoons minced fresh parsley
3 tablespoons snipped fresh chives
1 clove garlic, minced
1 tablespoon minced fresh tarragon

1 tablespoon lemon juice
dash of Worcestershire sauce
salt and coarse pepper to taste

In a bowl, gently fold all of the ingredients together. Cover and refrigerate until serving time. Serve spooned over torn lettuce or mixed salad greens.

Nutritional Analysis

Calories	16.62 Kcal.	Protein	0.29 gm.
Fat	0.55 gm.	Carbohydrate	2.57 gm.
Sodium	78.80 mg.	Cholesterol	0.30 mg.
Saturated Fat	0.04 gm.		

Horseradish Salad Dressing

Yield: About ⅔ cup

1 tablespoon lemon juice
2 tablespoons rice wine vinegar
2 tablespoons fresh, grated horseradish
1 teaspoon honey
½ cup plain nonfat yogurt

In a bowl, stir together all the ingredients until well mixed.

Nutritional Analysis

Calories	11.20 Kcal.	Protein	0.72 gm.
Fat	0.02 gm.	Carbohydrate	2.08 gm.
Sodium	9.16 mg.	Cholesterol	0.22 mg.
Saturated Fat	0.01 gm.		

A Salad a Day . . .

Nothing beats a salad for low fat and high nutritional eating. And sometimes the very best salads are very simple recipes. For example consider how good thick slices of juicy tomatoes sprinkled with fresh basil, coarsely ground black pepper, and freshly chopped chives taste.

Salads can also be meals unto themselves. Start with fresh greens including dark-green spinach leaves, soft Bibb lettuce, curly red-tipped leaf lettuce and add crisp carrots, thinly sliced cucumbers, tomatoes, fresh mushrooms, green peppers, fresh zucchini, or even broccoli, and cauliflower. Add cold pasta or rice and serve with a hearty bread! A crunchy, crispy, delicious low-fat meal!

THE EVERYTHING LOW-FAT HIGH-FLAVOR COOKBOOK

Sandwiches

CHAPTER FIVE

Amount Per Chapter

21 Recipes

	% Daily Value
Easy to Prepare	**100%**
Low Fat / High Flavor	**100%**
Simple to Understand	**100%**

DELICIOUS, EASY, LOW-FAT RECIPES

With all of the delicious bread varieties available today in supermarkets and in bakeries, there's no excuse for a boring low-fat sandwich anymore. And having an equally diverse choice of tasty and exotic vegetables available, such as red- and green-leaf lettuces, fresh basil, and vine-ripened tomatoes year-round, doesn't hurt either.

You can use the recipes I've provided here as a springboard for countless sandwiches, a different one every day of the year. For instance, if you're a mustard connoisseur, experiment with some of the recipes here by substituting a whole-grain Dijon for the low-fat mayonnaise.

Use your imagination, and you'll look forward to having wonderfully creative sandwiches for lunch—and dinner, too.

French Bread Pizzas

Serves: 4

1 loaf French bread
2 tablespoons olive oil
1 large onion, chopped
1 green bell pepper, chopped
2 garlic cloves, minced
2 teaspoons dried basil, crumbled
2 teaspoons dried oregano, crumbled
2 cups spaghetti sauce, from a jar or
    homemade
2 large tomatoes, sliced
1 cup pitted black olives, sliced
2 cups finely grated carrots
1/3 cup grated Parmesan cheese

Preheat oven to 450°F.
Slice the bread in half lengthwise. Drizzle the cut sides of both halves with 1 tablespoon of the

oil and place on a baking sheet. In a skillet, heat the remaining tablespoon of oil over medium heat. Add the onion, bell pepper, garlic, basil, and oregano and cook for 5 minutes, or until softened. Remove from the heat. Spoon 1 cup of the spaghetti sauce on each piece of bread. Top evenly with the onion-pepper mixture, tomatoes, and black olives. Then sprinkle evenly with the carrots and Parmesan cheese.

Bake for 12 to 15 minutes, or until bubbly and the bread is lightly browned. Cut crosswise to serve. Serve hot.

Nutritional Analysis

Calories	655.70 Kcal.	Protein	17.86 gm.
Fat	22.34 gm.	Carbohydrate	99.40 gm.
Sodium	1758.23 mg.	Cholesterol	5.21 mg.
Saturated Fat	4.27 gm.		

Grilled Chicken Breast Sandwiches with Onions

Serves: 4

> 1 tablespoon butter
> 4 large onions, sliced
> 1/2 cup oil-packed sun-dried tomatoes, drained and chopped
> 2 cloves garlic, minced
> 1 tablespoon water
> 2 boneless, skinless whole chicken breasts, split
> 4 hamburger buns

Prepare a fire in a charcoal grill.

In a large skillet, melt the butter over medium heat. Add the onions and cook, stirring occasionally, for 10 minutes, or until translucent. Add the tomatoes, garlic, and water and cook for 5 minutes, stirring occasionally.

Meanwhile, place the chicken over medium-hot coals and grill, turning once, until done, about 10 minutes. Spread some of the onion mixture over the bottom half of each bun. Top with a piece of the chicken, the remaining onion mixture, and then the tops of the buns. Serve hot.

Nutritional Analysis

Calories	436.66 Kcal.	Protein	35.63 gm.
Fat	10.87 gm.	Carbohydrate	49.69 gm.
Sodium	473.81 mg.	Cholesterol	76.20 mg.
Saturated Fat	2.73 gm.		

Grilled Vegetable Sandwich

Serves: 6

Dressing:

> 1 cup plain nonfat yogurt
> 3 tablespoons Dijon mustard
> pepper to taste
> 2 tablespoons nonfat cottage cheese
> 1/3 teaspoon Tabasco sauce
> 2 tablespoons minced shallot
> 1 clove garlic, minced
> 1 teaspoon lemon juice

Sandwiches:

> 1 small eggplant, cut into 1/4-inch-thick rounds
> 1 medium-sized yellow squash, cut into 1/4-inch-thick rounds
> 1 medium-sized zucchini, cut into 1/4-inch-thick rounds
> 1 medium onion
> 1 tablespoon Italian seasoning
> 1/4 teaspoon cayenne pepper
> 2 baguettes
> 1 large tomato, sliced
> pepper to taste
> 2 tablespoons chopped jalapeño pepper
> 8 fresh basil leaves
> 8 arugula leaves
> 2 red bell peppers, roasted and quartered

To make the dressing, combine all the ingredients and blend until smooth. Transfer to a bowl, cover, and refrigerate.

Preheat broiler.

(continued)

Low-Fat Grilled Sandwiches

The grilled cheese sandwiches of my childhood—a pat of butter on each bread slice, a big hunk of American cheese in the middle, and sometimes a slice of bologna, too—have rightfully earned the moniker of high-fat cooking.

Today, however, you can grill a sandwich on a griddle or in a skillet that has been sprayed with nonstick cooking spray, resulting in a wonderful melted cheese sandwich without a heavy, greasy taste. One bite and you will be transported back to a childhood when a rainy day meant sitting down to a mug of tomato soup and a grilled cheese sandwich.

Spray a baking sheet with nonstick cooking spray. Arrange the eggplant, yellow squash, zucchini and onion in a single layer on the baking sheet. Sprinkle the Italian dressing and cayenne pepper over all of the rounds. Broil, turning once, for about 5 minutes on each side, or until browned. Remove the baking sheet, but leave the broiler on.

Cut each of the baguettes in half lengthwise and scoop out the soft inner dough. Place in the broiler and toast for 2 minutes on each side.

Put a few slices of tomato into the well in each baguette half. Dust with black pepper and sprinkle with the jalapeño pepper.

Place 4 basil leaves, 4 arugula leaves, and 4 pieces of roasted pepper onto the bottom half of each baguette. Layer slices of eggplant, yellow squash, zucchini, and onion on top. Coat the inside of the remaining half of each baguette with the dressing and place it on top of the vegetables. Cut each baguette crosswise into 3 equal pieces and serve.

Nutritional Analysis

Calories	286.41 Kcal.	Protein	11.35 gm.
Fat	2.64 gm.	Carbohydrate	53.11 gm.
Sodium	706.29 mg.	Cholesterol	1.16 mg.
Saturated Fat	0.56 gm.		

California-Style Turkey Burger

Serves: 6

> 1 pound ground turkey breast
> 1 cup old-fashioned or quick-cooking rolled
>   oats
> 1/4 cup ketchup
> 1 egg, beaten
> 1/4 cup minced onion
> 1 1/2 teaspoons garlic salt
> 1/2 teaspoon pepper
> 1 teaspoon Worcestershire sauce
> 1/4 teaspoon Tabasco sauce
> 6 hamburger buns

Prepare a fire in a charcoal grill.

Combine all the ingredients except the buns in a large bowl. Mix well and shape into 6 patties. Place the patties on the grill rack and grill for about 6 minutes on each side, or until done; the timing with depend on the thickness. Serve plain or on buns.

Nutritional Analysis

Calories	285.45 Kcal.	Protein	25.73 gm.
Fat	4.40 gm.	Carbohydrate	34.32 gm.
Sodium	778.18 mg.	Cholesterol	82.32 mg.
Saturated Fat	1.05 gm.		

Chicken Pocket Sandwich

Serves: 5

> 1 2/3 cup diced cooked chicken
> 1 cup plain low-fat yogurt
> 1/2 cup chopped almonds
> 1/4 cup chopped nectarine
> 1/3 cup chopped scallions
> 1 tablespoon lemon juice
> 1/8 teaspoon pepper
> 1/8 teaspoon dried dill, crumbled
> 5 large pita breads
> 10 lettuce leaves

In a bowl, combine all the ingredients except the pita bread and lettuce. Toss gently to mix well. Using a sharp knife, cut each pita bread in half, forming 10 pockets. Line each pita half with 1 lettuce leaf. Spoon in the chicken mixture, dividing it evenly. Serve at once.

Nutritional Analysis

Calories	437.05 Kcal.	Protein	26.61 gm.
Fat	12.04 gm.	Carbohydrate	55.29 gm.
Sodium	532.44 mg.	Cholesterol	44.33 mg.
Saturated Fat	2.18 gm.		

Corn Dogs

Serves: 8

> 1 cup all-purpose flour
> 2 tablespoons sugar
> 1 1/2 teaspoons baking powder
> 1 teaspoon salt
> 2/3 cup cornmeal

(continued)

2 tablespoons shortening
1 egg
3/4 cup milk
1 pound Healthy Choice Frankfurters
ketchup
mustard

Preheat oven to 350°F.

In a bowl, sift together the flour, sugar, baking powder, and salt. Stir in the cornmeal. Using a pastry blender or 2 knives, cut in the shortening until the mixture resembles coarse meal. In a separate bowl, whisk together the egg and milk until blended and stir into the cornmeal mixture, again mixing until blended. Insert a wooden skewer into the end of each hot dog. Working in batches, coat the hot dogs evenly with the batter and arrange on a cookie sheet sprayed with nonstick spray. Bake for 15 minutes or until batter is lightly browned. Serve immediate with ketchup and mustard.

Nutritional Analysis

Calories	233.87 Kcal.	Protein	11.08 gm.
Fat	6.53 gm.	Carbohydrate	30.34 gm.
Sodium	930.10 mg.	Cholesterol	59.62 mg.
Saturated Fat	1.99 gm.		

Grilled Chicken Sandwich with Tarragon Mayonnaise

Serves: 6

2 tablespoons red wine vinegar
2 tablespoons dried tarragon, crumbled

2 tablespoons butter
4 teaspoons minced shallots
1 cup low-fat mayonnaise
1/2 teaspoon white pepper
3 boneless whole chicken breasts, 1/2 pound
   each, skin and visible fat removed
salt and pepper to taste
6 sandwich buns, split
6 lettuce leaves
6 slices tomato

Prepare a fire in a charcoal grill.

In a small saucepan, combine the vinegar and tarragon, and bring to a boil. Cook until reduced by half and set aside. In a small skillet, melt the butter over medium heat. Add the shallots and sauté for 10 minutes, or until tender. Transfer to a small bowl and add the mayonnaise, tarragon reduction, and white pepper. Mix well.

Pound the chicken breasts lightly with the fine side of meat-tenderizing mallet. Cut in half down the natural seam, eliminating any cartilage at the center. Season with salt and pepper.

Place the chicken on the grill rack on medium fire and grill, turning once and basting each side with 1 tablespoon of the mayonnaise mixture, for about 7 minutes on each side, or until done. Just before the chicken is ready, place the buns, cut sides down, on the grill rack to warm.

Spread the cut sides of the buns generously with the flavored mayonnaise. Place one chicken piece on the bottom of each bun. Top with lettuce and tomato and then the bun top. Serve immediately.

Nutritional Analysis

Calories	369.65 Kcal.	Protein	29.65 gm.
Fat	11.75 gm.	Carbohydrate	34.53 gm.
Sodium	716.58 mg.	Cholesterol	79.80 mg.
Saturated Fat	3.71 gm.		

Curried Chicken Pockets

Serves: 4

> 1 cup plain low-fat yogurt
> 1/2 teaspoon curry powder
> 1/4 teaspoon ground mace
> 1 1/2 cups deboned, cubed, cooked chicken
>   breasts
> 1/2 cup low-fat Italian dressing
> 1 green apple, cored and cubed
> 1/4 cup thinly sliced celery
> 1/4 cup sliced almonds, toasted
> 4 tablespoons raisins
> 1 avocado, pitted, peeled, and cubed
> 4 pita breads
> 8 curly lettuce leaves

In small bowl, stir the yogurt until smooth and creamy. Add the curry powder and mace and mix well. Cover and refrigerate for at least 4 hours or up to 24 hours to blend the flavors.

Meanwhile, in a medium bowl, combine the chicken and Italian dressing. Cover and marinate in the refrigerator for at least 4 hours or up to 8 hours.

Add the apple, celery, almonds, and raisins to the chicken. Stir the curry-yogurt dressing into the chicken mixture. Add the avocado cubes and fold in gently. Cut the pita breads in half, forming 8 pockets. Line each pocket with 1 lettuce leaf, then spoon in the chicken mixture, dividing it evenly. Serve immediately.

Nutritional Analysis

Calories	507.66 Kcal.	Protein	23.49 gm.
Fat	13.26 gm.	Carbohydrate	57.77 gm.
Sodium	654.75 mg.	Cholesterol	34.23 mg.
Saturated Fat	2.38 gm.		

Peach Pita Sandwiches

Serves: 2

> 2 pita breads
> 4 curly lettuce leaves
> 1 cup 1% low-fat cottage cheese
> 4 tomato slices
> 4 extra-lean smoked ham slices
> 1 can (16 ounces) cling peach slices, drained

Cut the pita breads in half, forming 4 pockets. Line each pocket with 1 lettuce leaf. Fill the pockets with the cottage cheese, tomato slices, ham slices, and peach slices, dividing them evenly. Serve at once.

Nutritional Analysis

Calories	427.92 Kcal.	Protein	32.23 gm.
Fat	4.85 gm.	Carbohydrate	64.85 gm.
Sodium	1603.11 mg.	Cholesterol	31.16 mg.
Saturated Fat	1.74 gm.		

Roast Beef Pita Bread Sandwich with Tomato

Serves: 6

¹/₂ cup chopped fresh basil
¹/₈ cup prepared horseradish
¹/₂ cup plain low-fat yogurt
³/₄ pound delicatessen-style sliced roast beef
1 head butter lettuce, separated into leaves
3 pita breads
1 large tomato, cored and cut into 12 slices

In a large bowl, stir together the basil, horse-radish, and yogurt. Spread the horseradish-yogurt mixture on the beef slices and wrap each slice in a lettuce leaf. Cut the pita breads in half, forming 6 pockets. Put the lettuce-wrapped beef and 2 slices of tomato into each half. Serve immediately.

Nutritional Analysis

Calories	174.20 Kcal.	Protein	15.76 gm.
Fat	2.85 gm.	Carbohydrate	21.54 gm.
Sodium	761.34 mg.	Cholesterol	26.10 mg.
Saturated Fat	1.03 gm.		

Bruschetta with Basil

Serves: 16 to 20

¹/₂ pound plum tomatoes, sliced lengthwise
¹/₄ cup diced red onion
1 tablespoon olive oil
2 tablespoons chopped fresh parsley
1 tablespoon chopped fresh basil
1 clove garlic, minced

salt and pepper to taste
1 sourdough baguette, about 10 ounces, cut
  on the diagonal into 1-inch slices and lightly
  toasted
16 to 20 small fresh basil leaves

In a medium bowl, combine the tomatoes, onion, olive oil, parsley, chopped basil, garlic, salt, and pepper. Mix gently. Top each toasted bread slice with about 1 heaping tablespoon of the tomato-avocado mixture. Garnish each with a small basil leaf.

Nutritional Analysis

Calories	53.76 Kcal.	Protein	1.52 gm.
Fat	1.26 gm.	Carbohydrate	9.03 gm.
Sodium	97.46 mg.	Cholesterol	0.00 mg.
Saturated Fat	0.20 gm.		

Black Bean and Vegetable Dip

Serves: 6

Black Bean Dip:
³/₄ cup dried black beans, picked over and
  soaked for 2 hours in water to cover
¹/₂ cup chopped fresh basil
¹/₂ cup plain nonfat yogurt
pepper to taste

Corn Tortilla Chips:
1 teaspoon olive oil
6 corn tortillas, each 6 inches in diameter

6 flour tortillas, each 6 inches in diameter
6 ounces low-fat mozzarella cheese, shredded

1/2 cup diced green bell pepper
1/2 cup diced red bell pepper
1/2 cup chopped tomatoes
1/2 cup chopped fresh basil
1 avocado, pitted, peeled, and diced

To make the black bean dip, drain the beans and place them in a saucepan with water to cover by 2 inches. Bring to boil, cover, reduce the heat to low, and cook until tender, about 1 hour. Drain and mash with a fork. Let cool, then add the basil, yogurt, and pepper.

To make the tortilla chips, preheat the oven to 300°F. Brush the corn tortillas on both sides with the olive oil. Place on a baking sheet. Cut each tortilla into 6 wedges. Bake until crispy. Leave the oven set at 300°F.

Place a nonstick skillet over medium heat. One at a time, heat the flour tortillas, turning once, until crispy. Remove and top each one with equal portions of the grated cheese, green and red bell peppers, tomato, and basil. Place the tortillas on a baking sheet and bake until cheese is melted and bubbly, about 10 minutes. Remove from the oven and cut each tortilla into 6 wedges. Top each with a slice of avocado.

Serve the tortillas, bean dip, and chips together.

Nutritional Analysis

Calories	325.78 Kcal.	Protein	19.73 gm.
Fat	8.43 gm.	Carbohydrate	45.16 gm.
Sodium	366.99 mg.	Cholesterol	3.36 mg.
Saturated Fat	1.31 gm.		

Pita Bread

Although pita bread has long been a Middle Eastern staple, Americans have only recently become familiar with this pocket bread.

It's not surprising that it has caught on so quickly. You can stuff a pita with everything from vegetables to peanut butter and, unlike a conventional sandwich, the filling won't fall out of the sides. That makes a pita sandwich a genuinely portable meal. In addition, pita bread is virtually fat free. Try some of the new flavors, from onion to sourdough.

Lemon-Sesame Tuna Sandwiches

Serves: 4

2 tablespoons lemon juice
1 tablespoon soy sauce
1 tablespoon Asian sesame oil
4 tuna fillets, about ⅓ pound each
3 scallions, minced
pinch of pepper
4 hamburger buns, split and toasted
4 green leaf lettuce leaves

In a small bowl, stir together the lemon juice, soy sauce, and sesame oil to form a marinade. Place the tuna steaks on a baking sheet and drizzle the marinade over the fish. Chill for 1 hour.

Preheat oven to 400°F. Bake the fish until it is opaque throughout, about 10 minutes, or until done to your liking. Sprinkle with the scallions and pepper and serve on the buns with the lettuce.

Nutritional Analysis

Calories	379.55 Kcal.	Protein	39.42 gm.
Fat	13.04 gm.	Carbohydrate	23.61 gm.
Sodium	560.96 mg.	Cholesterol	57.36 mg.
Saturated Fat	2.89 gm.		

Greek Lamb Pita Sandwiches

Serves: 4

½ pound lean ground lamb
1 onion, minced
3 cloves garlic, minced
1 celery stalk, chopped

1 package (10 ounces) chopped frozen
   spinach, thawed and well drained
1 teaspoon dried oregano, crumbled
salt and pepper to taste
½ cup crumbled feta cheese
4 pita breads
8 lettuce leaves
1 tomato, diced
¼ cup plain low-fat yogurt

In a large nonstick skillet, combine the lamb, onion, garlic, and celery over medium heat. Sauté until the vegetables are tender, about 5 minutes. Drain off any liquid. Add the spinach, oregano, salt, and pepper, and cook, stirring, for 5 minutes until heated through and the flavors are blended. Remove from the heat and add the feta. Cut each pita bread in half, forming 8 pockets. Slip the lettuce leaves, some tomato, and 1 tablespoon yogurt into each pocket. Spoon the lamb mixture into the pita halves, then serve.

Nutritional Analysis

Calories	385.20 Kcal.	Protein	22.14 gm.
Fat	12.78 gm.	Carbohydrate	45.91 gm.
Sodium	628.11 mg.	Cholesterol	54.15 mg.
Saturated Fat	6.08 gm.		

Sweet-and-Sour Turkey Burgers

Serves: 6

1 tablespoon soy sauce
1 tablespoon honey
4 scallions, minced

1 pound ground turkey, lean
6 slices canned pineapple
6 hamburger buns, split and toasted

Stir the soy sauce and honey together in a bowl until blended. Add the ground turkey and scallions and mix well. Shape into 4 patties. In a nonstick skillet over medium heat, fry the patties, turning once, until done, about 8 minutes. To serve, place a burger on the base of each bun and top with a pineapple ring.

Nutritional Analysis

Calories	299.79 Kcal.	Protein	17.71 gm.
Fat	9.85 gm.	Carbohydrate	34.61 gm.
Sodium	460.41 mg.	Cholesterol	38.11 mg.
Saturated Fat	2.58 gm.		

Mozzarella Sandwiches with Basil and Tomato

Serves: 4

2/3 cup chopped dry-packed sun-dried tomatoes
2 cloves garlic, chopped
1/4 teaspoon salt
1 tablespoon olive oil
1 tablespoon lemon juice
1/4 teaspoon red pepper flakes
4 black olives, chopped
8 slices sourdough French bread
1/4 pound low-fat mozzarella cheese, sliced
pepper to taste
3 tomatoes, sliced
salt to taste
2 teaspoons balsamic vinegar
1 cup fresh basil leaves, torn

Place the sun-dried tomatoes in a bowl and cover with boiling water. Let stand for 10 minutes. Drain.

In a medium bowl, mash together the garlic and salt. Add the oil, lemon juice, and red pepper flakes. Mix well. Add the rehydrated tomatoes and the olives and again mix well. Divide among 4 of the bread slices, spreading evenly. Top with the cheese slices, and sprinkle with the pepper. Place the tomato slices on top and season with salt and vinegar. Top with the basil and then the remaining bread slices. Cut in half to serve.

Nutritional Analysis

Calories	298.54 Kcal.	Protein	18.11 gm.
Fat	5.91 gm.	Carbohydrate	44.75 gm.
Sodium	755.36 mg.	Cholesterol	3.00 mg.
Saturated Fat	0.90 gm.		

A Year in Provence Sandwich

Serves: 2

1 teaspoon olive oil
1 onion, chopped
1 teaspoon dried oregano, crumbled
1 teaspoon dried basil, crumbled
1 tablespoon water
1/4 cup pitted black olives, sliced
2 tablespoons grated Parmesan cheese
8 to 12 spinach leaves
2 French rolls, split
4 ounces low-fat mozzarella cheese, sliced
2 plum tomatoes, sliced

(continued)

Heat the oil in a large skillet over medium heat. Add onion, oregano, and basil and cook, stirring, for 2 minutes. Add the water, reduce the heat to low, cover, and cook until the onion is tender, about 5 minutes. Remove from the heat and stir in the olives and Parmesan.

Arrange 2 or 3 spinach leaves on bottom half of each French roll. Spoon half the onion mixture onto each, top with the cheese slices, and then the tomato slices. Arrange the remaining spinach leaves on top and then the tops of the rolls. Cut in half to serve.

Nutritional Analysis

Calories	348.10 Kcal.	Protein	27.10 gm.
Fat	8.39 gm.	Carbohydrate	42.44 gm.
Sodium	1026.64 mg.	Cholesterol	9.94 mg.
Saturated Fat	2.08 gm.		

Portobello, Basil, and Tomato Sandwich

Serves: 4

1 tablespoon low-fat mayonnaise
1/2 teaspoon lemon juice
2 large portobello mushrooms
1 teaspoon olive oil
2 cloves garlic, minced
4 kaiser rolls, split
1 tomato, sliced
2/3 cup fresh basil leaves, minced
4 leaves green leaf lettuce

Preheat broiler.

In a small bowl, mix together the mayonnaise and lemon juice. Brush the mushrooms with the oil and place on a broiler pan. Broil until tender, about 5 minutes.

Spread the garlic over the bottom halves of the rolls. Spread the mayonnaise mixture on top of the garlic, and then top with the grilled mushrooms, tomato, basil, and lettuce. Put the top half of each roll in place and serve.

Nutritional Analysis

Calories	215.01 Kcal.	Protein	7.93 gm.
Fat	4.30 gm.	Carbohydrate	37.16 gm.
Sodium	352.33 mg.	Cholesterol	0.00 mg.
Saturated Fat	0.54 gm.		

Steak Subs

Serves: 6

1 pound boneless beef sirloin steak, all fat
    trimmed
shredded lettuce
1 loaf French bread, 1 pound, split lengthwise
1 jar (7 ounces) roasted red peppers, drained
salt and pepper to taste
1/2 cup shredded fat-free mozzarella cheese

Prepare a fire in a charcoal grill. Grill the steak until done to your liking. In the meantime, spread the lettuce over the bottom half of the split bread loaf. Spread the peppers over the lettuce. Carve the steak into thin slices, and season with salt and pepper. Spread the steak slices over the peppers; top with the cheese. Put

the top on the loaf, and cut into 6 portions. Serve at once.

Nutritional Analysis

Calories	339.02 Kcal.	Protein	26.86 gm.
Fat	6.35 gm.	Carbohydrate	41.94 gm.
Sodium	611.24 mg.	Cholesterol	51.46 mg.
Saturated Fat	2.06 gm.		

Lean, Juicy Burgers

Serves: 6

3/4 pound lean top round, trimmed of fat and ground
2 tablespoons canola or safflower oil
1/2 cup finely chopped onion
1/2 cup finely chopped celery
2 tablespoons seasoned dried bread crumbs
1 tablespoon Worcestershire sauce
salt and pepper to taste
6 hamburger buns
1/4 cup low-fat mayonnaise
6 tomato slices
6 onion slices

Prepare a fire in a charcoal grill or preheat a broiler.

In a large bowl, mix together the beef, oil, onion, celery, bread crumbs, Worcestershire sauce and salt and pepper. Shape into 6 patties.

Place the patties on a grill rack or broiler pan. Grill or broil, turn once, until done as desired, 7 to 8 minutes on each side for medium. Just before the burgers are ready, toast the buns on the grill or in the broiler. Spread the mayonnaise

on the buns and top with the burgers. Place the tomato and onion slices on the burgers and then the tops of the buns. Serve at once.

Nutritional Analysis

Calories	270.49 Kcal.	Protein	17.96 gm.
Fat	8.93 gm.	Carbohydrate	28.09 gm.
Sodium	440.78 mg.	Cholesterol	35.59 mg.
Saturated Fat	1.55 gm.		

Steak-Vegetable Pockets

Serves: 4

3/4 pound top round
3 tablespoons soy sauce
1/4 cup water
1 1/2 teaspoons cornstarch
1 1/2 cup broccoli florets
1 small carrot, diced
1 small onion, chopped
1/2 green bell pepper, chopped
8 snow peas, halved crosswise
6 mushrooms, sliced
1 small tomato, chopped
1 tablespoon olive oil
4 pita bread rounds, halved

Thinly slice the beef into bite-sized strips. Set aside.

In a small bowl, stir together the soy sauce, water, and cornstarch until the cornstarch dissolves; set aside.

(continued)

Spicing up a Sandwich

For extra tasty low-fat sandwiches use spices. Use a spicy brown mustard on sliced turkey rather than mayonnaise. Sprinkle tomatoes in sandwiches with garlic powder and dried basil.

Also when making sandwiches, experiment using different kinds of bread such as whole wheat or cracked wheat, rye or pumpernickel. Special breads such as dill bread make for great tasting sandwiches. Pita bread and lavash rollup bread make for especially low-fat sandwiches and make sandwich eating convenient, with no chance of the stuffing falling out.

Spray a wok or large skillet with nonstick cooking spray and place over high heat. Add broccoli, carrot, onion, green pepper and stir-fry until carrot is tender, about 7 minutes. Add the snow peas, mushrooms, and tomato and stir-fry for 2 minutes. Remove the vegetables from the pan and set aside. Add the oil and heat over high heat. Add the beef and stir-fry until beef is tender, about 3 minutes. Quickly stir the cornstarch mixture and add to the pan. Cook and stir until bubbly and the pan juices thicken. Return the vegetables to the pan and heat through.

To serve, cut the pita breads in half, forming 8 pockets. Spoon the vegetable-beef mixture into the pockets and serve.

Nutritional Analysis

Calories	405.91 Kcal.	Protein	27.53 gm.
Fat	12.86 gm.	Carbohydrate	45.16 gm.
Sodium	1165.82 mg.	Cholesterol	51.92 mg.
Saturated Fat	3.73 gm.		

THE EVERYTHING LOW-FAT HIGH-FLAVOR COOKBOOK

Side Dishes

CHAPTER SIX

Amount Per Chapter

53 Recipes

% Daily Value

Easy to Prepare	**100%**
Low Fat / High Flavor	**100%**
Simple to Understand	**100%**

DELICIOUS, EASY, LOW-FAT RECIPES

Too many people regard side dishes to be either a scoop of mashed potatoes or a spoonful of soggy green beans. It is no wonder that so many diners tend to ignore the side dishes on their dinner plates in favor of the main course.

The great thing about cooking low-fat side dishes is that you learn to rely on the crunch and flavor of fresh vegetables—and fruits—in order to avoid the fat. Here are a number of delicious side dishes that depend on such ingredients as onion, garlic, apples, and herbs to deliver taste with little fat.

Apple–Sweet Potato Bake

Serves: 4

> 3 Red Delicious apples, peeled, cored, and
>   sliced
> 1 tablespoon lemon juice
> 2 pounds sweet potatoes, peeled and sliced
> 1/3 cup apple juice
> 1 tablespoon butter, melted

Preheat oven to 350°F.

In a bowl, toss the apple slices with the lemon juice. In a 1 1/2-quart flameproof baking dish, alternate layers of the sweet potatoes and apples. Pour the apple juice and the melted butter over the layers. Cover and bake until tender and juice is bubbling, about 1 1/4 hours.

Remove from the oven. Turn the oven to broil. Uncover the baking dish and slip in under the broiler until top is lightly browned, about 5 minutes.

Nutritional Analysis

Calories	262.13 Kcal.	Protein	2.88 gm.
Fat	3.68 gm.	Carbohydrate	56.54 gm.
Sodium	51.91 mg.	Cholesterol	7.76 mg.
Saturated Fat	1.91 gm.		

Green Beans with Garlic

Serves: 6

> l pound green beans
> 1/2 tablespoon olive oil
> 1 small onion, chopped
> 1 tablespoon chopped garlic
> 1 tablespoon all-purpose flour
> 1 can (16 ounces) tomatoes, drained, liquid
>   reserved, and chopped

Steam the green beans until tender, about 5 minutes, then plunge them into cold water to cool. Drain and set aside.

In a medium nonstick saucepan, heat the oil over medium heat. Add the onion and garlic and sauté for a few minutes. Stir in the flour and cook for 1 minute. Stir in the liquid from the tomatoes. Cook the mixture, stirring, until slightly thickened. Add the tomatoes and green beans, mixing well. Cook, stirring, over medium heat for a couple of minutes until the beans are done but still crisp and the flavors are blended.

Nutritional Analysis

Calories	62.91 Kcal.	Protein	2.51 gm.
Fat	1.43 gm.	Carbohydrate	11.81 gm.
Sodium	128.62 mg.	Cholesterol	0.00 mg.
Saturated Fat	0.20 gm.		

Risotto with Vegetables

Serves: 4

> 2 tablespoons butter
> 1 onion, chopped
> 1 cup Arborio rice
> 4 cups reduced-sodium, fat-free chicken broth, heated
> 1 cup green beans, cut in 1/2-inch lengths
> 1 cup chopped zucchini
> 1/3 cup minced fresh parsley
> 1/4 cup grated Parmesan cheese
> salt and pepper to taste

Melt 1 tablespoon of the butter in a large skillet over medium heat. Add the onion and sauté until softened. Add the rice and stir to coat with the butter. Reduce the heat to low and add 1/2 cup of the broth. Cook, stirring, until it is absorbed. Add 1 1/2 cups more broth, 1/2 cup at a time, cooking and stirring until each addition is absorbed. Add the green beans and zucchini and cook for 2 minutes. Add the remaining broth, again 1/2 cup at a time. Simmer for about 15 minutes more. The risotto is done when the kernels are still slightly firm at the center and mixture is creamy. Add the parsley, Parmesan, the remaining butter, and salt and pepper.

(continued)

About Risotto

Although it may sound exotic, risotto is considered a simple rice dish in Italy. It is made by adding a hot broth in increments to uncooked rice in a saucepan over low heat. You must stir the rice continuously, and wait until the rice has absorbed all of the broth before adding more. Risotto is typically creamy and served in a shallow puddle of broth. The average cooking time is about 25 minutes.

Nutritional Analysis

Calories	269.44 Kcal.	Protein	9.59 gm.
Fat	7.87 gm.	Carbohydrate	40.07 gm.
Sodium	718.72 mg.	Cholesterol	19.47 mg.
Saturated Fat	4.53 gm.		

Indian Rice

Serves: 8

1 tablespoon butter
2 large onions, sliced
4 cups reduced-sodium, fat-free chicken broth
2 cups sliced mushrooms
1½ cups white rice
1 cup lentils
1 tablespoon peeled and minced fresh ginger
1 teaspoon curry powder
¼ teaspoon ground cinnamon
2 cloves garlic, minced
½ cup chopped fresh parsley
salt and pepper to taste

In a heavy skillet, melt the butter over low heat. Add the onions and cook, stirring occasionally, until tender, about 20 minutes. Meanwhile, in a saucepan, combine the broth, mushrooms, rice, lentils, ginger, curry powder, cinnamon, and garlic. Bring to a boil, reduce the heat to low, cover, and cook until the rice and lentils are tender and the liquid is absorbed, about 30 minutes.

Uncover and mix in the parsley, salt, and pepper. Serve at once.

Nutritional Analysis

Calories	257.76 Kcal.	Protein	11.88 gm.
Fat	2.08 gm.	Carbohydrate	47.93 gm.
Sodium	303.60 mg.	Cholesterol	3.88 mg.
Saturated Fat	1.00 gm.		

Vegetable Fried Rice

Serves: 6

1 tablespoon peanut oil
2 cups sliced zucchini
1 cup minced celery
4 cups cold cooked rice
1 red bell pepper, diced
2 eggs, lightly beaten
2 cups bean sprouts
⅓ cup oyster sauce
1 onion, chopped

In a large, deep skillet, heat the oil over medium-high heat. Add the zucchini and celery and stir-fry for 2 minutes. Add the rice and stir-fry for another minute. Add the bell pepper and stir-fry for another minute. Add the eggs and cook, stirring, for 30 seconds. Add the bean sprouts and stir-fry for 1 minute longer, or until the eggs are set. Add the oyster sauce and stir until evenly distributed. Sprinkle with chopped onion and serve.

Nutritional Analysis

Calories	221.04 Kcal.	Protein	8.34 gm.
Fat	4.40 gm.	Carbohydrate	37.30 gm.
Sodium	672.15 mg.	Cholesterol	70.83 mg.
Saturated Fat	0.98 gm.		

Wild Rice Pilaf

Serves: 6

1 tablespoon olive oil
1 onion, diced
3 cups reduced-sodium, fat-free chicken broth
1/2 cup wild rice
1 cup white rice
1/4 cup chopped fresh parsley
1 teaspoon dried basil, crumbled
salt and pepper to taste

In a large skillet, heat the oil over medium heat for 1 minute. Add the onion and sauté until tender, about 5 minutes. Add the chicken broth, stir in wild rice, and bring to a boil. Add the white rice. Reduce the heat to low, cover, and cook until the rices are done, about 20 minutes. Mix in the parsley, basil, salt, and pepper and serve.

Nutritional Analysis

Calories	199.76 Kcal.	Protein	6.05 gm.
Fat	2.63 gm.	Carbohydrate	37.39 gm.
Sodium	285.00 mg.	Cholesterol	0.00 mg.
Saturated Fat	0.37 gm.		

Texan Rice

Serves: 6

1/2 pound lean ground beef
1 medium onion, chopped
2 cups hot cooked white rice
1 can (10 ounces) corn kernels, drained and heated
1/2 cup barbecue sauce

In a large nonstick skillet, cook the beef until browned, about 5 minutes. Drain off any fat. Add the onion and continue to cook until the onion is soft, about 8 minutes longer. Drain again.

Place the beef-onion mixture in a serving bowl. Add the rice, corn, and barbecue sauce and mix well.

Nutritional Analysis

Calories	195.81 Kcal.	Protein	9.54 gm.
Fat	6.06 gm.	Carbohydrate	25.90 gm.
Sodium	260.89 mg.	Cholesterol	22.89 mg.
Saturated Fat	2.17 gm.		

Indian Raita

Serves: 10

2 cups plain fat-free yogurt
2 medium cucumbers, chopped
1 clove garlic, minced
2 teaspoons minced fresh dill
1 tablespoon olive oil
2 teaspoons distilled white vinegar

In a bowl, combine all the ingredients. Cover and chill for at least 1 hour before serving. Serve as a side dish with curry.

Nutritional Analysis

Calories	55.10 Kcal.	Protein	3.58 gm.
Fat	1.85 gm.	Carbohydrate	6.26 gm.
Sodium	44.37 mg.	Cholesterol	1.13 mg.
Saturated Fat	0.31 gm.		

Black Beans with Rice

Serves: 8

2 cans (19 ounces each) black beans, drained
4 cups hot cooked white rice
2 teaspoons ground cumin
4 cloves garlic, minced
2 bay leaves
2 teaspoons dried oregano, crumbled
1 teaspoon salt
1 medium onion, chopped
1 green bell pepper, chopped
2 tablespoons lemon juice
1 can (16 ounces) tomatoes, drained and cut up
1 cup shelled green peas, blanched
1 cup chopped fresh tomatoes
2 scallions, thinly sliced
2 tablespoons low-fat sour cream

In a large saucepan, combine the beans, cumin, garlic, bay leaves, oregano, salt, onion, bell pepper, lemon juice, and canned tomatoes. Bring to a boil, reduce the heat to medium, cover, and cook until the vegetables are done, about 30 minutes.

Discard the bay leaves. Mix the beans with the hot rice and stir in the green peas, chopped fresh tomatoes, scallions, and sour cream and serve.

Nutritional Analysis

Calories	259.96 Kcal.	Protein	11.78 gm.
Fat	1.97 gm.	Carbohydrate	50.50 gm.
Sodium	808.86 mg.	Cholesterol	1.25 mg.
Saturated Fat	0.28 gm.		

Baked Acorn Squash

Serves: 4

1 acorn squash
1 tablespoon buttery light, reduced-fat margarine
1 teaspoon brown sugar (optional)

Preheat oven to 400°F.

Cut the squash in half and scoop out the seeds. (Save and bake for snacks, if you like.) Bake the squash on an ungreased cookie sheet for 30 to 40 minutes, or until tender. Scoop out the pulp and mix with the margarine or butter and the brown sugar, if desired. (For a lower-calorie, lower-fat alternative, try a little ground cinnamon and nutmeg.) Return the mixture to the shells or place in a baking dish and heat thoroughly, about 15 minutes.

Nutritional Analysis

Calories	78.55 Kcal.	Protein	1.03 gm.
Fat	0.12 gm.	Carbohydrate	17.08 gm.
Sodium	31.80 mg.	Cholesterol	0.00 mg.
Saturated Fat	0.51 gm.		

Potato-Cheese Casserole

Serves: 6

6 russet potatoes
2 cups 1% low-fat cottage cheese
2 tablespoons olive oil
1 onion, chopped
2 tablespoons all-purpose flour

1 teaspoon dried parsley flakes
1 teaspoon dried thyme, crumbled
$1/8$ teaspoon salt
pepper to taste
$1/3$ cup nonfat milk
$1/2$ cup fine dried bread crumbs
2 tablespoons grated Parmesan cheese
2 tablespoons buttery light, reduced-fat
   margarine, cut into bits

Place the potatoes in a saucepan with water to cover. Bring to a boil, reduce the heat to medium, and simmer until tender, about 25 minutes. Drain and, when cool enough to handle, peel and slice.

Preheat oven to 350°F. Grease a $1/2$-quart baking dish.

In a bowl, beat together the cottage cheese and oil with a rotary beater until fluffy. Mix in the onion. In a small bowl, stir together the flour, parsley, thyme, salt, and pepper. Make a layer of one-third of the sliced potatoes in the prepared baking dish. Cover with a layer of half of the cottage cheese. Sprinkle with half of the seasoned flour. Repeat the layers, then end with a layer of potatoes. Pour the milk evenly over the potato-cheese layers. Mix the bread crumbs with the Parmesan cheese and sprinkle over the potatoes. Dot with margarine.

Bake until cheese is lightly browned, about 30 minutes. Serve hot directly from the dish.

Adding Heat

Whenever I am making a dish that calls for Tabasco sauce and I know I will be serving it to guests, I forego adding the Tabasco during cooking and instead just place the bottle of sauce on the table.

People have different expectations of what constitutes "hot" today. One person's hot is another person's tepid. Evidence of that fact is the difference between the hot curry I've encountered in Manhattan and the hot curry I might order in an Indian restaurant in my home state of New Hampshire.

In other words, play it safe. Let guests add their own heat.

(continued)

Calories	326.80 Kcal.	Protein	15.16 gm.
Fat	11.13 gm.	Carbohydrate	41.37 gm.
Sodium	527.74 mg.	Cholesterol	4.58 mg.
Saturated Fat	2.30 gm.		

Orangey Sweet Potatoes

Serves: 6

3 large sweet potatoes
1/4 cup orange juice
1 tablespoon buttery light, reduced-fat margarine
1/8 teaspoon salt
1/4 teaspoon pepper
1/4 teaspoon ground ginger
3 oranges, peeled and cut into small pieces
1/4 cup toasted almonds, slivered (optional)

Preheat oven to 400°F.

Pierce potatoes with fork and bake until tender, about 1 hour. Remove from the oven and leave the oven set at 400°F. Halve the sweet potatoes lengthwise and scoop out the pulp into a bowl, being careful to keep the skins intact. Set the skins aside. Mash the pulp, then add the orange juice, margarine, salt, pepper, and ginger. Stir the orange pieces into the mixture. Spoon into the skins and place on a baking sheet. Top with the almonds, if desired.

Bake until heated through, about 15 minutes. Serve hot.

Variations: Use 8 ounces canned crushed pineapple and its juice in place of the oranges

and orange juice. You may add 1/2 cup raisins to either mixture. The sweet potato mixture can be baked in a baking dish instead of being stuffed into the skins. The mixture can be prepared up to a day in advance and refrigerated until ready to be heated.

Nutritional Analysis

Calories	171.23 Kcal.	Protein	2.40 gm.
Fat	2.37 gm.	Carbohydrate	36.39 gm.
Sodium	85.42 mg.	Cholesterol	0.00 mg.
Saturated Fat	0.39 gm.		

Asian Rice

Serves: 10

1 1/2 cups water
1 cup defatted reduced-sodium, fat-free chicken broth
1 1/3 cups long-grain white rice
1 tablespoon buttery light, reduced-fat margarine
2 tablespoons finely chopped onion
2 tablespoons finely chopped green bell pepper
1/4 teaspoon ground sage
1 cup finely chopped celery
1/2 cup chopped pecans
1/2 cup sliced water chestnuts
1/4 teaspoon ground nutmeg
1/8 teaspoon pepper

In a medium saucepan, bring the water and broth to a boil. Add the rice, stir, cover, reduce the heat to low, and simmer for 20 minutes.

Remove from the heat. Let stand, covered, until all the liquid is absorbed, about 5 minutes. Meanwhile, melt the margarine in a large nonstick skillet over medium heat. Add the onion, celery, and peppers and sauté until tender, about 3 minutes. Stir in the pecans, water chestnuts, nutmeg, and pepper and heat through. Add the rice and fluff with a fork to distribute all the ingredients evenly, then serve.

Nutritional Analysis

Calories	145.42 Kcal.	Protein	2.68 gm.
Fat	4.98 gm.	Carbohydrate	22.47 gm.
Sodium	82.30 mg.	Cholesterol	0.00 mg.
Saturated Fat	0.52 gm.		

Wonderful Stuffed Potatoes

Serves: 8

4 baking potatoes
³/₄ cup 1% low-fat cottage cheese
¹/₄ cup 1% milk
2 tablespoons buttery light, reduced-fat margarine
1 teaspoon dill weed, dried
³/₄ teaspoon herb seasoning
4 to 6 drops Tabasco sauce
2 teaspoons grated Parmesan cheese

Preheat oven to 425°F.

Prick the potatoes with a fork. Bake until easily pierced with a fork, about 1 hour. Remove from the oven and leave the oven set at 425°F. Halve the potatoes lengthwise and scoop out the pulp

into a bowl, leaving shells about ¹/₂ inch thick. Mash the pulp, then mix in all the remaining ingredients except the Parmesan cheese. Spoon into the potato shells. Place on a baking sheet, and sprinkle the top of each with ¹/₄ teaspoon Parmesan cheese. Bake until tops are golden brown, 15 to 20 minutes.

Nutritional Analysis

Calories	130.95 Kcal.	Protein	5.60 gm.
Fat	3.38 gm.	Carbohydrate	20.10 gm.
Sodium	139.99 mg.	Cholesterol	1.46 mg.
Saturated Fat	0.74 gm.		

Lemony Asparagus and Carrots

Serves: 6

¹/₂ pound baby carrots
1 package (8 ounces) frozen asparagus spears
2 tablespoons lemon juice
1 teaspoon lemon pepper

Steam the carrots until crisp tender, about 15 minutes, then plunge into cold water to cool. Drain and place in a bowl.

Meanwhile, cook the frozen asparagus spears according to the package directions, then plunge into cold water to cool, and drain. Add to the carrots, cover, and chill for 30 minutes.

To serve, arrange the carrots and asparagus on a platter. Sprinkle with a little lemon juice and lemon pepper.

(continued)

Dijon Coleslaw

Serves: 6

1 small head cabbage, shredded
4 scallions, chopped
1 small yellow onion, sliced
1/2 green bell pepper, sliced
2 carrots, shredded or sliced
1/4 cup golden or dark raisins
1/2 teaspoon celery seeds
1/2 cup low-fat mayonnaise
1/4 cup nonfat sour cream
1/2 cup nonfat buttermilk
1 tablespoon Dijon or other prepared mustard
1 to 3 tablespoons cider vinegar
2 teaspoons sugar

In a large bowl, combine the cabbage, scallions, yellow onion, bell pepper, carrots, raisins, and celery seeds. In a small bowl, whisk together all the remaining ingredients. Add the mayonnaise mixture to the cabbage mixture and stir to combine. Refrigerate for 15 minutes in the refrigerator (so liquid will drain to bottom). Pour off any liquid, mix well again, and serve cold.

Nutritional Analysis

Calories	109.64 Kcal.	Protein	3.69 gm.
Fat	0.35 gm.	Carbohydrate	23.56 gm.
Sodium	264.67 mg.	Cholesterol	1.41 mg.
Saturated Fat	0.02 gm.		

Nutritional Analysis

Calories	26.39 Kcal.	Protein	1.62 gm.
Fat	0.16 gm.	Carbohydrate	5.69 gm.
Sodium	87.46 mg.	Cholesterol	0.00 mg.
Saturated Fat	0.02 gm.		

Pineapple-Pear Mold

Serves: 6

2 envelopes unflavored gelatin
2 1/2 cups orange juice
1 can (20 ounces) crushed pineapple
2 medium pears, cored, peeled, and diced

In a small saucepan, soften the gelatin in 1/2 cup of the orange juice for 5 minutes. Place over low heat and stir until the gelatin dissolves. Stir in the undrained crushed pineapple and the remaining 2 cups orange juice. Cover and chill until partially set, about 30 minutes.

Fold the pears into the pineapple mixture and transfer to a 6-cup mold.

Cover and chill until firm, about 30 minutes. To unmold, dip the bottom of the mold in hot water for 10 seconds, then invert onto a plate.

Nutritional Analysis

Calories	143.80 Kcal.	Protein	3.29 gm.
Fat	0.35 gm.	Carbohydrate	34.36 gm.
Sodium	6.54 mg.	Cholesterol	0.00 mg.
Saturated Fat	0.02 gm.		

Potato Gratin

Serves: 6

3 medium russet potatoes, thinly sliced
2 tablespoons all-purpose flour
1 medium onion, thinly sliced into rings
1/8 teaspoon cayenne pepper
1 teaspoon paprika
1/2 teaspoon pepper
1/4 cup grated Parmesan cheese
1 small zucchini, thinly sliced
1/4 teaspoon nutmeg
1 can (12 ounces) evaporated milk
2 teaspoons chopped fresh parsley

Preheat oven to 400°F.

Coat a 9-inch pie dish or a similar-sized gratin dish with 3 sprays of cooking spray. Layer one-third of the potatoes over the bottom of the prepared dish, overlapping the slices in a spiral pattern. Sprinkle 1 tablespoon of the flour over the potatoes and arrange the onion rings on top. Dust with the cayenne pepper and 1/2 teaspoon of the paprika. Layer another third of the potatoes, adding the remaining flour, all the black pepper, and 2 tablespoons of the Parmesan cheese. Scatter the zucchini over top, and dust with the nutmeg. Top with a spiral layer of the remaining potatoes. Pour the evaporated milk evenly over the gratin and sprinkle on the remaining 1/2 teaspoon paprika and 2 tablespoons Parmesan cheese. Cover the dish with foil.

Bake for 45 minutes. Uncover, reduce the oven temperature to 350°F and continue to bake until

the top is golden brown, about 15 minutes longer. Remove from the oven and let cool for 10 minutes. Garnish with the parsley and serve.

Nutritional Analysis

Calories	196.52 Kcal.	Protein	8.15 gm.
Fat	6.54 gm.	Carbohydrate	27.03 gm.
Sodium	137.21 mg.	Cholesterol	20.90 mg.
Saturated Fat	3.52 gm.		

Herbed Rice Pilaf

Serves: 4

1 tablespoon olive oil
1 onion, chopped
2 celery stalks, chopped
1 clove garlic, minced
1 teaspoon dried thyme, crumbled
1 bay leaf
2 1/2 cups water
1 cup long-grain white rice
1 fresh thyme sprig

In a medium saucepan, heat the oil over medium heat. Add the onion, celery, garlic, and thyme and sauté until the onion is translucent, about 5 minutes. Add the bay leaf and water, bring to a boil, and add the rice. Cover, reduce the heat to low, and simmer until all the water is absorbed and rice is tender, about 20 minutes.

Remove and discard the bay leaf. Spoon pilaf into a serving bowl. Garnish with the thyme sprig.

(continued)

Nutritional Analysis

Calories	221.24 Kcal.	Protein	4.02 gm.
Fat	3.79 gm.	Carbohydrate	42.08 gm.
Sodium	21.40 mg.	Cholesterol	0.00 mg.
Saturated Fat	0.54 gm.		

Risotto with Winter Squash

Serves: 6

>   1 tablespoon olive oil
>   1 cup finely chopped shallots or onions
>   1 teaspoon dried sage, crumbled
>   1½ cups Arborio rice
>   3½ to 4 cups vegetable broth
>   1 small butternut squash, about 1 pound,
>   peeled, seeded, and cut into 1-inch cubes
>   (about 3 cups)
>   1 teaspoon salt, or to taste
>   ¼ cup grated Parmesan cheese or balsamic
>   vinegar to taste
>   pepper to taste
>   2 tablespoons minced fresh parsley

Heat the oil in a pressure cooker over medium-high heat. Add the shallots and sauté, stirring frequently, for 1 minute. Add the sage and rice and stir to coat the rice with the oil. Stir in 3 ½ cups of the broth and bring to a boil. Add the squash and salt. Secure the lid in place and bring to high pressure over high heat. Adjust the heat to maintain high pressure and cook for 5 minutes. Reduce the pressure with the quick-release

method. Remove the lid, tilting it away from you to allow excess steam to escape.

If the risotto isn't creamy, stir in the remaining ½ cup broth. Cook over medium heat, stirring constantly, until the rice achieves the desired consistency. Stir in the Parmesan cheese or vinegar, pepper, and parsley. Serve immediately in shallow soup bowls.

Nutritional Analysis

Calories	246.13 Kcal.	Protein	6.94 gm.
Fat	3.83 gm.	Carbohydrate	47.04 gm.
Sodium	612.92 mg.	Cholesterol	2.63 mg.
Saturated Fat	0.94 gm.		

Mediterranean Vegetable Couscous

Serves: 6

>   1 to 2 tablespoons olive oil
>   2 teaspoons minced garlic
>   1 cup coarsely chopped onions
>   1½ cups boiling water
>   1 small fennel bulb, cut into ½-inch strips
>   (about 2½ cups; chop and reserve fronds),
>   or 2 large celery stalks, cut into ½-inch-
>   thick slices, plus ½ teaspoon fennel seeds
>   1 large red bell pepper, thinly sliced
>   1 large carrot, cut on diagonal into ½-inch-
>   wide slices
>   ¼ pound mushrooms, halved
>   2 medium zucchini, cut into 1½-inch chunks

1¹/₂ cups coarsely chopped plum tomatoes
¹/₃ cup pitted oil-cured black olives
1¹/₂ teaspoons dried basil leaves, crumbled
1¹/₂ teaspoons dried oregano leaves, crumbled
1 teaspoon salt or to taste
¹/₄ teaspoon ground cinnamon
¹/₈ teaspoon pepper
1 to 3 tablespoons balsamic vinegar or lemon juice
1¹/₂ cups instant whole-wheat couscous
¹/₄ cup minced fresh basil or parsley

Heat 1 tablespoon oil in a pressure cooker over medium-high heat. Add the garlic and cook, stirring constantly, until just browned. Add the onions and cook, stirring frequently, for 1 minute. Add the water, fennel bulb strips or celery and fennel seeds, bell pepper, carrot, mushrooms, zucchini, tomatoes, olives, dried basil, oregano, salt, cinnamon, and pepper.

Secure the lid in place and bring to high pressure over high heat. Adjust the heat to maintain high pressure and cook for 2 minutes. Reduce the pressure with the quick-release method. Remove the lid, tilting it away from you to allow excess steam to escape.

Stir in 1 tablespoon vinegar or lemon juice and the couscous. Replace the lid and let stand until couscous is tender, about 5 minutes. Add the fennel fronds, if using, the fresh basil or parsley, the remaining 1 tablespoon oil, and additional vinegar or lemon juice to taste. Stir well and serve.

Note: Leftovers are terrific at room temperature. Drizzle with olive oil and lemon juice and garnish with olives.

Nutritional Analysis

Calories	323.84 Kcal.	Protein	10.99 gm.
Fat	7.69 gm.	Carbohydrate	57.88 gm.
Sodium	707.99 mg.	Cholesterol	0.00 mg.
Saturated Fat	0.80 gm.		

Southwest Succotash

Serves: 6

1 tablespoon safflower or canola oil
³/₄ teaspoon cumin seeds
2 teaspoons finely minced garlic
1 cup coarsely chopped onions
1 medium red bell pepper, diced
1 or 2 jalapeño peppers, seeded and diced; 1 chipotle pepper, seeded and chopped into bits; or 1 generous pinch of red pepper flakes
1 cup water
2 tablespoons tomato paste
1 butternut or kabocha squash, 1¹/₂ pounds, halved, seeded, peeled, and cut into 1-inch pieces
2 cups fresh or frozen corn kernels
salt to taste
2 cups frozen baby lima beans, thawed
¹/₄ to ¹/₃ cup minced fresh coriander

(continued)

Heat the oil in a pressure cooker over medium-high heat. Add the cumin seeds and let sizzle for 5 seconds. Add the garlic and cook, stirring frequently, until light brown, about 5 to 7 minutes. Add the onions, bell pepper, and jalapeño or chipotle pepper and continue cooking, stirring frequently, for 1 minute.

Add water, tomato paste, squash, corn, and salt. Secure the lid in place and bring to high pressure over high heat. Adjust the heat to maintain high pressure and cook for 2 minutes. Reduce the pressure with the quick-release method. Remove the lid, tilting it away from you to allow excess steam to escape. If the squash is not quite tender, replace but do not lock the lid; allow the squash to steam for a few more minutes in the residual heat.

Stir in the lima beans, cover, and simmer until tender, 2 to 3 minutes. Stir in the coriander just before serving.

Nutritional Analysis

Calories	205.41 Kcal.	Protein	7.53 gm.
Fat	3.17 gm.	Carbohydrate	41.17 gm.
Sodium	79.08 mg.	Cholesterol	0.00 mg.
Saturated Fat	0.27 gm.		

Coriander Carrots

Serves: 6

1 tablespoon oil
1/2 cup chopped leeks or onions
3/4 to 1 cup water
1/4 cup dried currants or raisins
1 tablespoon ground coriander
1 bay leaf
1/2 teaspoon salt, or to taste
1 1/2 pounds carrots, cut on the diagonal into 1/2-inch-thick slices
1 to 2 tablespoons lemon juice (optional)
1 tablespoon minced fresh parsley

Heat the oil in a pressure cooker over medium-high heat. Add the leeks or onions and cook, stirring frequently, for 1 minute. Add the water (use the amount recommended by the cooker manufacturer), currants or raisins, coriander, bay leaf, salt, and carrots.

Secure the lid in place and bring to high pressure over high heat. Adjust the heat to maintain high pressure and cook for 2 minutes. Reduce the pressure with the quick-release method. Remove the lid, tilting it away from you to allow excess steam to escape. If the carrots are not quite tender, replace but do not lock the lid. Let them continue to cook in residual steam another minute or two.

Just before serving, stir in lemon juice, if desired, and the parsley.

Nutritional Analysis

Calories	92.31 Kcal.	Protein	1.58 gm.
Fat	2.52 gm.	Carbohydrate	17.40 gm.
Sodium	235.56 mg.	Cholesterol	0.00 mg.
Saturated Fat	0.31 gm.		

Indian-Style Rice

Serves: 6

2 cups water
2 teaspoons curry powder
1/2 teaspoon ground turmeric
1/4 teaspoon ground cinnamon
1 cup long-grain white rice
1 package (9 ounces) frozen green beans
1 onion, chopped
1 clove garlic, minced
2 peaches, pitted, peeled, and coarsely
*   chopped*
1/2 cup plain low-fat yogurt
1 peach, pitted, peeled, and sliced
1/4 cup raisins

In a saucepan, combine the water, curry powder, turmeric, and cinnamon. Bring to a boil, add the rice, cover, reduce the heat to low, and cook until the liquid is absorbed and the rice is tender, about 20 minutes.

Meanwhile, place the frozen beans in a colander. Run hot water over them to thaw; drain well. Preheat oven to 375°F.

When the rice is ready, mix the onion and garlic in it. Spoon half of the rice into a 1½-quart baking dish. Scatter the chopped peaches and green beans over the rice. Top with the remaining rice mixture. Cover the dish with foil.

Bake for 30 minutes. Serve immediately. Pass the yogurt, sliced peaches, and raisins at the table, if desired.

(continued)

Exotic Rices

Although many of the rice recipes in *The Everything Low-Fat, High-Flavor Cookbook* can be made with ordinary white rice, you can easily add a bit of interest to these dishes by using an exotic rice, such as Arborio, jasmine, basmati, or brown rice.

Arborio rice is from Italy and is used most often in risotto dishes. Jasmine is a faintly aromatic Thai white rice that cooks up as easily as regular long-grain white rice and adds a bit of sweetness to your dish. Basmati is a Middle Eastern rice of long, slender grains that adds a hint of perfume to a dish. Finally, brown rice contains a good deal more fiber than white rice and has a nutty taste.

Nutritional Analysis

Calories	199.45 Kcal.	Protein	5.02 gm.
Fat	0.77 gm.	Carbohydrate	44.42 gm.
Sodium	18.14 mg.	Cholesterol	1.13 mg.
Saturated Fat	0.25 gm.		

Mushroom-Pineapple Rice

Serves: 4

> 1 can (8½ ounces) crushed pineapple,
>   drained, with liquid reserved
> 1 teaspoon salt
> 1 cup long-grain white rice
> 1 tablespoon butter
> ¼ cup minced scallions
> ¼ pound mushrooms, sliced
> 2 teaspoons soy sauce
> ½ teaspoon ground ginger
> ¼ cup cashews

Pour the pineapple liquid into a measuring pitcher and add enough water to measure 2½ cups. Pour into a medium saucepan, add the salt, and bring to a boil. Stir in the rice. Cover, reduce the heat to low, and cook until the liquid is absorbed and the rice is tender, about 20 minutes.

Meanwhile, melt the butter in a skillet over medium heat. Add the scallions and mushrooms and sauté until tender, about 5 minutes. Stir in the soy sauce, ginger, and pineapple, mixing well. Keep hot.

When the rice is ready, add the mushroom mixture and the nuts to it, stirring to distribute them evenly, then serve.

Nutritional Analysis

Calories	290.99 Kcal.	Protein	5.75 gm.
Fat	7.30 gm.	Carbohydrate	51.38 gm.
Sodium	790.07 mg.	Cholesterol	7.76 mg.
Saturated Fat	2.65 gm.		

Brown Rice with Pears

Serves: 8

> 3 tablespoons lemon juice
> 2 teaspoons finely chopped garlic
> ¼ teaspoon ground ginger
> ¼ teaspoon pepper
> 2 Bartlett pears, cored, peeled, and diced
> 3½ cups cooked brown rice, at room
>   temperature
> ½ cup sliced scallions
> ½ cup grated carrots
> ½ cup thinly sliced celery
> 2 tablespoons vegetable oil

In a bowl, combine the lemon juice, garlic, ginger, and pepper. Add the pears, toss to coat, and set aside. In a separate bowl, combine all the remaining ingredients, mixing well. Gently fold in the pears. Cover and chill before serving.

Nutritional Analysis

Calories	158.23 Kcal.	Protein	2.66 gm.
Fat	4.36 gm.	Carbohydrate	27.97 gm.
Sodium	15.54 mg.	Cholesterol	0.00 mg.
Saturated Fat	0.58 gm.		

Rancho California Rice

Serves: 6

2 tablespoons butter
1 cup chopped onions
4 cups cooked white rice
1 cup low-fat sour cream
1 cup 1% cottage cheese
1 bay leaf, crumbled
salt and pepper to taste
1 can (16 ounces) whole green chile peppers,
*   drained, seeded, and cut into strips*
1 cup shredded fat-free cheddar cheese

Preheat oven to 375°F. Grease a 2-quart baking dish.

In a skillet, melt the butter over low heat. Add the onions and sauté until translucent, about 5 minutes. Remove from the heat. Add the rice, sour cream, cottage cheese, bay leaf, salt, and pepper. Mix well. Layer one-third of the rice mixture in the prepared dish. Top with a layer of the chiles and then 1/3 cup of the cheddar cheese. Repeat the layers, ending with a layer of rice.

Bake for 25 minutes. Top with the remaining cheddar cheese and bake until cheese is lightly browned, about 10 minutes longer. Serve hot.

Nutritional Analysis

Calories	310.44 Kcal.	Protein	16.51 gm.
Fat	7.99 gm.	Carbohydrate	44.38 gm.
Sodium	835.47 mg.	Cholesterol	27.17 mg.
Saturated Fat	4.87 gm.		

Wonderful Risotto

Serves: 2

2 tablespoons butter
1 medium onion, diced
1 cup medium-grain white rice
1¾ cups reduced-sodium, fat-free chicken broth
½ cup sherry
½ cup grated Parmesan cheese

In a large skillet, melt butter over medium heat. Add the onion and sauté until golden brown, about 10 minutes. Add the rice and stir until the rice turns yellow. Add the broth and sherry, bring to a boil, cover, reduce the heat to low, and cook until the liquid is absorbed and the rice is tender, about 20 minutes. Stir in the cheese and serve.

Nutritional Analysis

Calories	318.11 Kcal.	Protein	9.33 gm.
Fat	9.10 gm.	Carbohydrate	44.55 gm.
Sodium	496.57 mg.	Cholesterol	23.42 mg.
Saturated Fat	5.56 gm.		

Soulful Black-Eyed Peas

Serves: 8

1 tablespoon olive oil
1 cup chopped onion
2 cloves garlic, crushed
4 cups water
1 teaspoon salt
1 teaspoon dried thyme, crumbled
2 bay leaves
1/4 teaspoon cracked red or black pepper
1 pound dried black-eyed peas, picked over, soaked in water to cover for 1 hour, and drained

In a large, heavy saucepan, heat the oil over medium heat. Add the onion and sauté until almost browned, about 5 minutes. Stir in the garlic, water, salt, thyme, bay leaves, and pepper. Bring to a boil, add the drained peas, and return to a boil. Cover, reduce the heat to low, and cook until peas are tender, 45 minutes to 1 hour.

Nutritional Analysis

Calories	215.35 Kcal.	Protein	13.62 gm.
Fat	2.44 gm.	Carbohydrate	36.25 gm.
Sodium	301.18 mg.	Cholesterol	0.00 mg.
Saturated Fat	0.40 gm.		

Zesty Spanish Rice

Serves: 6

2 tablespoons olive oil
1 bunch fresh parsley, finely chopped

1 large onion, finely chopped
1 tablespoon finely chopped garlic
3 cups water
2 tablespoons tomato paste
1 cup peeled and chopped tomatoes
1/8 teaspoon salt
1/8 teaspoon pepper
1 package (10 ounces) spinach, stemmed and chopped
1 cup white rice

In a large saucepan, heat the oil over medium-high heat. Add the parsley, onion, and garlic, and sauté until translucent, 3 to 4 minutes. Add the water and bring to a boil. Add the tomato paste, chopped tomatoes, salt, and pepper. Mix thoroughly. Add the spinach and rice, reduce the heat to low, and cook, covered, until the liquid is absorbed and the rice is tender, about 30 minutes. Serve at once.

Nutritional Analysis

Calories	189.26 Kcal.	Protein	4.14 gm.
Fat	5.00 gm.	Carbohydrate	32.49 gm.
Sodium	122.79 mg.	Cholesterol	0.00 mg.
Saturated Fat	0.68 gm.		

Wild Rice Casserole

Serves: 6

1 tablespoon olive oil
1 cup chopped onions
1 cup sliced mushrooms
3 celery stalks, chopped

1 cup wild rice
1 teaspoon seasoned salt
4¹/₂ cups reduced-sodium, fat-free chicken broth
salt and pepper to taste

Preheat oven to 325°F.

In a sauté pan, heat the oil over medium heat. Add the onions and sauté until translucent, about 5 minutes. Add the mushrooms and celery and sauté until warmed through. Transfer to a 2-quart baking dish and add the rice, seasoned salt, broth, salt, and pepper. Cover the dish with foil.

Bake until the rice is tender, about 1 hour. Serve hot.

Nutritional Analysis

Calories	142.58 Kcal.	Protein	6.86 gm.
Fat	2.63 gm.	Carbohydrate	23.54 gm.
Sodium	652.11 mg.	Cholesterol	0.00 mg.
Saturated Fat	0.34 gm.		

Glazed Baby Carrots

Serves: 8

2 pounds baby carrots
1 tablespoon butter
2 tablespoons chopped fresh herbs (such as dill, parsley, or rosemary)
1 bunch fresh mint, minced
salt and pepper to taste

Place the carrots in a heavy saucepan and add water to barely cover. Add the butter, cover, and bring to a boil. Reduce the heat to low and

cook until still firm but easy to pierce with a fork, about 15 minutes.

Remove the cover, bring to a boil, and boil until the liquid has evaporated and carrots are coated with butter, about 12 to 15 minutes. Watch the carrots carefully, as they burn easily. Add the herbs, season with salt and pepper, and serve.

Nutritional Analysis

Calories	63.10 Kcal.	Protein	1.28 gm.
Fat	1.66 gm.	Carbohydrate	11.79 gm.
Sodium	55.49 mg.	Cholesterol	3.88 mg.
Saturated Fat	0.92 gm.		

"Creamed" Spinach

Serves: 6

1 package (10 ounces) fresh spinach, chopped
1 small onion, finely chopped
1 teaspoon olive oil
3 tablespoons all-purpose flour
1¹/₄ cups 1% milk
1 teaspoon salt
¹/₂ teaspoon pepper

Place the spinach in a heavy skillet over medium heat, cover, and steam, stirring occasionally, until wilted, about 5 minutes. (There is no need to add water other than what clings to the leaves from washing.) Place in a sieve and press with the back of a spoon to remove as much moisture as possible.

(continued)

In a nonstick saucepan, sauté the onion in the olive oil over medium heat until translucent, about 7 to 10 minutes. Stir in the flour until a smooth paste forms. Gradually add milk, stirring constantly. Bring just to a boil, reduce the heat to low, and simmer, stirring often, until thickened, about 10 minutes. Add the salt and pepper. Grind the spinach fine in a blender or food processor and add to the cream sauce. Serve hot.

Nutritional Analysis

Calories	60.23 Kcal.	Protein	3.64 gm.
Fat	1.50 gm.	Carbohydrate	8.79 gm.
Sodium	451.78 mg.	Cholesterol	2.03 mg.
Saturated Fat	0.45 gm.		

Potato Parsnip Purée

Serves: 6

3 parsnips, peeled and quartered
2 russet potatoes, peeled and quartered
1/2 onion, cut into wedges
2 cloves garlic
4 cups water
salt and pepper to taste

In a saucepan, combine the parsnips, potatoes, onion, and garlic. Pour in the water, cover, and bring to a boil. Reduce the heat to medium and cook until all the vegetables are tender, about 20 minutes. Drain the vegetables, then purée with a handheld blender or pass through a potato ricer. Season with salt and pepper and serve immediately.

Yogurt: The Secret Weapon

One of the best tips for successfully pursuing a low-fat diet is to have a container of plain low-fat yogurt in your refrigerator at all times. Just a few spoonfuls of yogurt can add creaminess and a bit of zip to nearly any recipe.

You can forget about sugared, flavored yogurts for the most part. If you hanker for a bit of variety, however, a cup of lemon-flavored low-fat yogurt can add flavor and a lemony zest to rice or even to Indian Raita.

Nutritional Analysis

Calories	93.19 Kcal.	Protein	1.87 gm.
Fat	0.28 gm.	Carbohydrate	20.91 gm.
Sodium	10.18 mg.	Cholesterol	0.00 mg.
Saturated Fat	0.02 gm.		

Sparkling Carrots

Serves: 8

> 2 tablespoons buttery light, reduced-fat
>   margarine
> 1 small onion, chopped
> 1 1/2 pounds carrots, thinly sliced
> 1 cup lemon-lime carbonated soda
> salt and pepper to taste
> 1 tablespoon sugar

In a large saucepan, melt the margarine over medium heat. Add the onion and sauté until translucent, about 5 minutes. Add the carrots and carbonated beverage, and season with salt and pepper. Add the sugar, raise the heat to high, and cook until the liquid is absorbed and carrots are slightly glazed, 8 to 10 minutes. Serve hot.

Nutritional Analysis

Calories	72.79 Kcal.	Protein	1.03 gm.
Fat	1.68 gm.	Carbohydrate	14.60 gm.
Sodium	47.34 mg.	Cholesterol	0.00 mg.
Saturated Fat	0.39 gm.		

Steamed Sweet Potatoes with Yogurt-Herb Sauce

Serves: 8

> 1 1/2 pounds sweet potatoes, peeled and sliced
>   1/4 inch thick
> 1 tablespoon buttery light, reduced-fat
>   margarine
> 1 cup chopped onions
> 1 clove garlic, crushed
> 3/4 teaspoon dried dill, crumbled
> 3/4 teaspoon paprika
> 1/4 teaspoon salt
> dash of pepper
> 1/2 cup plain nonfat yogurt
> 1 tablespoon lemon juice
> dried parsley flakes

Steam the sweet potatoes until just tender, 6 to 10 minutes. Transfer to a warmed serving dish and keep hot. Meanwhile, melt the margarine in a small saucepan over medium heat. Add the onions, garlic, dill, paprika, salt, and pepper. Sauté until the onions are tender, 6 to 8 minutes. Remove from the heat and stir in the yogurt and lemon juice. Return to low heat and cook until heated through, about 1 minute.

Pour the yogurt sauce over the potatoes and stir to coat. Sprinkle with the parsley and serve immediately.

(continued)

Nutritional Analysis

Calories	94.45 Kcal.	Protein	2.12 gm.
Fat	1.67 gm.	Carbohydrate	18.11 gm.
Sodium	108.26 mg.	Cholesterol	0.28 mg.
Saturated Fat	0.28 gm.		

Sesame Garlic Kasha

Serves: 4

1 tablespoon Asian sesame oil
³/₄ cup kasha
1 egg, lightly beaten
1³/₄ cups boiling water
1 clove garlic, minced
1 tablespoon soy sauce

In a saucepan, heat the sesame oil over medium heat. Add the kasha and sauté for 5 minutes. Add the egg and stir until the egg is cooked. Pour in the boiling water, stir well, and cook, uncovered, for 3 minutes. Add the garlic and soy sauce, cover, and cook over low heat until kasha is tender, about 10 minutes. Remove from the heat and let stand, covered, for 5 minutes before serving.

Nutritional Analysis

Calories	184.99 Kcal.	Protein	6.63 gm.
Fat	5.54 gm.	Carbohydrate	29.12 gm.
Sodium	276.78 mg.	Cholesterol	53.12 mg.
Saturated Fat	0.86 gm.		

Orange Pilaf

Serves: 4

¹/₂ cup raisins
¹/₃ cup slivered blanched almonds
grated zest and juice of 1 orange
¹/₂ tablespoon Asian sesame oil
³/₄ cup bulgur
1 small onion, chopped
1¹/₂ cups water

Combine the raisins, nuts, orange zest, and orange juice in a blender. Blend for 5 seconds.

In a nonstick saucepan, heat the oil over medium heat. Add the bulgur and onion and sauté for 3 minutes. Reduce the heat to low and add the orange mixture. Add the water. Cover and cook until the bulgur is tender, 15 to 20 minutes. Fluff with a fork before serving.

Nutritional Analysis

Calories	248.80 Kcal.	Protein	6.60 gm.
Fat	8.10 gm.	Carbohydrate	41.75 gm.
Sodium	8.90 mg.	Cholesterol	0.00 mg.
Saturated Fat	0.88 gm.		

Pesto Potatoes

Serves: 3

12 red new potatoes
2 tablespoons pesto, homemade or
  commercially prepared
salt and pepper to taste

Steam the potatoes until tender, about 15 minutes. Remove from the steamer, place in a bowl, and add the pesto. Toss well, season with salt and pepper, and serve.

Nutritional Analysis

Calories	173.83 Kcal.	Protein	3.89 gm.
Fat	5.26 gm.	Carbohydrate	28.00 gm.
Sodium	84.80 mg.	Cholesterol	1.66 mg.
Saturated Fat	0.83 gm.		

Ginger Carrots

Serves: 3

1/4 cup distilled white vinegar
1 tablespoon honey
1 tablespoon water
1 tablespoon soy sauce
1 tablespoon peeled and grated fresh ginger
2 carrots, julienned

In a bowl, stir together the vinegar, honey, water, soy sauce, and ginger. Add the carrots and toss thoroughly to coat.

Nutritional Analysis

Calories	49.07 Kcal.	Protein	0.85 gm.
Fat	0.10 gm.	Carbohydrate	12.49 gm.
Sodium	360.44 mg.	Cholesterol	0.00 mg.
Saturated Fat	0.01 gm.		

Fresh Ginger

Fresh ginger is readily available these days, and it's so tangy and flavorful that I don't know why everyone isn't using it.

One of my favorite ways to use grated fresh ginger is to add it to ice cream. People aren't expecting to taste it in their dessert bowls, and they immediately discover what a great flavor it imparts. It's also an effective breath freshener. A former landlady of mine always chewed fresh ginger before she went out ballroom dancing. She never lacked partners, so I figure it worked.

Curried Cauliflower

Serves: 4

1 cauliflower, cut into florets
1 cup peeled and sliced potato
4 cups 1% milk
1 tablespoon butter
1 teaspoon salt
1 teaspoon curry powder
1 teaspoon ground cumin
2 tablespoons minced onion

In a large saucepan, combine the cauliflower, potato, and milk. Bring to a boil, cover, reduce the heat to medium, and cook until the cauliflower is tender, about 20 minutes.

Remove from the heat and, working in batches if necessary, purée in a food processor. Add the butter, salt, curry powder, and cumin, mixing well. Pour into a bowl, cover, and chill overnight. Adjust the seasonings before serving. Garnish with the onion.

Nutritional Analysis

Calories	184.21 Kcal.	Protein	10.77 gm.
Fat	5.81 gm.	Carbohydrate	23.70 gm.
Sodium	750.58 mg.	Cholesterol	17.52 mg.
Saturated Fat	3.42 gm.		

Open Sesame Carrots

Serves: 6

1 tablespoon sesame seeds
¼ cup orange juice

Asian Sesame Oil

Asian sesame oil, which is widely available in supermarkets, is not like the big bottles of vegetable oils that line the market shelves. Because sesame oil is generally used only in small amounts, it is typically available in glass bottles holding 10 ounces or less.

Asian sesame oil is made from roasted seeds, and it has an intense nutty taste that brings out the earthy flavor of a brown rice or wild rice. Indeed, whenever you want to add a nutty taste to a dish without using nuts that are rich in fats, choose sesame oil. You'll get robust flavor with a minimum of fat and calories.

1 tablespoon peeled and grated fresh ginger
1 teaspoon Asian sesame oil
1 teaspoon soy sauce
1 pound carrots, julienne
salt and pepper to taste

In a small skillet, heat the sesame seeds over medium heat, stirring occasionally, until golden brown, about 1 minute. Transfer to a plate. In a small bowl, mix together the orange juice, ginger, sesame oil, and soy sauce; set aside.

Steam the carrots until tender, about 5 to 8 minutes. Transfer to a bowl and add the sesame seeds and ginger mixture. Toss well, season with salt and pepper, and serve.

Nutritional Analysis

Calories	53.70 Kcal.	Protein	1.16 gm.
Fat	1.63 gm.	Carbohydrate	9.36 gm.
Sodium	84.13 mg.	Cholesterol	0.00 mg.
Saturated Fat	0.22 gm.		

Roasted Potatoes with Rosemary and Garlic

Serves: 8

2 pounds red new potatoes, sliced
2 tablespoons olive oil
3 cloves garlic, minced
2 teaspoons dried rosemary
salt and pepper to taste

Preheat oven to 325°F.
In a large baking dish, toss the potatoes with the oil, garlic, rosemary, salt, and pepper. Bake

until the potatoes are tender when pierced with a fork, about 1 hour. Serve at once.

Nutritional Analysis

Calories	124.12 Kcal.	Protein	2.25 gm.
Fat	3.62 gm.	Carbohydrate	20.92 gm.
Sodium	9.05 mg.	Cholesterol	0.00 mg.
Saturated Fat	0.47 gm.		

Buttermilk Mashed Potatoes

Serves: 12

3 pounds potatoes, peeled and quartered
2 cups buttermilk, heated
2 tablespoons butter
1 onion, chopped
pinch of ground nutmeg
salt and pepper to taste

Place the potatoes in a large saucepan with water to cover. Bring to a boil, cover, reduce the heat to medium, and cook until tender, about 20 minutes. Drain, return to the pan, and mash until smooth. Gradually add the buttermilk, stirring constantly. Stir in the butter, then add the onion, nutmeg, salt, and pepper. Serve immediately.

Nutritional Analysis

Calories	105.94 Kcal.	Protein	3.29 gm.
Fat	2.36 gm.	Carbohydrate	18.47 gm.
Sodium	67.91 mg.	Cholesterol	6.80 mg.
Saturated Fat	1.43 gm.		

Oven-Baked Fries

Serves: 6

4 large potatoes, cut into fries
1 tablespoon vegetable oil
½ teaspoon paprika
½ teaspoon chili powder

Preheat oven to 475°F.

In a medium bowl, toss together the potatoes, oil, paprika, and chili powder. Spread out on a baking sheet. Bake, turning occasionally, until golden, about 30 minutes. Serve hot.

Nutritional Analysis

Calories	132.87 Kcal.	Protein	3.35 gm.
Fat	2.48 gm.	Carbohydrate	25.33 gm.
Sodium	12.74 mg.	Cholesterol	0.00 mg.
Saturated Fat	0.32 gm.		

Sweet Potato and Apple Purée

Serves: 12

3 pounds sweet potatoes, peeled and cubed
2 large apples, cored, peeled, and chopped
½ cup water
1 tablespoon butter
ground nutmeg to taste
salt and pepper to taste
2 tablespoons sunflower seeds, toasted

In a medium saucepan, combine the potatoes with water to cover. Cover, bring to a boil, reduce the heat to medium, and cook until tender, about 15 minutes. Drain.

Meanwhile, in a small saucepan, combine the apples with the ½ cup water. Bring to a simmer over medium heat and cook until tender, about 5 minutes. Transfer the potatoes and undrained apples to a food processor and purée until smooth. Transfer to a warmed serving bowl. Add the butter, nutmeg, salt, and pepper and stir to mix and melt the butter. Sprinkle with the sunflower seeds and serve.

Nutritional Analysis

Calories	114.97 Kcal.	Protein	1.72 gm.
Fat	1.99 gm.	Carbohydrate	23.28 gm.
Sodium	20.41 mg.	Cholesterol	2.58 mg.
Saturated Fat	0.71 gm.		

Macaroni and Cheese

Serves: 8

2 cups macaroni
1 onion, chopped
2 cups 1% milk
2 tablespoons cornstarch
1 teaspoon dry mustard
1 cup shredded fat-free cheddar cheese
1 cup shredded low-fat mozzarella cheese
salt and pepper to taste
½ cup seasoned dried bread crumbs
2 tablespoons grated Parmesan cheese
1 tablespoon butter, melted

In a large pot, bring water to a boil. Add the macaroni and cook for 5 minutes. Add the onion and cook for another 5 minutes, or until the macaroni is nearly al dente. Drain and set aside.

Preheat oven to 350°F.

In a large saucepan, combine the milk, cornstarch, and mustard together, stirring to dissolve the cornstarch and mustard. Place over medium heat and cook, stirring, until thickened. Add the cheddar and mozzarella cheeses and cook, stirring, until the cheeses melt. Add the cooked macaroni, and season with salt and pepper. Pour into a 9 x 13-inch baking dish. In a small bowl, stir together the bread crumbs, Parmesan cheese, and butter. Scatter over the macaroni.

Bake until bubbly, about 20 minutes. Serve hot.

Nutritional Analysis

Calories	244.24 Kcal.	Protein	15.67 gm.
Fat	5.40 gm.	Carbohydrate	32.90 gm.
Sodium	440.90 mg.	Cholesterol	17.02 mg.
Saturated Fat	3.06 gm.		

Tomato Potatoes

Serves: 8

 1 tablespoon olive oil
 1 teaspoon butter
 2 onions, chopped
 6 cloves garlic, minced
 1 can (35 ounces) tomatoes, well drained and
   diced
 salt and pepper to taste

 2 tablespoons minced fresh parsley
 1 teaspoon dried basil, crumbled
 1 teaspoon dried oregano, crumbled
 2 1/2 pounds russet potatoes, thinly sliced
 1/2 cup grated Parmesan cheese

Preheat oven to 325°F. Spray a 3-quart baking dish with nonstick cooking spray.

In a skillet, heat the oil and the butter over medium heat. Add the onions and garlic and sauté for 1 minute. Cover, reduce the heat to low, and cook until the onions are translucent, about 5 minutes. Remove from the heat and add the tomatoes, salt, pepper, parsley, basil, and oregano. Mix well.

Spread one-third of the onion mixture in the prepared dish. Spread half of the sliced potatoes on top. Sprinkle salt and pepper and 1/4 cup of the Parmesan over the potatoes. Repeat the layers. Top with the remaining onion mixture. Cover with foil.

Bake for 1 1/4 hours. Uncover and continue to bake until the potatoes are tender, about 30 minutes longer. Serve hot.

Nutritional Analysis

Calories	205.27 Kcal.	Protein	6.56 gm.
Fat	4.80 gm.	Carbohydrate	35.30 gm.
Sodium	312.97 mg.	Cholesterol	5.24 mg.
Saturated Fat	1.64 gm.		

Spicy Sweet Potato Salad

Serves: 8

2 pounds sweet potatoes
1 small onion, chopped
2 celery stalks, minced
1/2 cup chopped fresh parsley
1 tablespoon olive oil
2 tablespoons lemon juice
1 teaspoon soy sauce
pepper to taste

In a saucepan, combine the sweet potatoes with water to cover. Cover, bring to a boil, reduce the heat to medium, and cook until tender, 30 to 40 minutes. Drain and let cool.

Peel and dice the sweet potatoes and place in a large bowl. Add the onion, celery, and parsley and stir to mix. In a small bowl, whisk together the olive oil, lemon juice, soy sauce, and pepper to form a dressing. Add the dressing to the potato mixture, toss gently, and serve warm.

Nutritional Analysis

Calories	110.10 Kcal.	Protein	1.69 gm.
Fat	1.97 gm.	Carbohydrate	21.97 gm.
Sodium	64.93 mg.	Cholesterol	0.00 mg.
Saturated Fat	0.26 gm.		

Scallion Tabbouleh

Serves: 8

1 cup bulgur
2 cups boiling water

1/2 cup chopped fresh parsley
2/3 cup raisins
1 cup chopped scallions
1/3 cup lime juice
2 tablespoons olive oil
salt and pepper to taste

In a medium bowl, mix together the bulgur and boiling water. Allow to stand for up to 1 hour, or until tender. Drain the bulgur in a colander to remove excess moisture, then transfer to a serving bowl. Add the parsley, raisins, and scallions. Toss to mix well. In a small bowl, stir together the lime juice, oil, salt, and pepper. Add to the bulgur mixture, toss well, and serve.

Nutritional Analysis

Calories	133.48 Kcal.	Protein	2.86 gm.
Fat	3.70 gm.	Carbohydrate	24.71 gm.
Sodium	9.50 mg.	Cholesterol	0.00 mg.
Saturated Fat	0.50 gm.		

Dilled Summer Green Beans

Serves: 6

1 pound green beans
3 cloves garlic, minced
12 fresh dill sprigs, chopped
1 teaspoon red pepper flakes
1/2 teaspoon dry mustard
1 cup cider vinegar
1 cup water
2 tablespoons sugar
1/2 teaspoon salt

Steam the beans until tender, about 5 minutes, then immediately plunge in cold water to cool. Drain.

Place beans in a bowl. Add the garlic, dill, red pepper flakes, and mustard. Combine the vinegar, water, sugar, and salt in a small saucepan and bring to a boil. Pour the hot marinade over the beans and let cool. Cover and chill overnight before serving.

Nutritional Analysis

Calories	48.85 Kcal.	Protein	1.56 gm.
Fat	0.21 gm.	Carbohydrate	12.51 gm.
Sodium	199.92 mg.	Cholesterol	0.00 mg.
Saturated Fat	0.01 gm.		

Baked Lima Bean Casserole

Serves: 6

1 tablespoon olive oil
1 onion, chopped
1 large apple, peeled, cored, and chopped
1 can (6 ounces) tomato paste
$1/2$ teaspoon dry mustard
3 tablespoons red wine vinegar
1 teaspoon dried oregano, crumbled
3 tablespoons honey
1 package (10 ounces) frozen lima beans, cooked and drained

Preheat oven to 350°F. Spray a 2-quart baking dish with nonstick cooking spray.

(continued)

Eyes on the Potato

Whenever you cook potatoes, try not to peel them if there is a choice. Potato skins can add a nice crunch to the overall texture of a dish, plus they carry valuable dietary fiber and vitamins.

If you're in a hurry and need precooked potato chunks for a recipe, cut them into thin slices. They'll cook faster than larger pieces.

In a skillet, heat the oil over medium heat. Add the onion and apple and sauté until the onion is translucent, about 5 minutes. Transfer to the prepared dish and add all the remaining ingredients, mixing well. Cover with foil. Bake until beans are tender, about 30 minutes. Serve hot.

Nutritional Analysis

Calories	154.35 Kcal.	Protein	4.52 gm.
Fat	3.00 gm.	Carbohydrate	29.92 gm.
Sodium	252.67 mg.	Cholesterol	0.00 mg.
Saturated Fat	0.37 gm.		

Baked Sweet Potatoes with Lime

Serves: 6

6 sweet potatoes
juice of 1 to 2 limes, to taste

Preheat oven to 350°F.

Prick the sweet potatoes with a fork. Place on a baking sheet and bake until tender when pierced with a fork, about 45 minutes. Remove from the oven and slice in half lengthwise almost all the way through. Sprinkle with the lime juice. Cover and chill overnight.

To serve, reheat in a 350°F oven for 30 minutes.

Nutritional Analysis

Calories	173.68 Kcal.	Protein	2.72 gm.
Fat	0.49 gm.	Carbohydrate	40.37 gm.
Sodium	21.31 mg.	Cholesterol	0.00 mg.
Saturated Fat	0.09 gm.		

Don't Forget the Herbs

When preparing side dishes don't forget fresh herbs and spices. Use fresh herbs whenever possible. Use a mortar and pestle to grind them for the freshest and fullest flavor. Add dried herbs such as ginger, thyme, rosemary and marjoram to dishes for a more pungent flavor, but use them sparingly. For example, chives, garlic, ginger, dill, onion, pimiento or saffron make for mouthwatering potatoes.

THE EVERYTHING
LOW-FAT HIGH-FLAVOR COOKBOOK

Pasta Dishes

CHAPTER SEVEN

Amount Per Chapter
41 Recipes

	% Daily Value
Easy to Prepare	**100%**
Low Fat / High Flavor	**100%**
Simple to Understand	**100%**

DELICIOUS, EASY, LOW-FAT RECIPES

onventional wisdom tells us that pasta is a natural low-fat food—the fat is in the sauce. For once, conventional wisdom is right. According to the National Pasta Association, a 2-ounce portion, the recommended serving size, has only 211 calories and 1 gram of fat. Even if 4 ounces is a more realistic helping, pasta is a calorie and fat bargain. To keep sauces in the same category takes some awareness. But with a few common-sense techniques, sauces can be kept low fat without sacrificing taste and texture.

It is also good to remember that the pasta itself is delicious, nutty in flavor, chewy, and pleasantly filling. Digging into a hot dish of noodles with just a touch of olive oil, salt, and garlic is so satisfying that forgoing more fattening ingredients really isn't difficult at all.

Penne with Chicken, Broccoli, and Rosemary

Serves: 4

1 tablespoon olive oil
1 clove garlic, minced
2 shallots, minced
1/2 teaspoon dried rosemary, crumbled
3/4 pound skinless chicken breast meat, cut into
*   bite-sized strips*
2 cups broccoli florets, separated into bite-sized
*   pieces*
1/2 cup reduced-sodium, fat-free chicken broth
1/4 cup dry white wine
2 tablespoons fresh parsley, chopped
1/2 pound penne
salt and pepper to taste
2 tablespoons grated Parmesan cheese

In a large, deep skillet, heat the oil over medium heat. Add garlic, shallots, and rosemary and cook for 1 minute. Add the chicken and sauté, tossing well, until lightly browned, about 3 minutes. Add the broccoli, broth, wine, and parsley. Simmer to heat through.

Meanwhile, cook the penne in boiling salted water until al dente. Drain.

Add the penne to the skillet with the chicken. Raise the heat to high and boil, stirring, until the liquid reduces enough to glaze the pasta lightly. Season with salt and pepper. Transfer to a warmed platter, sprinkle with the Parmesan, and serve.

Nutritional Analysis

Calories	382.67 Kcal.	Protein	30.69 gm.
Fat	6.43 gm.	Carbohydrate	47.03 gm.
Sodium	496.50 mg.	Cholesterol	51.34 mg.
Saturated Fat	1.38 gm.		

Summer Vegetable Spaghetti

Serves: 8

2 cups small onions, cut into eighths
2 cups peeled and chopped tomatoes
1 cup thinly sliced yellow squash
1 cup thinly sliced zucchini squash
1½ cups green beans, cut into ½-inch lengths
⅔ cup water
2 tablespoons minced fresh parsley
1 clove garlic, minced
½ teaspoon chili powder
¼ teaspoon salt
⅛ teaspoon pepper
1 can (6 ounces) tomato paste
1 pound spaghetti
½ cup grated Parmesan cheese

In a large saucepan, combine all the ingredients except the tomato paste, spaghetti, and cheese. Place over low heat and cook, stirring often, for 10 minutes, then stir in the tomato paste. Cover and cook gently, stirring occasionally, until the vegetables are tender, about 15 minutes. Meanwhile, cook the spaghetti in boiling unsalted water until al dente. Drain and place in a large bowl. Spoon the sauce over the spaghetti and then sprinkle the Parmesan over the top. Serve immediately.

Nutritional Analysis

Calories	289.00 Kcal.	Protein	11.71 gm.
Fat	2.86 gm.	Carbohydrate	54.96 gm.
Sodium	539.61 mg.	Cholesterol	3.95 mg.
Saturated Fat	1.13 gm.		

Broccoli-Pasta Toss

Serves: 6

2 cups broccoli florets
¼ pound eggless fettuccine, broken up
1 tablespoon olive oil
3 tablespoons grated Parmesan cheese
1 teaspoon sesame seeds, toasted
⅛ teaspoon garlic powder
pepper to taste

In a large saucepan, cook the broccoli and pasta in boiling salted water until the pasta is al dente, stirring once or twice. Drain and place in a bowl.

Add the oil to the pasta mixture and toss well. Add the cheese, sesame seeds, garlic powder, and pepper. Toss gently to coat. Serve immediately.

Nutritional Analysis

Calories	117.84 Kcal.	Protein	4.98 gm.
Fat	3.76 gm.	Carbohydrate	16.53 gm.
Sodium	130.94 mg.	Cholesterol	1.97 mg.
Saturated Fat	0.87 gm.		

Stuffed Pasta Triangles

Serves: 8

Pasta Triangles:
4 eggs
2 teaspoons oil
1/2 teaspoon salt
2 cups all-purpose flour

Tomato Sauce:
2 tablespoons olive oil
1 medium onion, minced
5 cloves garlic, crushed
2 cans (14 ounces each) plum tomatoes,
  undrained
8 fresh basil sprigs
2 teaspoons salt
pepper to taste
1 tablespoon sugar

Filling:
1 1/2 pounds part-skim ricotta cheese
3/4 pound spinach, cooked, chopped, and well
  drained
1 teaspoon ground nutmeg
4 eggs, lightly beaten
1/4 cup grated Parmesan cheese
salt and pepper to taste

1 tablespoon olive oil
2 tablespoons grated Parmesan cheese

To make the pasta, combine the eggs, oil, and salt in a large bowl and whisk until well blended. Add the flour, a little at a time, beating after each

Those Pasta Names!

Ruote! Radiatori! Capellini!

You don't need a degree in Italian to tell the different types of pasta apart in the supermarket, and serving these more unusual shapes is a great way to liven up a dish of pasta—in addition to using garlic, that is. Learn by studying the boxes, and have some fun when you tell your family you're serving little radiators (radiatori), angel hair (capellini), or wagon wheels (ruote).

addition. Turn out onto well-floured work surface and knead for several minutes until the dough is firm and smooth but not dry. Add more flour if necessary to reduce stickiness. Cover and let stand at slightly warm temperature for about 30 minutes to ripen.

Cut the dough in 2-inch portions. Flatten each portion slightly with a rolling pin so it will fit easily into the pasta machine. Working with 1 portion at a time and with the pasta machine set at its widest setting, roll the dough through the machine. Continue rolling out the dough while gradually narrowing the setting on the machine until the dough has passed through the next-to-finest setting. The pasta will be very thin (expansion takes place during cooking). Place on a floured work surface and sprinkle lightly with flour. Repeat until all the dough is rolled out into strips. Cut the strips into 4-inch squares and let rest for 10 minutes before cooking and filling.

To make the sauce, in a large skillet, heat the oil over medium-high heat. Add the onion and garlic and sauté until golden, about 5 minutes. Add the undrained tomatoes, basil, salt, and pepper. Bring to a boil and simmer about 15 minutes. Add the sugar at the last minute.

To make the filling, in a bowl, combine the ricotta cheese, spinach, nutmeg, eggs, and Parmesan and mix well. Season with salt and pepper.

Preheat oven to 400°F.

Bring a large pot of generously salted water to a boil. Add the 1 tablespoon oil. Drop the plain pasta squares, a few at a time, into the boiling water and cook just until they float to the surface, 3 to 4 minutes. Remove at once and plunge into a bowl filled with ice water; let stand for 1 minute. Transfer the squares to a clean kitchen towel to prevent sticking. Place 1 tablespoon filling in the center of each pasta square. Fold the square into a triangle, then again into a smaller triangle. Press edges together to seal.

Spoon a layer of the tomato sauce in a large baking dish. Arrange the pasta triangles on the sauce in rows, slightly overlapping them. Cover with the remaining sauce and sprinkle with additional Parmesan cheese.

Bake, uncovered, until cheese is lightly browned, 5 to 7 minutes. Serve hot.

 Nutritional Analysis

Calories	397.20 Kcal.	Protein	25.90 gm.
Fat	13.13 gm.	Carbohydrate	40.45 gm.
Sodium	1453.00 mg.	Cholesterol	215.45 mg.
Saturated Fat	3.22 gm.		

Pasta Shells with Zucchini
Serves: 4

2 teaspoons butter
1 clove garlic, minced
4 zucchini, sliced
1 teaspoon dried rosemary, crumbled
salt and pepper to taste
1 pound large pasta shells
2 tablespoon chopped fresh parsley
1/3 cup grated Parmesan cheese

(continued)

In a large skillet or shallow saucepan, melt the butter over medium heat. Add the garlic and zucchini and cook until crisp-tender, about 5 to 7 minutes. Add the rosemary and season with salt and pepper. Raise the heat and cook for a few minutes to blend the flavors. Remove from the heat.

Meanwhile, cook the pasta in boiling salted water until al dente. Drain thoroughly and add to the zucchini mixture. Return the pan to the heat and toss until the shells are well coated with sauce, 2 to 3 minutes. Add the parsley and cheese and toss again. Serve at once.

Nutritional Analysis

Calories	494.58 Kcal.	Protein	19.32 gm.
Fat	5.95 gm.	Carbohydrate	90.47 gm.
Sodium	544.04 mg.	Cholesterol	10.39 mg.
Saturated Fat	2.77 gm.		

Corkscrew Pasta with Spinach Pesto

Serves: 4

Pesto:

1 package (10 ounces) spinach, stemmed
4 cloves garlic, cut up
salt and pepper to taste
2 tablespoons olive oil

Pasta:

1 pound corkscrew pasta
1/2 cup low-fat mayonnaise
2 tablespoons olive oil
2 tablespoons pine nuts
diced pimiento

To make the pesto, combine spinach, garlic, salt, and pepper in a food processor. Process to chop finely. With the machine running, gradually add the 1/4 cup oil in a thin, steady stream, processing until the pesto is the consistency of thin mayonnaise. Set aside.

Cook the pasta in boiling salted water until al dente. Drain, then transfer to a large bowl. Add the mayonnaise and olive oil. Mix well. Add the pesto and stir and toss until well mixed. Cover and chill before serving. Garnish with the pine nuts and pimiento.

Nutritional Analysis

Calories	630.66 Kcal.	Protein	17.28 gm.
Fat	19.75 gm.	Carbohydrate	96.47 gm.
Sodium	717.36 mg.	Cholesterol	0.00 mg.
Saturated Fat	2.46 gm.		

California Fettuccine

Serves: 4

1/2 pound eggless fettuccine
1/2 avocado, pitted, peeled, and cut into chunks
1 can (8 ounces) marinated artichoke hearts, drained
1 large tomato, diced
2 cloves garlic, minced
1 tablespoon olive oil
2 scallions, thinly sliced
1/2 pound cooked shrimp
2 tablespoons grated Parmesan cheese

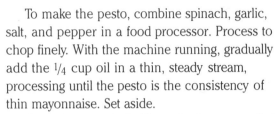

Cook the fettuccine in boiling salted water until al dente. Drain and place in a bowl. Add all the remaining ingredients except the Parmesan cheese and toss well. Serve warm or chilled. Top with the Parmesan just before serving.

Variations: Chopped fresh basil or coriander or toasted sesame seeds are nice additions to this dish.

Nutritional Analysis

Calories	418.93 Kcal.	Protein	22.69 gm.
Fat	13.98 gm.	Carbohydrate	52.41 gm.
Sodium	672.48 mg.	Cholesterol	112.63 mg.
Saturated Fat	2.42 gm.		

Italian-Style Pistachio Pasta

Serves: 4

1 tablespoon butter or buttery light, reduced-fat margarine
1 onion, cut into thin wedges
1/4 cup finely diced green bell pepper
1/4 cup finely diced yellow bell pepper
1/4 cup finely diced red bell pepper
2 tablespoons minced garlic
1/4 pound prosciutto, sliced 1/8 inch thick and then diced
1 cup pistachios, coarsely chopped
1 1/2 teaspoons dried rosemary, crumbled
3 tablespoons extra-virgin olive oil
1 pound penne

In a skillet, melt the butter or margarine over low heat. Add the onion and sauté until nearly

tender. Add all the bell peppers, the garlic, prosciutto, pistachios, rosemary, and olive oil. Continue to cook, stirring, until thoroughly heated.

Meanwhile, cook the penne in boiling salted water until al dente. Drain and place in a bowl. Spoon the hot sauce over the top and serve.

Nutritional Analysis

Calories	816.16 Kcal.	Protein	30.08 gm.
Fat	34.81 gm.	Carbohydrate	99.47 gm.
Sodium	953.85 mg.	Cholesterol	30.78 mg.
Saturated Fat	6.54 gm.		

Savory Pastitsio

Serves: 10

1 teaspoon olive oil
1 large onion, finely chopped
1 1/2 pounds lean ground beef or ground turkey
1 cup water
3/4 cup dry white wine
1 can (6 ounces) tomato paste
1/2 cup bulgur
3/4 teaspoon cinnamon
3/4 teaspoon nutmeg
3/4 teaspoon allspice
1 1/2 teaspoons salt, plus more to taste
1/2 teaspoon black pepper, plus more to taste
2 cups 1% cottage cheese
2 tablespoons all-purpose flour
1 cup reduced-sodium, fat-free chicken broth
1 can (12 ounces) evaporated skim milk
3/4 cup plus 2 tablespoons freshly grated Parmesan cheese

(continued)

1 pound elbow macaroni
1 teaspoon olive oil
2 tablespoons chopped fresh parsley (optional)

In a large nonstick skillet, heat oil over medium heat; add onion and sauté until softened, about 5 minutes. Add ground meat and cook, breaking it up with a wooden spoon, until no longer pink, about 5 minutes. Drain off fat. Add water, wine, tomato paste, bulgur, spices, 1 teaspoon of the salt, and 1/2 teaspoon of the pepper. Simmer, uncovered, over low heat, stirring occasionally, until the bulgur is tender, about 20 minutes. Taste and adjust seasonings.

In a food processor or blender, purée cottage cheese until completely smooth. Set aside. In a small bowl, stir together flour and 1/4 cup cold chicken broth until smooth. In a medium-sized heavy saucepan, combine evaporated skim milk and the remaining chicken broth. Heat over medium heat until scalding. Stir the flour mixture into the hot milk mixture and cook, stirring constantly, until thickened, about 2 minutes. Remove from the heat and whisk in the puréed cottage cheese and the 1/2 cup of grated cheese. Season with salt and a generous grinding of pepper to taste. To prevent a skin from forming, place wax paper or plastic wrap directly over the surface and set aside.

In a large pot of boiling salted water, cook macaroni until al dente, 8 to 10 minutes. Drain and return to the pot. Toss with 1/4 cup of the grated cheese, oil, and 1/2 teaspoon of the salt.

Preheat oven to 350°F. Spray a 9 x 13-inch baking dish with nonstick cooking spray. Spread half of the pasta mixture over the bottom of the prepared dish. Top with one third of the cream sauce. Spoon all of the meat sauce over, spreading evenly. Cover with another third of the cream sauce. Top with the remaining pasta mixture and cover with the remaining cream sauce. Sprinkle with the remaining 2 tablespoons of the grated cheese. Bake for 40 to 50 minutes, or until bubbling and golden. Sprinkle with parsley, if using, and serve.

Nutritional Analysis

Calories	470.06 Kcal.	Protein	31.98 GM.
Fat	14.49 GM.	Carbohydrate	51.94 GM.
Sodium	1086.83 MG.	Cholesterol	51.28 MG.
Saturated Fat	5.91 gm.		

Pasta with Sautéed Artichokes

Serves: 1

1 artichoke
1 lemon, halved
2 tablespoons olive oil
1 cup sliced mushrooms
2 tablespoons dry white wine
1/4 cup thinly sliced scallions
1/2 teaspoon dried basil, crumbled
salt to taste
1/4 pound mostaccioli

1 tablespoon grated Parmesan cheese
cracked pepper to taste

Bend back the outer leaves of the artichoke until they snap off easily near base. Edible portion of the leaf should remain on the artichoke base or heart. Continue to snap off and discard the thick, dark leaves until central core of pale green leaves is reached. Cut off the top 2 inches of artichoke; discard. Cut off the stem; reserve. Using a paring knife, trim the dark green outer layer from the artichoke bottom and the stem. Rub all cut surfaces with a lemon half to prevent discoloration. Quarter the artichoke lengthwise. Scoop or cut out the prickly center petals and choke and discard. Rub again with a lemon half. Cut the artichoke and stem lengthwise into very thin slices.

In a large skillet, heat the oil over medium heat. Add the artichoke and mushrooms and sauté for 2 minutes. Add the wine, scallions, and basil; cover and simmer until the liquid has evaporated and the artichokes are tender, about 5 minutes. Season with salt.

Meanwhile, cook the pasta in boiling salted water until al dente. Drain and place in a bowl. Spoon the sauce over the pasta and sprinkle with Parmesan and pepper.

Nutritional Analysis

Calories	790.78 Kcal.	Protein	22.78 gm.
Fat	30.83 gm.	Carbohydrate	104.37 gm.
Sodium	617.49 mg.	Cholesterol	3.95 mg.
Saturated Fat	4.94 gm.		

Fusilli with Chicken and Coriander Pesto

Serves: 4

2 whole chicken breasts, halved
3 ounces cilantro
4 cloves garlic, cut up
$1/2$ cup slivered blanched almonds
4 serrano chile peppers, seeded
2 tablespoons olive oil
1 cup low-fat mayonnaise
1 pound fusilli pasta, cooked, drained, and chilled

Preheat oven to 375°F.

Place the chicken breasts in a baking pan. Bake until cooked through and tender, 15 to 20 minutes. Remove from the oven and let cool. Remove and discard the skin and bones and shred the meat. Place in a bowl, cover, and chill.

In a food processor or blender, combine the cilantro, garlic, almonds, and chiles. Process until finely chopped. With the motor running, add the oil in a thin, steady stream, processing until the pesto is the consistency of a thick paste.

Place the pesto in a bowl. Whisk in the mayonnaise.

In a large bowl, combine the chilled pasta, shredded chicken, and the pesto. Stir to mix well. Cover and chill for 1 hour before serving.

Nutritional Analysis

Calories	833.08 Kcal.	Protein	45.44 gm.
Fat	24.60 gm.	Carbohydrate	106.10 gm.
Sodium	1027.79 mg.	Cholesterol	73.10 mg.
Saturated Fat	2.87 gm.		

Pasta Salad Niçoise

Serves: 4

- 1/4 cup low-fat Italian dressing
- 1/4 cup chopped fresh basil
- 2 cloves minced garlic
- 1/4 teaspoon red pepper flakes
- 2 cups small shell pasta, cooked, drained, and chilled
- 1 can (6 ounces) water-packed albacore tuna, drained and flaked
- 3/4 cup diced tomato
- 1/2 avocado, peeled and diced
- 1/4 cup thinly sliced red onion
- 2 tablespoons chopped black olives
- 4 lettuce leaves

In a small bowl, stir together the dressing, basil, garlic, and red pepper flakes to form a dressing. In a large bowl, combine the pasta, tuna, tomato, avocado, red onion, and olives. Add dressing and toss well. Line 4 plates with the lettuce leaves. Spoon the pasta mixture on the lettuce, dividing evenly. Serve at once.

Nutritional Analysis

Calories	236.73 Kcal.	Protein	14.57 gm.
Fat	5.82 gm.	Carbohydrate	22.94 gm.
Sodium	370.63 mg.	Cholesterol	16.61 mg.
Saturated Fat	0.97 gm.		

Pistachio Pasta Salad Florentine

Serves: 4

- 1 1/2 cups frozen peas
- 6 ounces small tubular pasta
- 2 tablespoons honey
- 2 1/2 tablespoons Dijon mustard
- 3 tablespoons red wine vinegar
- 1 egg white
- 1 1/2 teaspoons dried oregano, crumbled
- 1/2 teaspoon garlic powder
- 2 cups spinach leaves, torn
- 2 cups halved cherry tomatoes
- 1/2 cup pistachio nuts

Place the peas in a sieve and rinse with running hot water to thaw; drain well and set aside. Cook the pasta in boiling salted water until al dente.

Meanwhile, in a small bowl, stir together the honey, mustard, vinegar, egg white, oregano, and garlic powder to form a dressing.

When the pasta is ready, drain and place in a bowl. Add the spinach, tomatoes, peas, pistachios, and the dressing. Toss well and serve warm.

Nutritional Analysis

Calories	358.43 Kcal.	Protein	13.76 gm.
Fat	8.90 gm.	Carbohydrate	56.20 gm.
Sodium	475.65 mg.	Cholesterol	0.00 mg.
Saturated Fat	1.14 gm.		

Jumbo Shells Stuffed with Cheese

Serves: 6

12 jumbo pasta shells
2 tablespoons grated Parmesan cheese
1/4 teaspoon chili powder
1 1/2 cups low-fat cheddar cheese, shredded
2 cloves garlic, pressed
1 tablespoon chopped fresh parsley
1/4 cup low-fat sour cream
1/4 cup chopped black olives

Cook the pasta shells in a large pot of boiling salted water until al dente. Drain into a colander and let stand for at least 10 minutes, or until completely drained. (Shells may be prepared in advance and stored in a covered container in the refrigerator.)

In a shallow bowl, mix together the Parmesan cheese and chili powder. Roll the pasta shells in the mixture. In a mixing bowl, combine cheddar cheese, garlic, parsley, sour cream, and olives. Mix well. Stuff the shells with the cheese mixture. The shells can be eaten as they are, or you can bake them. To do the latter, preheat an oven to 400°F. Arrange the shells on a baking sheet, propping their open ends up with crumpled foil so the filling won't run out during baking. Bake until the cheese is melted, 8 to 10 minutes. Serve hot.

Nutritional Analysis

Calories	154.37 Kcal.	Protein	13.95 gm.
Fat	2.11 gm.	Carbohydrate	20.58 gm.
Sodium	378.06 mg.	Cholesterol	7.64 mg.
Saturated Fat	0.93 gm.		

A Pasta Fallacy

It seems that nearly every pasta recipe I see—whether it's on the side of a pasta package or in another cookbook—instructs the cook to add a tablespoon of oil to the pasta cooking water to prevent the pasta strands from sticking together.

I conducted an experiment in which I cooked two pots of pasta side by side, using the same amount of pasta and water in each pot and adding the oil to only one of the pots. I did not notice any difference between the two. If you've been cooking your pasta with oil in the water, I think it's safe to say that you can cut down on the fat in your pasta dishes by eliminating the oil.

Garden Pasta

Serves: 6

> 5 tomatoes, peeled and chopped
> 2 carrots, chopped
> 2 celery stalks, chopped
> 1 medium onion, chopped
> 8 scallions, chopped
> 1 teaspoon dried basil, crumbled
> 1/2 teaspoon salt
> 1/2 teaspoon dried oregano, crumbled
> 1/4 teaspoon garlic powder
> 1/2 teaspoon pepper
> 1 tablespoon olive oil
> 1 pound spaghetti

In a large saucepan, combine the tomatoes, carrots, celery, onions, and scallions. Cover tightly and cook over medium heat, stirring occasionally, for 10 minutes. Add the basil, salt, oregano, garlic powder, and pepper. Cover and cook over medium-low heat for 5 minutes. Add the oil and simmer until the carrots are tender, about 30 minutes.

Meanwhile, cook the spaghetti in boiling salted water until al dente. Drain and place in a bowl. Add the sauce and toss well, then serve.

Nutritional Analysis

Calories	351.98 Kcal.	Protein	11.53 gm.
Fat	3.89 gm.	Carbohydrate	68.13 gm.
Sodium	489.33 mg.	Cholesterol	0.00 mg.
Saturated Fat	0.52 gm.		

Linguine Stir-Fry with Asparagus and Garlic

Serves: 4

> 1 pound linguine
> 2 tablespoons olive oil
> 1 pound skinless chicken breast meat, slivered
> 1 pound asparagus, trimmed and cut on the
>   diagonal into 1-inch lengths
> 2 red bell peppers, diced
> 4 cloves garlic, minced
> 1/4 cup teriyaki sauce
> 1 cup reduced-sodium, fat-free chicken broth

Cook the linguine in boiling salted water until al dente.

Once the water is put on to boil, in a wok or large, deep skillet, heat 1 tablespoon of the oil over high heat. Add the chicken and stir-fry until firm and cooked through, about 4 minutes. Remove the chicken and set aside. Add the remaining tablespoon oil to the pan. When it is hot, add the asparagus and bell pepper and stir-fry until crisp-tender, about 5 minutes. Add the garlic and stir-fry for 30 seconds. Stir in the teriyaki sauce and the broth.

As the pasta finishes cooking, return the chicken to the wok and heat through. Drain the pasta and toss with the chicken and sauce. Transfer to a warmed platter and serve at once.

Nutritional Analysis

Calories	658.90 Kcal.	Protein	45.79 gm.
Fat	10.21 gm.	Carbohydrate	94.35 gm.
Sodium	1302.60 mg.	Cholesterol	65.83 mg.
Saturated Fat	1.58 gm.		

Curried Tonnarelli and Vegetables

Serves: 4

1 tablespoon vegetable or peanut oil
1 small onion, diced
6 scallions, thinly sliced
1 tablespoon chopped garlic
1 jalapeño pepper, seeded, if desired, and finely chopped
1 tablespoon curry powder, or to taste
1 large tomato, cut into 1/2 inch cubes
1 tablespoon soy sauce
1/2 cup grated carrots
1/2 cup diced zucchini
1/2 cup broccoli florets
1/2 cup shelled peas
3/4 pound tonnarelli or penne pasta
2 tablespoons honey
1/2 cup raisins

In a large skillet, heat the oil over medium heat. Add the onion, scallions, garlic, and jalapeño pepper and sauté until the onion is wilted and begins to brown, about 4 minutes. Stir in the curry powder and cook for 1 minute. Add the tomato and soy sauce, reduce the heat to low, and cook until the tomato begins to give off liquid, about 12 to 15 minutes. Stir in the carrots, zucchini, broccoli, and peas and cook until crisp-tender, 3 to 5 minutes. Remove from heat.

Meanwhile, cook the pasta in boiling salted water until al dente. Just before it is ready to drain, scoop out 1/4 cup of the cooking water and stir it into the curry mixture. Return the skillet to low heat and cook until heated through.

Drain the pasta and transfer to a warmed bowl. Add the curry mixture and stir well to coat with the sauce. Fold in the honey and raisins and serve at once.

Nutritional Analysis

Calories	502.66 Kcal.	Protein	15.17 gm.
Fat	5.46 gm.	Carbohydrate	101.11 gm.
Sodium	580.53 mg.	Cholesterol	0.00 mg.
Saturated Fat	0.82 gm.		

Pasta with Yellow Summer Squash and Roasted Garlic

Serves: 4

8 cloves garlic
1/2 teaspoon dried thyme, crumbled
1/2 teaspoon dried basil, crumbled
2 tablespoons olive oil
1 pound rotini or fusilli
3 yellow squash, coarsely grated
salt and pepper to taste

Preheat oven to 450°F. Place the whole garlic cloves in the center of a large piece of foil. Sprinkle with the thyme and basil. Pour the oil over the garlic and herbs. Fold the foil to form a well-sealed packet and place in the center of the oven. Bake until the garlic is soft, 20 to 30 minutes.

Meanwhile, cook the pasta in boiling salted water until al dente. About 2 minutes before it is ready, add the squash to the pasta cooking water. When the pasta is ready, scoop out 1/2 cup of the cooking water. Drain the pasta and squash and place in a warmed bowl.

(continued)

Open the foil and, in a small bowl, mash the garlic lightly with a spoon. Add from 1/4 cup to 1/2 cup of the reserved pasta water and stir to form a thick, slightly liquid sauce. Pour over the pasta and squash, toss well, season with salt and pepper, and serve immediately.

Nutritional Analysis

Calories	514.87 Kcal.	Protein	16.10 gm.
Fat	8.88 gm.	Carbohydrate	92.12 gm.
Sodium	399.24 mg.	Cholesterol	0.00 mg.
Saturated Fat	1.23 gm.		

Capellini with Super Low-Fat Tomato Sauce

Serves: 4

1 can (28 ounces) plum tomatoes, undrained
1/2 cup diced onion
2 cloves garlic, finely chopped
1 teaspoon dried basil, crumbled
1 teaspoon dried parsley, crumbled
1 teaspoon dried oregano, crumbled
1/4 to 1/2 teaspoon red pepper flakes
salt to taste
1 pound capellini

In a 2-quart saucepan, combine the tomatoes, onion, garlic, basil, parsley, oregano, and red pepper flakes. Bring to a boil, reduce the heat to medium, and simmer until the liquid is reduced by half, 10 to 20 minutes. Season with salt. In a food processor or blender, purée the sauce, in batches, to desired consistency. Use quick on-off pulses for a chunky sauce and a steady action for a smoother sauce. Reheat to serving temperature, if necessary.

Meanwhile, cook the pasta in boiling salted water until al dente. Drain and transfer to a warmed bowl. Toss with the sauce and serve.

Nutritional Analysis

Calories	473.28 Kcal.	Protein	16.77 gm.
Fat	2.35 gm.	Carbohydrate	96.05 gm.
Sodium	720.17 mg.	Cholesterol	0.00 mg.
Saturated Fat	0.33 gm.		

Southwestern Radiatori

Serves: 4

3 medium tomatoes, minced
3 scallions, thinly sliced
1/2 cup lime juice
1 teaspoon salt
2 teaspoons olive oil
2 cloves garlic, minced
1 small red onion, chopped
1 jalapeño pepper, seeded and minced
1 large red bell pepper, cut into julienne
1 large green bell pepper, cut into julienne
1/2 teaspoon ground cumin
1/2 teaspoon chili powder
1 pound radiatori
2 tablespoons fresh coriander leaves, chopped

Place the tomatoes and scallions in a large bowl. Stir in the lime juice and salt.

In a large, deep skillet, heat the oil over medium heat. Add the garlic and cook until soft-

ened. Add the red onion and jalapeño pepper and sauté until softened, 2 to 3 minutes. Add the bell peppers and sauté until crisp-tender, about 5 minutes. Add the tomato mixture, cumin, and chili powder, and cook until sauce thickens slightly, about 10 minutes.

Meanwhile, cook the pasta in boiling salted water until al dente. Drain.

Add the pasta to the sauce in the skillet and toss well. Transfer to a warmed bowl, sprinkle with the coriander, and serve.

Nutritional Analysis

Calories	501.17 Kcal.	Protein	16.69 gm.
Fat	4.64 gm.	Carbohydrate	98.88 gm.
Sodium	1001.28 mg.	Cholesterol	0.00 mg.
Saturated Fat	0.60 gm.		

Fettuccine with Light Alfredo Sauce

Serves: 4

> 1 pound eggless fettuccine
> 1 cup evaporated skim milk
> 1/2 cup grated Parmesan cheese
> 1/2 cup finely chopped fresh parsley
> white pepper to taste
> pinch of red pepper flakes (optional)

Cook the fettuccine in boiling salted water until al dente.

While the pasta is cooking, heat the evaporated milk in a deep saucepan over medium heat. Bring to a simmer but do not boil. Add the Parmesan cheese and parsley. As soon as the

cheese has melted and the sauce is thick and creamy, remove from the heat. Drain the pasta and place in warmed bowl. Add the sauce and toss well. Season with white pepper and red pepper flakes, if using. Serve immediately.

Nutritional Analysis

Calories	519.34 Kcal.	Protein	23.63 gm.
Fat	4.93 gm.	Carbohydrate	92.98 gm.
Sodium	658.01 mg.	Cholesterol	10.45 mg.
Saturated Fat	2.23 gm.		

Ziti with Chicken, Pineapple, and Mint

Serves: 4

> 1 pound skinless chicken breast meat
> 1 tablespoon vegetable oil
> 1/4 cup dry white wine
> 1/4 teaspoon cayenne pepper
> 6 scallions, cut on the diagonal into 1-inch lengths
> 1 1/2 cups pineapple juice
> 1 tablespoon soy sauce
> 1 tablespoon peeled and grated fresh ginger
> 1 tablespoon honey
> 1 tablespoon orange juice
> 1 tablespoon buttery light, reduced-fat margarine, melted
> 1/2 pound ziti
> 1 can (10 ounces) mandarin oranges, drained
> 1 tablespoon chopped fresh mint

(continued)

Ricotta Cheese

I've always considered ricotta cheese one of the most delicious dairy products I've ever tasted. In fact, I sometimes use the part-skim type as a substitute for yogurt, mixing honey, coconut, and fruit into it for a great lunch.

Most people are familiar with ricotta as a primary ingredient in lasagna and stuffed shells, and although nonfat ricotta is available, it detracts from the dish. Choose part-skim instead, and beat in a few egg whites to give it volume and texture.

Preheat oven to 350°F. Place the chicken in a baking dish and brush with the oil. Sprinkle with wine, and season with the cayenne pepper. Cover with foil and bake until cooked through and tender, about 15 minutes. Do not overcook. During the last 2 to 3 minutes, add the scallions to the pan. Remove from the oven, let cool slightly, and cut the chicken into bite-sized pieces. Reserve the scallions.

While the chicken is cooking, combine the pineapple juice, soy sauce, ginger, and honey in a small saucepan. Bring to a boil over medium-high heat and cook until reduced by half, about 20 minutes. Add the orange juice. Remove from the heat and whisk in the margarine.

Meanwhile, cook the pasta in boiling salted water until al dente. Drain and transfer to a large warmed bowl. Top with the scallions, pour the sauce over the pasta, and toss well. Carefully fold in the mandarin oranges and mint. Serve at once.

Nutritional Analysis

Calories	512.80 Kcal.	Protein	34.91 gm.
Fat	8.70 gm.	Carbohydrate	73.13 gm.
Sodium	572.52 mg.	Cholesterol	65.83 mg.
Saturated Fat	1.39 gm.		

Fusilli with Fresh Herbs and Ricotta
Serves: 4

1 container (15 ounces) part-skim ricotta cheese
2/3 cup low-fat milk
1/4 grated Parmesan cheese
1 tablespoon olive oil

³/₄ cup chopped onion
4 cloves garlic, minced
¹/₂ cup chopped fresh basil leaves
¹/₄ cup chopped fresh chives
¹/₄ cup chopped fresh parley
salt and pepper to taste
1 pound fusilli

In a food processor or blender, combine the ricotta cheese, milk, and Parmesan. Process until smooth. In a large, deep skillet, heat the oil over medium heat. Add the onion and sauté until nearly browned, about 10 minutes. Add the garlic and cook until softened.

Add the ricotta mixture and fold in the basil, chives, and parsley. Cook until heated through. Season with salt and pepper.

Meanwhile, cook the pasta in boiling salted water until al dente. Drain and add to the skillet. Toss well so that the pasta is coated with the sauce. Transfer to a warmed bowl and serve.

Nutritional Analysis

Calories	614.45 Kcal.	Protein	27.42 gm.
Fat	11.50 gm.	Carbohydrate	96.43 gm.
Sodium	606.82 mg.	Cholesterol	31.29 mg.
Saturated Fat	4.49 gm.		

Vermicelli with Tuna, Anchovies, and Capers

Serves: 4

2 tablespoons olive oil
¹/₂ cup chopped onion
1 clove garlic, minced

1 can (16 ounces) plum tomatoes, drained
1 anchovy fillets, finely chopped
2 tablespoons buttery light, reduced-fat margarine, softened
1 pound vermicelli
3 tablespoons capers
1 can (6¹/₂ ounces) water-packed tuna, drained and flaked
2 tablespoons chopped fresh parsley

In a large, deep skillet, heat the oil over medium heat. Add onion and sauté until soft, about 5 to 7 minutes. Add the garlic and sauté briefly. Add the tomatoes, break them up with a wooden spoon, cover, and simmer until soft, about 10 minutes.

Place the anchovies in a small bowl and mash them with a spoon. (Alternatively, process them in a mini food processor.) Add the margarine to the anchovies and mash together with a fork.

Meanwhile, cook the pasta in boiling salted water until al dente. Scoop out ¹/₂ cup of the cooking water. Drain the pasta.

Stir enough of the reserved cooking water into the anchovy butter to make it thick and smooth and no longer a paste. Add the capers to the skillet and stir to blend. Add the tuna fish and heat through over medium heat. Add the pasta to the sauce and toss until the pasta is coated. Transfer to a warmed bowl, sprinkle with the parsley, and serve.

(continued)

Nutritional Analysis

Calories	623.37 Kcal.	Protein	28.35 gm.
Fat	14.83 gm.	Carbohydrate	92.51 gm.
Sodium	1165.01 mg.	Cholesterol	17.81 mg.
Saturated Fat	2.22 gm.		

Radiatore with Eggplant and Tomatoes

Serves: 4

2 tablespoons olive oil
3/4 cup chopped onion
3 cloves garlic, minced
1 eggplant, about 3/4 pound, peeled and cut into 1/2- to 1-inch cubes
2 tablespoons balsamic vinegar
1/2 cup reduced-sodium, fat-free chicken broth
1 can (16 ounces) plum tomatoes, undrained
1 tablespoon tomato paste
1/2 teaspoon dried oregano, crumbled
2 tablespoons chopped fresh basil
dash of red pepper flakes
salt to taste
3/4 pound radiatore

In a large, deep skillet, heat the oil over medium heat. Add the onion and sauté until soft, about 5 minutes. Add the garlic and sauté briefly. Add the eggplant, vinegar, and broth. Cover and cook until the eggplant is tender, about 10 minutes. Add the tomatoes and break them up with a wooden spoon. Stir in the tomato paste and oregano. Cook, uncovered, until the sauce thickens slightly, about 15 minutes. Stir in the basil and red pepper flakes and season with salt.

Meanwhile, cook the pasta in boiling salted water until al dente. Drain and transfer to a large warmed bowl. Add the sauce and toss well. Serve immediately.

Nutritional Analysis

Calories	438.50 Kcal.	Protein	13.76 gm.
Fat	8.52 gm.	Carbohydrate	77.32 gm.
Sodium	588.51 mg.	Cholesterol	0.00 mg.
Saturated Fat	1.15 gm.		

Turkey and Spinach Fettuccine Casserole

Serves: 4

2 teaspoons olive oil
3/4 pound mushrooms, sliced
3/4 pound boneless, skinless turkey breast, cut in 1/2-inch strips
1/2 cup dry white wine
3 tablespoons all-purpose flour
2 cups 1% milk
1/2 teaspoon dried marjoram, crumbled
1/2 cup grated Parmesan cheese
salt and pepper to taste
1/2 pound eggless spinach fettuccine
3 tablespoons slivered blanched almonds

Preheat oven to 400°F.

In a large, deep skillet, heat the oil over medium heat. Add the mushrooms and sauté until

they begin to soften, about 5 minutes. Add the turkey and sauté until just browned, about 10 minutes. Add the wine and cook for 3 minutes. Stir in the flour, mixing thoroughly. Gradually add the milk, stirring constantly, and cook until the mixture thickens slightly, about 10 minutes. Stir in the marjoram and 1/4 cup of the Parmesan cheese until blended. Season with salt and pepper.

Meanwhile, cook the pasta in boiling salted water until nearly al dente. Drain and combine with the turkey mixture, tossing well. Then transfer the contents of the skillet to an 11-by-7-inch baking dish. Top with remaining 1/4 cup Parmesan and sprinkle with the almonds.

Bake until heated through and the top is lightly browned, about 20 minutes. Serve at once.

Nutritional Analysis

Calories	502.83 Kcal.	Protein	40.33 gm.
Fat	11.66 gm.	Carbohydrate	58.49 gm.
Sodium	508.78 mg.	Cholesterol	65.55 mg.
Saturated Fat	3.66 gm.		

Baked Ziti with Meat

Serves: 4

2 tablespoons olive oil
1 cup chopped onion
4 cloves garlic, minced
1/2 pound lean ground beef
1/2 cup dry white wine
1 can (28 ounces) crushed tomatoes
1/2 teaspoon dried basil, crumbled

1/2 teaspoon dried oregano, crumbled
1 tablespoon tomato paste
2 tablespoons all-purpose flour
1/2 cup 1% milk
salt and pepper to taste
3/4 pound ziti
1 cup shredded low-fat mozzarella cheese
1/2 cup grated romano cheese

Preheat oven to 400°F.

In a large skillet, heat the oil over medium heat. Add the onion and sauté until soft, about 10 minutes. Add the garlic and sauté briefly. Stir in the beef, breaking it up with a wooden spoon and browning well. Drain off the oil from the pan. Stir in the white wine and scrape the bottom of pan as it cooks. Add the tomatoes, basil, oregano, and tomato paste, stirring to blend. Cook for 3 minutes. Add the flour and stir well until combined. Gradually add the milk and cook until slightly thickened, about 10 minutes. Season with salt and pepper.

Meanwhile, cook the pasta in boiling salted water until nearly al dente. Drain and place in a large warmed bowl. Add the meat mixture to the pasta, tossing well. Transfer to a 3-quart baking dish.

Bake until heated through, about 15 minutes. Distribute the mozzarella evenly over the top and sprinkle with the romano cheese. Return to the oven and bake until the cheese melts and the top has browned lightly, about 15 minutes. Serve immediately.

(continued)

Nutritional Analysis

Calories	690.85 Kcal.	Protein	36.89 gm.
Fat	23.52 gm.	Carbohydrate	82.54 gm.
Sodium	1007.50 mg.	Cholesterol	58.01 mg.
Saturated Fat	8.56 gm.		

Salmon with Fettucine

Serves: 4

1 cup reduced-sodium, fat-free chicken broth
1/2 cup dry white wine
1 pound salmon fillets, skinned and cut into 1/2-inch pieces
1 tablespoon vegetable oil
3 shallots, minced
6 scallions, thinly sliced
1 can (16 ounces) plum tomatoes, drained
2 tablespoons tomato paste
1/2 cup evaporated nonfat milk
1/4 cup snipped fresh dill
3/4 pound eggless fettuccine
4 fresh dill sprigs

In a large skillet, bring the broth and wine to a boil. Reduce the heat to a simmer and add the salmon. Cover and cook until the fish is opaque, about 5 minutes. Remove the fish with a slotted spoon. Set aside; cover to keep warm. Reserve 1/2 cup of the cooking liquid.

In a skillet, heat the oil over medium heat. Add the shallots and scallions and cook until soft, about 5 minutes. Add tomatoes, breaking them up with a wooden spoon. Stir in the tomato paste, evaporated milk, the 1/2 cup cooking liquid, and the dill. Simmer until the sauce thickens, about 10 minutes. Return the fish to the pan and heat through.

Meanwhile, cook the pasta in boiling salted water until al dente. Drain and place in a large warmed bowl. Pour the sauce over the pasta and toss gently. Serve on warmed individual plates. Garnish with dill sprigs.

Nutritional Analysis

Calories	622.74 Kcal.	Protein	38.16 gm.
Fat	17.49 gm.	Carbohydrate	76.51 gm.
Sodium	725.41 mg.	Cholesterol	68.23 mg.
Saturated Fat	3.17 gm.		

Orecchiette with Summer Tomato Sauce and Olives

Serves: 4

1 1/2 pounds tomatoes, peeled, seeded, and chopped into 1/2-inch pieces
1 teaspoon minced garlic
3 tablespoons olive oil
2 tablespoons shredded fresh basil leaves
pepper to taste
1 pound orecchiette or other round or shell-shaped pasta
1/3 cup Kalamata or other brine-cured black olives, pitted

In a large bowl, combine the tomatoes, garlic, oil, basil, and pepper. Stir to mix well. Set aside at room temperature for at least 30 minutes.

Cook the pasta in boiling salted water until al dente. Drain. Stir the olives into the tomatoes, add the pasta, toss well, and serve immediately.

Nutritional Analysis

Calories	578.61 Kcal.	Protein	15.93 gm.
Fat	15.40 gm.	Carbohydrate	93.84 gm.
Sodium	610.28 mg.	Cholesterol	0.00 mg.
Saturated Fat	2.06 gm.		

Sweet-and-Sour Chicken with Ruote

Serves: 4

1 can (8 ounces) pineapple chunks in
   unsweetened juice
1$\frac{1}{2}$ tablespoons tomato paste
2 tablespoons cider vinegar
2 tablespoons soy sauce
1 tablespoon sugar
2 teaspoons cornstarch
2 tablespoons vegetable oil
1 pound skinless chicken breast meat, cut into
   $\frac{1}{2}$-inch-wide slices
3 cloves garlic, minced
2 teaspoons peeled and grated fresh ginger
$\frac{1}{2}$ cup chopped onion
$\frac{1}{2}$ cup chopped green bell pepper
2 cups thinly sliced bok choy or other Asian
   cabbage
4 scallions, thinly sliced
$\frac{1}{2}$ pound ruote
2 tablespoons chopped fresh coriander   *(continued)*

Fresh or Dried Pasta?

Most of us grew up eating dried spaghetti out of a box. If you've ever eaten fresh pasta, it may actually seem mushy to you.

Fresh pasta can be heavenly in taste and texture, but since it is fresh, it needs only a minute or two of cooking, just to heat through. Nowadays, you can buy freshly made pasta in the supermarket, and although it's more expensive than the boxed variety, you can look at it as a special treat. Read the label, however; many fresh pastas contain more egg than dried pastas do.

Drain the pineapple, saving 1/2 cup of the juice. Pour the pineapple juice in a small bowl. Add the tomato paste, vinegar, soy sauce, sugar, and cornstarch. Stir well and reserve.

In a wok or large, deep skillet, heat the oil over medium heat. Add the chicken and stir-fry until firm and lightly browned, about 10 minutes. Add the garlic, ginger, onion, and bell pepper. Sauté until they soften, about 5 minutes. Add the cabbage and stir-fry until crisp-tender, about 3 minutes.

Stir the tomato-pineapple mixture and add to the skillet, mixing well. Add the pineapple and stir constantly so that the sauce coats the contents as it thickens. Add the scallions and toss to mix.

Meanwhile, cook the pasta in boiling salted water until al dente. Drain. Transfer to a large warmed bowl. Pour the sauce over the pasta and toss to combine completely. Sprinkle with the coriander and serve immediately.

Nutritional Analysis

Calories	482.24 Kcal.	Protein	35.66 gm.
Fat	9.34 gm.	Carbohydrate	63.24 gm.
Sodium	861.81 mg.	Cholesterol	65.83 mg.
Saturated Fat	1.37 gm.		

Shells with Scallops and Sun-Dried Tomato Pesto

Serves: 4

1 cup water
1/2 cup dry-packed sun-dried tomatoes
1 clove garlic, peeled
2 tablespoons pine nuts
2 tablespoons grated Parmesan cheese
2 tablespoons olive oil
1/4 teaspoon salt
1/4 cup dry white wine
2 teaspoons cornstarch
1 pound bay scallops
1/2 cup reduced-sodium, fat-free chicken broth
3/4 pound medium shells
2 tablespoons chopped fresh parsley

In a medium saucepan, bring the water to a boil. Add the sun-dried tomatoes and cook until softened, about 10 minutes. Add the garlic and cook for another 2 minutes. Pour the mixture into a food processor or blender. Add the pine nuts, Parmesan cheese, 1 tablespoon of the oil, and the salt. Process until smooth pesto forms. Reserve. In a small bowl, combine the wine and cornstarch, mixing well. Set aside.

In a large, deep skillet, heat the remaining 1 tablespoon oil over medium heat. Add the scallops and cook until slightly firm, about 5 minutes. Add the broth and cook for 1 minute. Stir in the tomato pesto. Heat through. Stir the cornstarch-wine mixture and add to the skillet. Cook, stirring constantly, until the sauce thickens slightly, about 1 minute.

Meanwhile, cook the pasta in boiling salted water until al dente. Drain. Add the shells to the skillet and toss to glaze the pasta with the sauce. Transfer to a warmed bowl. Sprinkle with the parsley and serve immediately.

Nutritional Analysis

Calories	558.64 Kcal.	Protein	34.48 gm.
Fat	11.98 gm.	Carbohydrate	74.64 gm.
Sodium	750.95 mg.	Cholesterol	39.42 mg.
Saturated Fat	2.01 gm.		

Rich Low-Fat Lasagna

Serves: 8

> 1 tablespoon olive oil
> 2 garlic cloves, minced
> 1 red onion, minced
> 1 can (19 ounces) kidney beans, drained
> 4 cups canned tomato purée
> 1 teaspoon dried oregano, crumbled
> 1 teaspoon dried basil, crumbled
> pepper to taste
> 1 pound lasagna noodles, cooked
> 2 cups part-skim ricotta cheese
> 1/2 pound low-fat mozzarella cheese, thinly
>   sliced
> 1/4 cup grated Parmesan cheese

Preheat oven to 350°F.

In a saucepan, heat the oil over medium heat. Add the garlic and onion and sauté until soft, about 5 minutes. Add the beans, and cook for 5 more minutes. Add the tomato purée, oregano, basil, and pepper. Bring to a boil, reduce the heat to medium, and cook for 5 minutes to blend the flavors.

Spoon some of the sauce onto the bottom of a 9 x 13-inch baking dish. Arrange a layer of noodles on top and then some of the ricotta and mozzarella. Repeat the layers, using up the ricotta, mozzarella, noodles, and sauce. Finish off with a layer of noodles topped with sauce. Sprinkle with the Parmesan cheese and cover with foil.

Bake until top is bubbly, about 45 minutes. Let stand for 10 minutes before serving.

Nutritional Analysis

Calories	471.29 Kcal.	Protein	30.25 gm.
Fat	8.73 gm.	Carbohydrate	69.13 gm.
Sodium	1116.24 mg.	Cholesterol	24.03 mg.
Saturated Fat	3.89 gm.		

Artichoke Lasagna

Serves: 10

> 12 ounces dried or 1 pound fresh lasagne
>   noodles
> 1/3 cup plus 1 teaspoon all-purpose flour
> 3 cups 1% milk
> 3 tablespoons reduced-fat cream cheese
> 1 cup freshly grated Parmesan cheese
> 1 tablespoon chopped fresh thyme or 1
>   teaspoon dried thyme leaves
> 2 teaspoons fresh lemon juice
> 1 teaspoon salt, plus more to taste
> 1/4 teaspoon freshly ground black pepper, plus
>   more to taste
> 2 teaspoons olive oil
> 1 1/2 cups chopped onions
> 1 1/2 cups finely chopped carrots
> 2 cloves garlic, minced

(continued)

2 packages (9 ounces each) frozen artichoke
   hearts, thawed and coarsely chopped, or
   two cans (8½ ounces each) artichoke
   hearts, drained, squeezed dry, and
   coarsely chopped
½ cup reduced-sodium, fat-free chicken broth

In a large pot of boiling salted water, cook
noodles until barely tender (8 minutes for dried, 1
minute for fresh). Drain and rinse under cold
water. Spread the noodles on clean kitchen
towels, cover with plastic wrap and set aside.

Place ⅓ cup of the flour in a small bowl and
gradually whisk in ½ cup of the milk until
smooth. Set aside. In a large saucepan, heat the
remaining milk over medium heat until the milk is
steaming. Whisk the flour and milk mixture into
the hot milk and stir constantly over the heat
until the sauce comes to a simmer and thickens.
Lower the heat. Continue cooking and stirring for
1 minute. Remove from the heat. Whisk in cream
cheese, then ½ cup of the Parmesan, thyme,
lemon juice, 1 teaspoon salt, and pepper. Set the
cheese sauce aside.

In a large nonstick skillet, heat oil over
medium-high heat. Add onions and carrots and
cook, stirring, until they begin to color and soften,
about 5 minutes. Add garlic and stir for 1 minute
longer. Add artichoke hearts and sprinkle with the
remaining 1 teaspoon flour, and chicken broth.
Stir well and cook until liquid is thick and
simmering, about 3 minutes. Remove from the
heat and season with salt and pepper.

Preheat oven to 400°F. Lightly oil a 9 x 13-inch
baking dish or coat it with nonstick cooking spray.

A Pasta Rainbow

Today, pasta comes in as many
shades as there are colors in the
rainbow. Many of these flavored
pastas contain exotic ingredients, from squid ink to pesto to
sun-dried tomatoes.

I think the exotic ingredients
should be *on* the pasta, not *in* it.
These colorful additions add to
the cost of the pasta without
adding much flavor. Dried
spinach pasta is always available if you want to try the
"exotic" at a fair price.

Smear the bottom of the prepared dish with ¹/₂ cup of the cheese sauce. Line the bottom with a single layer of noodles. Spread half of the artichoke mixture over the noodles. Spoon on another ¹/₂ cup cheese sauce and use a spatula to spread it evenly. Add another layer of noodles, and spread another ¹/₂ cup sauce on top. Add a third layer of noodles, the remaining artichoke mixture and spread with ¹/₂ cup sauce. Finish with the remaining noodles and sauce. Sprinkle with the remaining Parmesan.

Lightly oil a large piece of aluminum foil or spray it with nonstick cooking spray, and use it to tightly cover the dish. Bake the lasagne for 30 minutes. Uncover and bake for about 15 minutes more, or until the top is lightly browned. Let stand for 10 minutes before serving.

Nutritional Analysis

Calories	275.82 Kcal.	Protein	13.67 gm.
Fat	6.57 gm.	Carbohydrate	40.67 gm.
Sodium	646.71 mg.	Cholesterol	13.63 mg.
Saturated Fat	3.20 gm.		

Szechuan Noodle Salad

Serves: 4

1 pound thin spaghetti
¹/₄ cup white wine vinegar
¹/₄ cup water
2 tablespoons soy sauce
2 tablespoons peeled and minced fresh ginger
1 tablespoon Asian sesame oil
2 cloves garlic, minced
1 teaspoon sugar

1 teaspoon Tabasco sauce
1 cup grated carrot
1 cup frozen peas, thawed
1 red bell pepper, cut into narrow strips
2 cups bean sprouts
¹/₄ cup chopped fresh parsley

Cook the spaghetti in boiling salted water until al dente. Drain.

Meanwhile, in a large bowl, stir together the vinegar, water, soy sauce, ginger, oil, garlic, sugar, and Tabasco. Add the warm, cooked noodles and toss. Add the carrot, peas, bell pepper, bean sprouts, and parsley. Toss well and serve.

Nutritional Analysis

Calories	527.65 Kcal.	Protein	19.07 gm.
Fat	5.52 gm.	Carbohydrate	100.23 gm.
Sodium	972.92 mg.	Cholesterol	0.00 mg.
Saturated Fat	0.78 gm.		

Pad Thai

Serves: 4

¹/₄ pound dried rice noodles
2 teaspoons peanut oil
3 cloves garlic, minced
1 egg, lightly beaten
¹/₂ pound small shrimp, peeled and deveined
2 cups mung bean sprouts
¹/₂ cup sliced scallion greens
3 tablespoons rice vinegar
2¹/₂ tablespoons fish sauce
2 tablespoons sugar

(continued)

1 teaspoon Chinese chile paste with garlic
3 tablespoons chopped dry-roasted peanuts

In a large bowl, soak rice noodles in warm water to cover until they are limp and white, about 20 minutes. In a wok or large deep skillet, heat oil over high heat until very hot. Add the garlic and stir-fry until golden, about 10 seconds. Add the egg and cook, stirring, until scrambled, about 30 seconds. Add shrimp and stir-fry until they curl and turn pink, about 2 minutes.

Drain the noodles and add to the wok, tossing with tongs until they soften and curl, about 1 minute. Add bean sprouts, scallion greens, vinegar, fish sauce, sugar and chile paste. Toss until the shrimp are fully cooked and noodles are heated through, 1 to 2 minutes. Sprinkle with peanuts and serve immediately.

Nutritional Analysis

Calories	292.64 Kcal.	Protein	16.06 gm.
Fat	8.88 gm.	Carbohydrate	38.13 gm.
Sodium	545.53 mg.	Cholesterol	123.85 mg.
Saturated Fat	1.64 gm.		

Linguine with White Clam Sauce

Serves: 4

1 tablespoon olive oil
3 cloves garlic, minced
1 can (10 ounces) minced clams, drained with liquid reserved
1 teaspoon red pepper flakes

1 teaspoon dried oregano, crumbled
1 teaspoon dried basil, crumbled
2 tablespoons fresh chopped parsley
1/2 cup dry white wine
1 pound linguine

In a large skillet, heat the oil over medium heat. Add the garlic and sauté until soft, about 3 minutes. Add the clams, red pepper flakes, oregano, basil, parsley, wine, and reserved clam liquid. Cook over medium heat about 15 minutes.

Meanwhile, cook the linguine in boiling salted water until al dente. Drain and place in a warmed bowl. Add the sauce, toss well, and serve.

Nutritional Analysis

Calories	533.63 Kcal.	Protein	24.39 gm.
Fat	6.00 gm.	Carbohydrate	88.46 gm.
Sodium	439.67 mg.	Cholesterol	24.69 mg.
Saturated Fat	0.79 gm.		

Chicken and Seafood Pasta

Serves: 4

1 whole chicken breast, split, boned, and skinned
2 tablespoons olive oil
1/4 cup all-purpose flour
1/4 pound jumbo shrimp, peeled and deveined
1/4 pound scallops
4 cloves garlic, minced
1 cup reduced-sodium, fat-free chicken broth
1 cup stemmed spinach leaves
10 dry-packed, sun-dried tomatoes, chopped

1 teaspoon dried basil, crumbled
salt and pepper to taste
¹/₂ pound radiatori

Using a meat mallet, pound the chicken to create thin cutlets. In a skillet, heat 1 tablespoon of the oil over high heat. Add the chicken and cook, turning once, for 5 minutes. Remove from the pan and set aside. Lightly flour the shrimp and scallops. Return the skillet to medium heat. Add the shrimp and scallops and sauté until shrimp turns pink, 3 to 4 minutes. Remove from the pan and set aside.

To the same pan, add the remaining 1 tablespoon oil and the garlic; heat until the garlic is browned, about 5 minutes. Return the chicken, shrimp, and scallops to the pan and add the broth. Add the basil, oregano, salt, and pepper to taste. Add the sun-dried tomatoes and the spinach. Cook for 4 minutes and remove from the heat.

While the sauce is cooking, cook the pasta in boiling salted water until al dente. Drain and place in a large warmed bowl. Spoon the chicken and seafood mixture on top and serve immediately.

Nutritional Analysis

Calories	444.71 Kcal.	Protein	33.72 gm.
Fat	9.13 gm.	Carbohydrate	54.89 gm.
Sodium	473.83 mg.	Cholesterol	78.08 mg.
Saturated Fat	1.33 gm.		

Angry Ziti
Serves: 4

1 pound ziti
1 tablespoon olive oil
1 onion, chopped
4 cloves garlic, minced
2 hot peppers
1 cup sliced mushrooms
1 cup chopped fresh plum tomatoes
2 teaspoons dried basil, crumbled
¹/₄ cup dry white wine
1 can (28 ounces) crushed tomatoes
salt and pepper to taste
¹/₄ cup grated Parmesan cheese

Cook the pasta in boiling salted water until al dente.

Meanwhile, in a large skillet, heat the oil over medium heat. Add the onions and garlic and sauté until translucent, about 5 minutes. Add the hot peppers and mushroom and sauté for 2 minutes. Add the plum tomatoes, basil, white wine, crushed tomatoes, salt, and pepper and sauté until blended, about 2 minutes.

Drain the pasta and add to the skillet along with the cheese. Cook, stirring and tossing, for 1 minute, then serve.

Nutritional Analysis

Calories	562.75 Kcal.	Protein	20.09 gm.
Fat	7.44 gm.	Carbohydrate	102.26 gm.
Sodium	820.12 mg.	Cholesterol	3.95 mg.
Saturated Fat	1.77 gm.		

Quick Lasagna

Serves: 8

1/4 cup grated Parmesan cheese
1 cup part-skim ricotta cheese
1 cup shredded fat-free mozzarella cheese
1 jar (28 ounces) spaghetti sauce
1 package (12 ounces) no-cook lasagna
  noodles

Preheat oven to 350°F.

In a medium bowl, stir together the Parmesan cheese, ricotta cheese, and mozzarella. Spray a 9 x 13-inch baking dish. Spread some of the sauce in the bottom. Layer the noodles atop the sauce. Spread one-third of the cheese mixture over the noodles. Repeat the layers until the ingredients are used up, ending with sauce. Cover with foil.

Bake until heated through, about 45 minutes. Remove from the oven and let cool for 10 minutes before serving.

Nutritional Analysis

Calories	443.39 Kcal.	Protein	21.42 gm.
Fat	11.70 gm.	Carbohydrate	65.86 gm.
Sodium	909.55 mg.	Cholesterol	17.34 mg.
Saturated Fat	3.54 gm.		

Linguine Fra Diavolo

Serves: 4

1/2 pound linguine
2 tablespoons olive oil
3 cloves garlic, minced

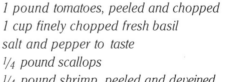

1 pound tomatoes, peeled and chopped
1 cup finely chopped fresh basil
salt and pepper to taste
1/4 pound scallops
1/4 pound shrimp, peeled and deveined
1/4 pound haddock fillet, cut into 1-inch chunks
8 mussels, well scrubbed and debearded

Cook the linguine in boiling salted water until al dente.

Meanwhile, in a large skillet, heat the oil over medium-high heat. Add the garlic and sauté until soft, about 5 minutes. Add the tomatoes, basil, salt, and pepper and cook, stirring occasionally, for 2 minutes. Add the scallops, shrimp, haddock, and mussels and cook until haddock is translucent, about 3 minutes.

Drain the linguine and place in a warmed bowl. Pour the sauce over the top, toss well, and serve.

Nutritional Analysis

Calories	388.43 Kcal.	Protein	25.42 gm.
Fat	9.26 gm.	Carbohydrate	50.28 gm.
Sodium	352.59 mg.	Cholesterol	64.51 mg.
Saturated Fat	1.27 gm.		

Fettuccine with Spinach Tomato Sauce

Serves: 4

3/4 pound eggless fettuccine
1 tablespoon olive oil
1 onion, chopped

2 cloves garlic, minced
1 package (10 ounces) frozen chopped spinach
¼ teaspoon salt
1 large tomato, chopped
1 cup part-skim ricotta cheese
¼ cup grated Parmesan cheese
salt and pepper to taste

Cook the fettuccine in boiling salted water until al dente.

Meanwhile, in a large skillet, heat the oil over medium heat. Add the onion and sauté until translucent, about 4 minutes. Add the garlic, spinach, and salt and cook for 5 minutes. Add the tomato and cook until soft, about 5 minutes longer. Drain the fettuccine and add to the skillet along with the ricotta cheese. Toss and cook until heated through, 1 to 2 minutes. Add the Parmesan, salt, and pepper, then toss well again. Transfer to a warmed bowl and serve immediately.

Nutritional Analysis

Calories	500.60 Kcal.	Protein	23.06 gm.
Fat	11.52 gm.	Carbohydrate	76.52 gm.
Sodium	668.67 mg.	Cholesterol	23.01 mg.
Saturated Fat	4.68 gm.		

Pasta Is Low-Fat

One cup of cooked spaghetti or elbow macaroni, without salt or oil has 0.1 grams of saturated fat, 0 mgs cholesterol and only 4 calories from fat with a total number of 197 calorie. That's something to think about when choosing a quick, low-fat meal. Spice up the pasta sprinkling garlic powder and fresh or dried basil on the hot pasta. Or for a really zesty pasta dish, add chopped hot peppers. Remember—a little hot pepper goes a long way.

Fish and Shellfish Dishes

CHAPTER EIGHT

Amount Per Chapter

23 Recipes

	% Daily Value
Easy to Prepare	**100%**
Low Fat / High Flavor	**100%**
Simple to Understand	**100%**

DELICIOUS, EASY, LOW-FAT RECIPES

Fish and shellfish are winners when it comes to a low-fat diet. High in protein and low in fat, fish provides low-fat diners with a tasty way to eat a filling, delicious main course without the fat of a piece of chicken or beef of comparable weight.

A wide variety of fish and shellfish from all over the world is now available in fish markets and supermarkets. This new bounty has convinced cooks and diners that dishes made from these fresh- and saltwater denizens are wonderful alternatives to heartier meat or poultry recipes.

To my mind, the only things a piece of fish usually needs is a sprinkling of minced garlic and a squeeze of juice from a lemon half. But the following recipes don't require much more effort than my garlic-and-lemon treatment, and they are certain to win raves even from people who insist they don't like fish or shellfish.

Seafood Rice

Serves: 8

2 tablespoons olive oil
6 scallions, thinly sliced
1 large onion, minced
1 clove garlic, chopped
¹/₂ pound bay scallops
¹/₂ pound shrimp, peeled and deveined
1 cup dry white wine, plus more if needed
¹/₂ cup bottled clam juice
1 tablespoon tomato paste
2 pounds mussels, well scrubbed and
   debearded
1¹/₂ cups white or brown rice
1 cup minced fresh parsley
pepper to taste
lemon wedges

In a large saucepan, heat the oil over medium heat for 1 minute. Add the scallions, onion, and garlic and sauté until soft, about 5 minutes. Transfer to a bowl. In the same pan, add the scallops and shrimp and cook, stirring, for a few minutes until the shrimp turn pink. Transfer the seafood to the bowl holding the scallion mixture. Keep warm.

Add the 1 cup wine, clam juice, and tomato paste to the pan over medium heat, stirring. Add the mussels, cover, and bring to a boil over high heat. Cook until the mussels open, about 5 minutes. Remove the mussels from the pan with a slotted spoon, reserving the sauce in the pan. When the mussels are cool enough to handle, discard any that did not open. Remove the meat from the opened shells and discard the shells. Add the mussels to the bowl with the seafood-scallion mixture; continue to keep warm.

Measure the liquid left in the pan and, if necessary, add wine to make 3 cups. Return the liquid to the pan and bring to a boil. Add the

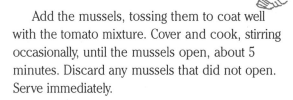

rice, stir, cover, reduce the heat to low, and cook until all the liquid is absorbed and the rice is tender, about 20 minutes for white rice and 30 minutes for brown rice.

Add the seafood mixture, parsley, and pepper to the cooked rice. Fluff with a fork and serve with lemon wedges.

Nutritional Analysis

Calories	254.85 Kcal.	Protein	16.71 gm.
Fat	5.02 gm.	Carbohydrate	34.32 gm.
Sodium	231.49 mg.	Cholesterol	53.93 mg.
Saturated Fat	0.74 gm.		

French Country Mussels

Serves: 6

> *1 tablespoon olive oil*
> *1 large onion, chopped*
> *2 tablespoons minced garlic*
> *1 can (16 ounces) peeled tomatoes, drained*
> *1/2 cup minced fresh parsley*
> *pepper to taste*
> *1 cup dry white wine*
> *4 pounds mussels, scrubbed and debearded*

In an 8-quart pot, heat the oil over medium heat. Add the onion and garlic and sauté until browned, about 10 minutes. Add the tomatoes, breaking them up with a wooden spoon. Add the parsley and pepper. Raise the heat to high and cook for about 2 minutes. Add the wine and cook for another 2 minutes.

Add the mussels, tossing them to coat well with the tomato mixture. Cover and cook, stirring occasionally, until the mussels open, about 5 minutes. Discard any mussels that did not open. Serve immediately.

Nutritional Analysis

Calories	158.20 Kcal.	Protein	11.92 gm.
Fat	4.47 gm.	Carbohydrate	11.48 gm.
Sodium	379.85 mg.	Cholesterol	24.57 mg.
Saturated Fat	0.71 gm.		

Tuna-Noodle Casserole, Italian Style

Serves: 6

> *1 can (13 ounces) water-packed solid white tuna*
> *3 tablespoons vegetable oil*
> *1 cup chopped celery*
> *1/2 cup chopped onion*
> *1 can (16 ounces) tomatoes, drained*
> *1 can (6 ounces) tomato paste*
> *1/2 cup water*
> *1/2 teaspoon garlic powder*
> *1 teaspoon dried oregano, crumbled*
> *1/2 teaspoon dried basil, crumbled*
> *1/4 teaspoon fennel seeds*
> *1/2 pound egg noodles*
> *2 tablespoons grated Parmesan cheese*

Drain the tuna. In a skillet, heat the oil over medium heat. Add the celery and onion and sauté

(continued)

until soft, about 10 minutes. Add the tomatoes, tomato paste, water, garlic powder, oregano, basil, and fennel seeds. Mix well, cover, and simmer over low heat, about 20 minutes. Add the tuna.

Preheat oven to 350°F. Spray a 2-quart baking dish with nonstick spray.

Cook the noodles in boiling salted water until nearly al dente. Drain. Layer half of the noodles in the prepared baking dish. Top with half of the tuna mixture and 1 tablespoon of the cheese. Repeat the layers.

Bake until firm, about 30 minutes. Serve immediately.

Nutritional Analysis

Calories	331.35 Kcal.	Protein	22.66 gm.
Fat	10.30 gm.	Carbohydrate	37.79 gm.
Sodium	726.23 mg.	Cholesterol	59.93 mg.
Saturated Fat	1.62 gm.		

Tomato-Seafood Stew

Serves: 6

1 tablespoon olive oil
1 cup chopped onion
2 cloves garlic, minced
1 can (16 ounces) tomatoes, chopped, juices reserved
1 can (8 ounces) tomato sauce
1 potato, peeled and diced
1 green bell pepper, chopped
1 celery stalk, chopped
1 carrot, shredded
1 teaspoon dried thyme, crumbled

1/4 teaspoon pepper
4 dashes of Tabasco sauce
1/2 pound shrimp, peeled, deveined, and halved lengthwise
1 can (20 ounces) whole baby clams, drained
2 tablespoons snipped fresh parsley

In a large saucepan, heat the oil over medium heat. Add the onion and garlic and sauté until soft, about 10 minutes. Stir in the tomatoes and their juice, tomato sauce, potato, bell pepper, celery, carrot, thyme, pepper, and Tabasco sauce. Bring to a boil, cover, reduce the heat to low, and simmer until the vegetables are tender, 20 to 25 minutes.

Stir in the shrimp, clams, and parsley. Bring to a boil, cover, reduce the heat to low, and simmer until the shrimp turn pink, about 2 minutes. Spoon into serving bowls and serve immediately.

Nutritional Analysis

Calories	191.20 Kcal.	Protein	21.16 gm.
Fat	4.08 gm.	Carbohydrate	17.72 gm.
Sodium	466.35 mg.	Cholesterol	80.07 mg.
Saturated Fat	0.52 gm.		

Quick Crab Cakes

Serves: 4

12 soda crackers, crushed
2 eggs, lightly beaten
2 tablespoons low-fat mayonnaise
1 teaspoon Worcestershire sauce
2 teaspoons Old Bay seasoning

¹/₄ teaspoon red pepper flakes
1 pound lump crabmeat, picked over for shells

In a large bowl, combine the crushed crackers, eggs, mayonnaise, Worcestershire sauce, Old Bay seasoning, and red pepper flakes. Mix well.

Add the crabmeat and, using a rubber spatula, gently fold mixture together. Form into 4 patties.

Spray a large skillet with nonstick cooking spray and heat over medium heat. Add the patties and cook, turning once, until browned and heated through, 12 to 15 minutes. Serve at once.

Nutritional Analysis

Calories	207.92 Kcal.	Protein	26.93 gm.
Fat	6.31 gm.	Carbohydrate	9.04 gm.
Sodium	879.74 mg.	Cholesterol	219.75 mg.
Saturated Fat	2.92 gm.		

Shrimp-Pear Pasta Salad

Serves: 4

1 cup plain low-fat yogurt
2 teaspoons Dijon mustard
¹/₂ teaspoon dried dill, crumbled
Tabasco sauce to taste
¹/₂ pound fusilli, cooked and drained
2 Bartlett pears, cored and sliced
¹/₂ cup chopped red bell pepper
¹/₂ cup chopped green bell pepper
2 scallions, chopped
¹/₄ pound cooked bay shrimp, peeled,
*   deveined, and cooked*
1 small head butter lettuce, leaves separated

In a small bowl, stir together the yogurt, mustard, dill, and Tabasco sauce to form a dressing. In a large bowl, combine the fusilli, pears, bell peppers, scallions, and shrimp. Stir to mix. Add the dressing and stir and toss to coat evenly.

Line a platter or individual plates with the lettuce leaves and spoon the pasta mixture on top. Serve at once.

Nutritional Analysis

Calories	339.25 Kcal.	Protein	17.23 gm.
Fat	2.50 gm.	Carbohydrate	61.83 gm.
Sodium	364.61 mg.	Cholesterol	58.73 mg.
Saturated Fat	0.78 gm.		

Crab Surprise

Serves: 4

¹/₄ cup olive oil
3 tablespoons all-purpose flour
²/₃ cup reduced-sodium, fat-free chicken broth
²/₃ cup 1% milk
¹/₄ cup ketchup
2 teaspoons Worcestershire sauce
1 teaspoon paprika
3 drops of Tabasco sauce
1 tablespoon lemon juice
1³/₄ pounds shelled crab claws
3 cups hot cooked white rice

In a saucepan, heat the oil over low heat. Add the flour and cook, stirring, for 2 minutes. Whisk in the broth and milk and simmer over low heat until thickened slightly, about 10 minutes.

(continued)

Whisk in the ketchup, Worcestershire sauce, paprika, Tabasco sauce, and lemon juice, and continue to simmer for 2 more minutes. Add the crabmeat and simmer until crabmeat is cooked, about 10 minutes.

Spoon the rice onto individual plates, top with crab mixture, and serve.

Nutritional Analysis

Calories	537.53 Kcal.	Protein	46.17 gm.
Fat	17.95 gm.	Carbohydrate	44.95 gm.
Sodium	876.76 mg.	Cholesterol	200.25 mg.
Saturated Fat	2.63 gm.		

Steamed Fish and Spinach

Serves: 4

1 tablespoon olive oil
1/2 cup chopped onion
1 clove garlic, minced
1/4 cup dry white wine
1/4 teaspoon dried tarragon or basil, crumbled
1/8 teaspoon salt
1/8 teaspoon pepper
1 package (10 ounces) frozen chopped spinach, thawed and drained
1 pound fish fillet such as haddock or cod, divided into 4 equal pieces
1 green bell pepper, cut into long, narrow strips

Prepare a fire in a charcoal grill.

In a small skillet, heat the oil over medium heat. Add the onion and garlic and sauté until soft, about 10 minutes. Remove from the heat. Stir in the wine, tarragon or basil, salt, and pepper. Return to the heat, bring to a boil, and boil gently until most of the liquid has evaporated, about 2 minutes. Remove from the heat and set aside.

Cut four 12-by-18-inch pieces of foil. Divide the spinach in half, and distribute one-half evenly among the pieces of foil. Place a piece of fish on each portion of spinach. Spoon the onion mixture evenly over the fish. Top with the remaining spinach, again dividing evenly, and then the bell pepper strips. Bring up the long edges of foil and, leaving a little space for steam expansion, seal tightly with a double fold. Then fold the short ends to seal.

Place the foil packets on the grill rack, seam side up, directly over medium-hot coals. Grill, turning the packets twice, until the fish flakes easily when tested with a fork, about 20 minutes. Serve at once.

Nutritional Analysis

Calories	160.26 Kcal.	Protein	23.98 gm.
Fat	4.45 gm.	Carbohydrate	6.16 gm.
Sodium	204.77 mg.	Cholesterol	64.69 mg.
Saturated Fat	0.62 gm.		

Citrus Shrimp and Scallops

Serves: 4

1/2 pound sea scallops
12 large shrimp, peeled and deveined (about 1/2 pound total)
1 teaspoon finely shredded orange zest
1/2 cup orange juice

1 teaspoon peeled and grated fresh ginger
¼ teaspoon cayenne pepper
2 tablespoons soy sauce
1 clove garlic, minced
12 fresh or frozen snow peas
1 orange, cut into 8 wedges

Halve any large scallops. Place the scallops and shrimp in a lock-top plastic bag set in a deep bowl. In a small bowl, stir together the orange zest, orange juice, ginger, cayenne pepper, soy sauce, and garlic. Pour over the seafood. Seal the bag. Marinate in the refrigerator for 30 minutes.

Prepare a fire in a charcoal grill.

Drain the seafood, reserving the marinade. If using fresh snow peas, cook in boiling water for about 2 minutes, then drain. If using frozen snow peas, thaw and drain well. Wrap 1 snow pea around each shrimp. Thread the shrimp onto four 10- to 12-inch-long skewers alternately with the scallops and orange wedges.

Place the skewers on the grill rack and grill over medium-hot coals for 5 minutes. Turn, brush with the reserved marinade, and grill until the shrimp turn pink and the scallops are opaque, 5 to 7 minutes longer. Brush the kabobs occasionally with the marinade as they cook. (These kabobs can also be broiled about 4 inches from the heat source. Plan on 4 minutes on the first side and 4 to 6 minutes on the second side.)

Cooking Fish

In most cases, fish requires only a few minutes of cooking time on each side. A white-fleshed fish such as sole or halibut takes less time than a firm steaklike fish such as salmon or tuna. Generally, the fish is done when the flesh is opaque and can be flaked easily with a fork.

(continued)

Nutritional Analysis

Calories	141.49 Kcal.	Protein	20.20 gm.
Fat	1.33 gm.	Carbohydrate	11.38 gm.
Sodium	675.47 mg.	Cholesterol	89.45 mg.
Saturated Fat	0.20 gm.		

Baked Sole with Bread Crumb Topping

Serves: 4

1¹/₂ pounds sole fillets
4 cups fresh bread crumbs
¹/₂ medium onion, minced
1 tablespoon lemon juice
¹/₂ teaspoon dried marjoram, crumbled
¹/₂ teaspoon salt
1 teaspoon pepper
2 tablespoons butter, melted
1 tomato, coarsely chopped
2 tablespoons grated Parmesan cheese

Preheat oven to 400°F. Spray a large baking dish in which all the fillets fit snugly with nonstick cooking spray.

Arrange the sole in a single layer in the prepared baking dish. In a small dish, stir together the bread crumbs, onion, lemon juice, marjoram, salt, pepper, and butter. Spread the mixture over the fish. Top with the tomato and sprinkle with the Parmesan cheese.

Bake until the fish is opaque throughout and flakes easily when tested with a fork, about 15 minutes. Serve immediately.

Nutritional Analysis

Calories	367.30 Kcal.	Protein	37.77 gm.
Fat	11.44 gm.	Carbohydrate	26.57 gm.
Sodium	759.91 mg.	Cholesterol	101.01 mg.
Saturated Fat	5.17 gm.		

Stuffed Fillet of Sole

Serves: 4

³/₄ cup seasoned dried bread crumbs
8 ounces cooked crabmeat, flaked
³/₄ cup dry sherry
1 teaspoon lemon juice
4 sole fillets, ¹/₄ pound each
paprika

Preheat oven to 350°F. Lightly grease a small baking dish with olive oil.

In a bowl, stir together the bread crumbs, crabmeat, sherry, and lemon juice. Place one-fourth of the stuffing on each fillet, and roll up the fillet. Secure with toothpicks. Place the rolls in the prepared baking dish, seam side down. Sprinkle with paprika.

Bake until the fish flakes easily when tested with a fork, about 10 minutes. Serve at once.

Nutritional Analysis

Calories	310.60 Kcal.	Protein	36.02 gm.
Fat	4.05 gm.	Carbohydrate	17.76 gm.
Sodium	850.68 mg.	Cholesterol	111.18 mg.
Saturated Fat	0.75 gm.		

Shrimp Scampi

Serves: 6

16 jumbo shrimp, peeled and deveined
1 pound eggless fettuccine
1 tablespoon olive oil
1/4 cup butter
3 cloves garlic, minced
16 clams, well scrubbed
1 cup dry white wine
1 teaspoon dried oregano, crumbled
1 teaspoon dried basil, crumbled

Split each shrimp along the back from the tail to the head, but not all the way through.

Cook the fettuccine in boiling salted water until al dente. Drain the fettuccine, place in a warmed bowl, and toss with the olive oil. Meanwhile, melt the butter in a large skillet over medium heat. Add the garlic and sauté until soft and translucent, about 10 minutes. Add the shrimp, clams, wine, oregano, and basil. Cook until the shrimp are pink and the clams have opened, 5 to 10 minutes. Discard any clams that did not open. Toss the shrimp and clams with the pasta and serve.

Nutritional Analysis

Calories	473.53 Kcal.	Protein	23.68 gm.
Fat	12.23 gm.	Carbohydrate	59.02 gm.
Sodium	429.58 mg.	Cholesterol	99.14 mg.
Saturated Fat	5.41 gm.		

Baked Boston Scrod

Serves: 4

4 scrod fillets, about 1/2 pound each
salt and pepper to taste
2 tablespoons lemon juice
1 1/2 cups dry white wine
1 cup seasoned dried bread crumbs

Preheat oven to 350°F. Lightly grease a baking pan with olive oil.

Place the scrod in the prepared pan and sprinkle with the salt, pepper, lemon juice, and add the wine.

Bake until the fish is opaque throughout and flakes easily when tested with a fork. Remove the pan from the oven. Preheat the broiler. Sprinkle the bread crumbs over the fish. Broil until lightly browned, 2 to 3 minutes. Serve immediately.

Nutritional Analysis

Calories	367.97 Kcal.	Protein	44.79 gm.
Fat	3.44 gm.	Carbohydrate	22.31 gm.
Sodium	923.59 mg.	Cholesterol	97.61 mg.
Saturated Fat	0.65 gm.		

Poached Cod with Spicy Buttermilk Sauce

Serves: 6

1 1/2 pounds cod fillets
3/4 teaspoon ground turmeric
pepper to taste

(continued)

**157**

3 cups buttermilk
1 tablespoon lemon juice
½ teaspoon salt
2 teaspoons ground cumin

Sprinkle the cod fillets with the turmeric and pepper. Pour the buttermilk into a heavy skillet and bring to a simmer. Slip the fish into the skillet, cover, and poach over low heat for 5 minutes.

Remove the fish from the skillet. Add the lemon juice and salt to the buttermilk, raise the heat to high, and boil for 5 minutes to blend flavors and reduce sauce. Stir in the cumin, reduce the heat to low, and return the fish to the pan. Cook until the fish is done, another 5 to 10 minutes. Spoon the sauce over the fish to serve.

Nutritional Analysis

Calories	146.10 Kcal.	Protein	24.40 gm.
Fat	1.99 gm.	Carbohydrate	6.49 gm.
Sodium	384.69 mg.	Cholesterol	53.70 mg.
Saturated Fat	0.81 gm.		

Curried Shrimp and Vegetables with Brown Rice

Serves: 6

1 tablespoon olive oil
1 large onion, sliced
3 cloves garlic, minced
1 tablespoon curry powder
½ teaspoon ground cinnamon
½ teaspoon salt, if desired

1½ cups water
2 large carrots, sliced
2 large potatoes, peeled and cubed
1 large zucchini, sliced
1 can (16 ounces) tomatoes, chopped, juice reserved
1 pound shrimp, peeled and deveined
4 cups hot cooked brown rice

In a large skillet, heat the oil over medium heat. Add the onion and garlic and sauté until translucent, about 5 minutes. Add the curry powder, cinnamon, salt, and water. Bring to a boil and add the carrots and potatoes. Reduce the heat, cover, and cook for 10 minutes. Add the zucchini, tomatoes with their juices, and shrimp, re-cover, and cook until shrimp are pink, about 10 minutes longer. Spoon the hot rice onto individual plates and top with the shrimp and vegetables.

Nutritional Analysis

Calories	329.19 Kcal.	Protein	19.08 gm.
Fat	5.02 gm.	Carbohydrate	52.81 gm.
Sodium	431.58 mg.	Cholesterol	93.16 mg.
Saturated Fat	0.80 gm.		

Lemon and Tarragon Sole

Serves: 4

¼ cup plain low-fat yogurt
1 teaspoon all-purpose flour
1 teaspoon dried tarragon, crumbled
1 teaspoon minced lemon zest
1 pound sole fillets

Preheat broiler. Spray a baking sheet with nonstick cooking spray.

In a small bowl, combine the yogurt, flour, tarragon, and lemon zest. Place the sole fillets on the prepared baking sheet. Spread the yogurt mixture on the fish. Place under the broiler until fish tests done, 5 to 10 minutes. Serve immediately.

Nutritional Analysis

Calories	117.86 Kcal	Protein	22.27 gm.
Fat	1.83 gm.	Carbohydrate	1.76 gm.
Sodium	102.13 mg.	Cholesterol	55.33 mg.
Saturated Fat	0.45 gm.		

Baked Sole Almandine

Serves: 4

1 egg
1/4 cup low-fat milk
1 cup seasoned dried bread crumbs
1 teaspoon dried basil, crumbled
salt and pepper to taste
1 pound sole fillets
2 tablespoons lemon juice
2 tablespoons water
1 tablespoon butter, melted
3 tablespoons blanched slivered almonds
3 scallions, chopped

Preheat oven to 425°F. Spray a baking sheet with nonstick cooking spray.

In a shallow dish, stir together the egg and milk until blended. On a separate plate, mix together the bread crumbs, basil, salt, and pepper.

Dip the sole fillets first in the egg mixture, and then in the crumbs. Place on the prepared baking sheet. In a small bowl, mix together the lemon juice, water, and butter. Sprinkle over the fish. Scatter the almonds over the top.

Bake until the fish flakes easily when tested with a fork, about 10 minutes. Sprinkle with the scallions and serve.

Nutritional Analysis

Calories	308.75 Kcal.	Protein	29.30 gm.
Fat	10.03 gm.	Carbohydrate	24.69 gm.
Sodium	943.71 mg.	Cholesterol	115.97 mg.
Saturated Fat	3.09 gm.		

Seafood Pasta Salad

Serves: 4

1/2 pound ziti
1/2 pound sea scallops
1/3 pound snow peas
1 cup plain low-fat yogurt
2 cloves garlic, minced
1 teaspoon dried oregano, crumbled
1/2 pound medium shrimp, cooked and peeled
1/4 pound crabmeat, picked over for bones and flaked
1 red bell pepper, diced
1 onion, chopped
salt and pepper to taste

Cook the ziti in boiling salted water until al dente. Drain and set aside.

(continued)

Cleaning Mussels

When you first open a bag of mussels, throw away any with cracked shells or those that do not close to the touch. With the rest, scrape off the beards with a sharp knife, and scrub well with a stiff brush under running water. Place in a large pot and add cold water to cover. Let stand for 20 to 30 minutes. Drain them, and then rinse once more before cooking.

Steam the scallops until opaque throughout, about 3 minutes. Remove from the steamer and set aside. Steam the snow peas until barely tender, about 1 minute. Set aside as well.

In a small bowl, stir together the yogurt, garlic, and oregano. In a large bowl, combine the ziti, scallops, snow peas, shrimp, crabmeat, bell pepper, onion, and the yogurt mixture. Toss to coat all the ingredients evenly. Season with salt and pepper and serve.

Nutritional Analysis

Calories	421.56 Kcal.	Protein	39.15 gm.
Fat	3.49 gm.	Carbohydrate	56.10 gm.
Sodium	538.52 mg.	Cholesterol	161.15 mg.
Saturated Fat	0.97 gm.		

Seafood, Louisiana Style

Serves: 4

> 2 cloves garlic, minced
> 2 shallots
> 1/4 cup dry white wine
> 10 large sea scallops
> 1 whole Maine lobster, 3 pounds, cooked and
>   shelled
> 4 jumbo shrimp, peeled and deveined
> 8 clams, well scrubbed
> 8 mussels, well scrubbed and debearded
> 1 tomato, chopped
> 2 cups hot cooked white rice

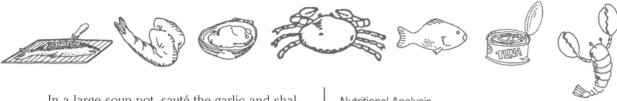

In a large soup pot, sauté the garlic and shallots in the white wine over medium heat until garlic softens, about 5 minutes. Add the scallops, lobster, and shrimp and sauté for 5 minutes. Add the clams, mussels, and tomato and cook until the clams and mussels open, about 7 minutes. Discard any clams or mussels that do not open. Spoon the rice onto individual plates and top with the seafood mixture.

Nutritional Analysis

Calories	312.27 Kcal.	Protein	38.76 gm.
Fat	2.20 gm.	Carbohydrate	28.89 gm.
Sodium	489.88 mg.	Cholesterol	116.31 mg.
Saturated Fat	0.33 gm.		

Quick Sole Florentine in the Microwave

Serves: 4

1 pound sole fillets
salt and pepper to taste
1/2 teaspoon paprika
2 cups stemmed spinach leaves

On a large microwave-safe plate, arrange the fillets. Season the fillets with salt, pepper, and paprika. Cover the plate with plastic wrap. Cut a small slit in the plastic wrap. Microwave on high for 5 minutes. Remove the plastic wrap. Drain off the juices and sprinkle spinach leaves over fillets. Serve at once.

Nutritional Analysis

Calories	110.26 Kcal.	Protein	22.22 gm.
Fat	1.47 gm.	Carbohydrate	1.13 gm.
Sodium	114.14 mg.	Cholesterol	54.48 mg.
Saturated Fat	0.32 gm.		

Scallop-and-Pepper Stir-Fry

Serves: 4

1 tablespoon olive oil
1 pound bay scallops
1 green bell pepper, chopped
1 red bell pepper, chopped
1 red onion, chopped
1 teaspoon red pepper flakes
2 cups cold cooked white rice
salt and pepper to taste

In a large skillet or a wok, heat the oil over medium-high heat. Add the scallops, bell peppers, onion, and red pepper flakes. Stir-fry until scallops are cooked and tender, about 5 minutes. Add the rice and cook and stir until heated through. Season with salt and pepper and serve.

Nutritional Analysis

Calories	252.61 Kcal.	Protein	22.05 gm.
Fat	4.61 gm.	Carbohydrate	29.63 gm.
Sodium	188.84 mg.	Cholesterol	37.45 mg.
Saturated Fat	0.60 gm.		

Curried Cod with Apricots

Serves: 4

1/4 cup minced fresh parsley
1 small onion, chopped
3 cloves garlic, minced
1 cup dry white wine
2 teaspoons curry powder
1/4 teaspoon dried thyme, crumbled
1 bay leaf
1 pound cod fillets
1/4 cup dried apricots, cut into strips

Coat a skillet with nonstick cooking spray and place over medium heat. Add parsley, onion, and garlic and sauté for 2 minutes. Add wine, curry powder, thyme, and bay leaf and bring to a boil. Reduce the heat to medium, add the fish, and cook for 5 minutes. Turn the fish over and continue to cook until the fish flakes easily when tested with a fork, about 5 minutes longer. Transfer the fillets to a warmed platter.

Add the apricots to the skillet and cook over high heat until apricots plump up slightly, about 2 minutes. Discard the bay leaf. Spoon the apricots and pan juices over the fish and serve immediately.

Nutritional Analysis

Calories	174.05 Kcal.	Protein	21.23 gm.
Fat	1.26 gm.	Carbohydrate	9.75 gm.
Sodium	68.37 mg.	Cholesterol	48.80 mg.
Saturated Fat	0.14 gm.		

Paella

Serves: 6

2 cups chicken stock
1/4 teaspoon saffron threads, crushed, or 1/4 teaspoon powdered saffron
1 1/2 tablespoons olive oil
1/2 pound medium shrimp, peeled and deveined
1/2 pound boneless, skinless chicken breast, trimmed of fat and cut into 1/2-inch-thick strips
salt and pepper to taste
1 onion, chopped
2 cloves garlic, minced
1 can (14 1/2 ounces) tomatoes, undrained
1/8 teaspoon red pepper flakes
1 cup arborio rice
1 cup artichoke hearts, canned in water or frozen and thawed
1 cup frozen peas, thawed
1/3 cup roasted red pepper, cut into strips
1/3 cup dry-packed smoked mussels (2 oz.)

In a small saucepan, combine chicken stock and saffron and bring to a simmer. Remove from the heat and set aside.

In a large nonstick skillet, heat 1 teaspoon of the oil over high heat. When the pan is hot, add shrimp and sauté until pink and curled, 3 to 4 minutes. Remove from the skillet and set aside. Add 1 teaspoon of the oil to the skillet. Add chicken and sauté until lightly browned on the outside and opaque inside, 3 to 4 minutes.

Remove from the skillet. Season the shrimp and chicken with salt and pepper and set aside.

Reduce heat to medium and add remaining 1 teaspoon oil to the skillet. Stir in onions and garlic. Sauté until softened, 3 to 5 minutes. Add 1 to 2 teaspoons of water if they become too dry. Stir in undrained tomatoes and red-pepper flakes and simmer, uncovered, for 3 minutes, breaking up tomatoes with a wooden spoon. Add rice and stir to coat well with the tomato mixture. Stir in the reserved chicken stock and bring to a simmer. Cover and cook over low heat for 20 minutes.

Gently stir artichoke hearts, peas, roasted red pepper, smoked mussels, and the reserved shrimp and chicken into the rice mixture. Cover and cook for 5 to 10 minutes longer, or until the rice is tender and the shrimp and chicken are heated through. (Stir occasionally to prevent scorching, if necessary.) Taste and season with salt and pepper. Serve immediately.

Nutritional Analysis

Calories	309.75 Kcal.	Protein	23.30 GM.
Fat	5.81 GM.	Carbohydrate	40.21 GM.
Sodium	462.30 MG.	Cholesterol	79.14 MG.
Saturated Fat	1.04 gm.		

Spicing up Low-Fat Cooking

Cooking low-fat style doesn't have to be tasteless. A creative cook can make low-fat cooking exciting and tantalizing. Experiment with seasonings. For fish and seafood use spices such as allspice, basil, cayenne, curry powder, cumin, fennel, garlic, green bell pepper, fresh lemon juice, marjoram, mint, dry mustard powder, paprika, saffron, sage, sesame seeds, tarragon, thyme, and turmeric. And for a real zing, add fresh hot peppers to your dishes. Remember to remove the membrane and the seeds before chopping finely. Warning: A small amount goes a long way.

Meat Dishes

CHAPTER NINE

Amount Per Chapter
15 Recipes

	% Daily Value
Easy to Prepare	**100%**
Low Fat / High Flavor	**100%**
Simple to Understand	**100%**

DELICIOUS, EASY, LOW-FAT RECIPES

When many people begin to consider a low-fat diet, the first thing they cross off their list of approved foods is meat. That's too bad, because if you get into the habit of choosing the leanest cuts of beef, pork, or lamb, you'll get a healthy dose of muscle-building protein along with a lower-than-average fat content.

Start to think about meat as a condiment or as an occasional treat when you eat out. Also, remember, even if you eat a succulent filet mignon, you won't be forced to go on a water-and-carrot diet for the rest of the week. In addition, once you get in the habit of eating less meat and meat with a lower fat content, you'll start to crave it less. The following recipes regard meat as a healthful, tasty part of your everyday low-fat diet.

Steak Stroganoff

Serves: 4

1 pound boneless round steak
3 tablespoons buttery light, reduced-fat margarine
½ cup chopped onions
½ pound mushrooms, sliced
2 tablespoons tomato paste
2 tablespoons water
½ teaspoon dried basil, crumbled
1 tablespoon cornstarch
1 cup plain low-fat yogurt
¼ cup sherry or beef broth
3 cups hot cooked noodles

Trim off any visible fat from the beef, then slice the beef into narrow strips.

In a skillet, melt 2 tablespoons of the margarine over medium heat. Add the onion and sauté until soft, about 5 minutes. Add the beef and cook, stirring occasionally, until browned, about 5 minutes. Remove the beef to a plate and keep warm. Add the remaining 1 tablespoon margarine to the skillet, melt over medium heat, and add the mushrooms. Sauté until mushrooms are soft, about 8 minutes. Stir in the tomato paste, water, and basil. Return the meat to the skillet and simmer briefly.

In a small saucepan, mix together the cornstarch with 1 tablespoon of the yogurt until thoroughly combined. Then stir in the remaining yogurt and cook over medium heat until thickened, about 10 minutes. Add to the meat mixture and heat through. Thin the sauce with the sherry or broth. Serve over cooked noodles.

Nutritional Analysis

Calories	475.54 Kcal.	Protein	36.34 gm.
Fat	15.25 gm.	Carbohydrate	43.47 gm.
Sodium	373.43 mg.	Cholesterol	107.69 mg.
Saturated Fat	3.65 gm.		

Hearty Meat Loaf

Serves: 6

1 pound lean top round, trimmed of fat and
ground
1/2 cup seasoned dried bread crumbs
2 egg whites or egg substitute equal to 2 eggs
1 tablespoon canola oil (optional)
1 cup chopped onion
1 cup chopped celery with leaf top
1/2 teaspoons Worcestershire sauce
salt and pepper to taste
1 cup ketchup

Preheat oven to 375°F.

In a large bowl, mix together the ground meat, bread crumbs, egg whites or egg substitutes, oil (if using), onion, celery, Worcestershire sauce, salt, and pepper. Mix well. Press the meat into a standard nonstick loaf pan. Spread the ketchup on top.

Bake until cooked through when tested with a knife, 1 to 1 1/4 hours. Serve hot or cold.

Variations: If you like, you can "stuff" the meat loaf. Put half of the meat mixture in the bottom of the loaf pan. Top with 1 1/2 cups sliced red, green, or yellow bell peppers; 1 1/2 cups julienned carrots; 1 cup chopped black olives; 4 hard-cooked egg whites, slivered; or 1 1/2 cups cooked sliced mushrooms. Then press the remaining meat on top and top with the ketchup. Bake as directed.

Nutritional Analysis

Calories	198.15 Kcal.	Protein	21.72 gm.
Fat	2.95 gm.	Carbohydrate	21.39 gm.
Sodium	834.90 mg.	Cholesterol	43.13 mg.
Saturated Fat	0.94 gm.		

Quick Pressure-Cooked Pot Roast

Serves: 8

1 bottom of the round beef roast, 2 to 2 1/2
pounds, all fat trimmed
all-purpose flour for dredging
salt and pepper to taste
1 tablespoon vegetable oil
1 large onion, cut into chunks
3 celery stalks, cut into chunks
1 teaspoon dried thyme, crumbled
1 teaspoon dried rosemary, crumbled
3 tablespoons honey
2 tablespoons cider vinegar
1/2 cup dry red wine
2 1/2 cups vegetable juice cocktail such as V8
brand

Dust the beef roast with flour that has been seasoned liberally with salt and pepper. In the bottom of a large pressure cooker, heat the oil over high heat. Brown the meat on all sides and transfer to a plate. Reduce the heat to medium. Add the onion and celery and cook until soft,

(continued)

about 1 minute, stirring frequently. Add the thyme, rosemary, honey, vinegar, and wine. Bring to a boil. Add the vegetable juice and heat just until the mixture simmers. Adjust seasoning with salt and pepper.

Return the beef to the pot. Secure the lid in place. Bring to high pressure over high heat. Adjust the heat to maintain high pressure and cook for 40 minutes. Remove from the heat and let rest for 10 minutes, then release the remaining steam through escape valve. Remove the lid, tilting it away from you to allow any excess steam to escape. Transfer the pot roast to a plate.

Slice the meat and serve with the juices from the cooker.

Nutritional Analysis

Calories	261.08 Kcal.	Protein	29.13 gm.
Fat	8.95 gm.	Carbohydrate	14.85 gm.
Sodium	326.82 mg.	Cholesterol	75.48 mg.
Saturated Fat	2.65 gm.		

Caribbean Beef

Serves: 10

1 tablespoon vegetable oil
3 pounds eye of round beef, cut in cubes
1 can (20 ounces) pineapple chunks
1 cup water
2/3 cup vinegar
1/2 cup brown sugar, packed
4 tablespoons cornstarch
1 teaspoon salt

2 tablespoons reduced-sodium soy sauce
1 cup thinly sliced green peppers
1 cup thinly sliced onions
8 cups hot cooked white rice
10 tomato wedges, for garnish
20 green pepper strips, for garnish

Heat the oil in a skillet over medium-high heat. Add cubed beef and brown meat slowly on all sides.

Drain pineapple, reserving syrup. In a large saucepan, combine water, vinegar, brown sugar, cornstarch, salt, soy sauce, and pineapple syrup. Cook over medium heat until thickened. Add meat and cover. Cook over low heat until meat is tender, approximately 45 minutes.

Add green pepper, onions, and pineapple chunks. Simmer for 30 minutes. Serve over hot rice. Garnish with tomato wedges and green pepper strips.

Nutritional Analysis

Calories	299.85 Kcal.	Protein	30.57 gm.
Fat	7.37 gm.	Carbohydrate	27.42 gm.
Sodium	433.55 mg.	Cholesterol	73.54 mg.
Saturated Fat	2.19 gm.		

Spicy Beef in Lettuce Cups

Serves: 4

3/4 pound top round beef steak
1/3 cup orange juice
2 tablespoons hoisin sauce
2 tablespoons reduced-sodium soy sauce

2 tablespoons rice vinegar
1 teaspoon cornstarch
1 teaspoon vegetable oil
1 tablespoon grated, peeled fresh ginger
1/4 teaspoon red pepper flakes
8- to 10-ounces shredded cabbage
1 3/4 cups shredded carrots
3 scallions, cut into 1/4-inch pieces
4 medium-size Boston-lettuce leaves

With sharp knife, trim all fat from round steak. Cut round steak lengthwise in half, then cut each half crosswise into 1/8-inch-thick slices.

In small bowl, combine orange juice, hoisin sauce, soy sauce, vinegar, and cornstarch.

In a 12-inch nonstick skillet over medium-high heat, heat vegetable oil. Add ginger and crushed red pepper and cook 20 seconds; add beef and cook 2 minutes or until beef just loses its pink color. Transfer beef to bowl; keep warm. Add orange-juice mixture, cabbage, carrots, and half the scallions to skillet and cook, stirring constantly, until sauce thickens slightly, about 1 minute. Return beef to skillet; heat through.

Line 4 plates with the lettuce leaves. Spoon beef mixture into the lettuce leaves and sprinkle with remaining scallions. Serve immediately.

Nutritional Analysis

Calories	213.88 Kcal.	Protein	23.44 gm.
Fat	4.50 gm.	Carbohydrate	19.96 gm.
Sodium	536.04 mg.	Cholesterol	48.52 mg.
Saturated Fat	1.16 gm.		

Orangey Beef and Broccoli Stir-Fry

Serves: 6

3 oranges
3 tablespoons reduced-sodium soy sauce
1 tablespoon rice wine or dry sherry
1 tablespoon cornstarch
1/2 teaspoon sugar
3 teaspoons sesame oil
1 pound lean beef sirloin, trimmed of fat and sliced against the grain into 1/8-inch slices
2 tablespoons minced garlic
2 tablespoons minced fresh ginger
6 to 8 small dried red chiles
2 pounds broccoli, broken into small florets (6 cups)
1/3 cup water
1 red bell pepper, seeded and sliced
1/2 cup sliced scallion greens

With a small sharp knife or vegetable peeler, carefully pare wide strips of zest from one of the oranges. Cut zest into 1-inch lengths and set aside. Squeeze juice from all the oranges into a small bowl (you'll have about 3/4 cup). Add soy sauce, rice wine (or sherry), cornstarch, and sugar; stir to combine and set aside.

In a wok or large skillet, heat 1 teaspoon of the oil over high heat until almost smoking. Add beef and stir-fry just until no longer pink on the outside, about 1 minute. Transfer to a plate lined with paper towels and set aside.

(continued)

Add the remaining oil to the pan and heat until very hot. Add garlic, ginger, chiles, and reserved orange peel. Stir-fry until fragrant, about 30 seconds. Add broccoli and water. Cover and simmer, stirring occasionally, until water has evaporated and broccoli sizzles, about 3 minutes. Add bell peppers and stir-fry for 1 minute more.

Stir the reserved orange sauce and pour into the wok. Bring to a boil, stirring; cook until sauce has thickened slightly, 1 to 2 minutes. Add scallions and reserved beef, toss to coat with sauce, and heat through.

Nutritional Analysis

Calories	229.51 Kcal.	Protein	22.21 gm.
Fat	6.53 gm.	Carbohydrate	23.04 gm.
Sodium	387.07 mg.	Cholesterol	46.15 mg.
Saturated Fat	1.60 gm.		

Thai-Style Beef Salad

Serves: 4

3 tablespoons soy sauce
1½ tablespoons brown sugar
2 tablespoons water
¾ pound top round steak, trimmed of fat and cut into strips 2 inches long by ¼ inch wide by ¼ inch thick
2 tablespoons seasoned rice vinegar
1 tablespoon lemon juice
1 large clove garlic, minced
1 teaspoon Asian sesame oil

¼ teaspoon red pepper flakes
4 cups shredded Chinese cabbage or iceberg lettuce
1½ cups coarsely grated carrots
1 cup thinly sliced scallions
1 cup cooked spaghetti
¼ cup loosely packed fresh coriander leaves

In a small bowl, combine 1 tablespoon of the soy sauce, 1 tablespoon of the brown sugar, and the water. Place the beef in a shallow bowl and pour the soy mixture over it. Toss to coat. Marinate for 30 minutes. Drain the beef, discarding the marinade. In a nonstick skillet, stir-fry the beef over high heat until browned, about 3 minutes. Remove from the pan and let cool to room temperature.

In a small bowl, stir together the remaining 2 tablespoons soy sauce and the remaining ½ tablespoon brown sugar with the vinegar, lemon juice, garlic, sesame oil, and red pepper flakes. In a large bowl, combine the beef, cabbage or lettuce, carrots, scallions, spaghetti, and coriander leaves. Toss to mix. Pour on the dressing, toss well, and serve.

Nutritional Analysis

Calories	233.19 Kcal.	Protein	23.52 gm.
Fat	4.44 gm.	Carbohydrate	24.82 gm.
Sodium	960.95 mg.	Cholesterol	48.52 mg.
Saturated Fat	1.19 gm.		

Beef Stew

Serves: 4

> 1 teaspoon olive oil
> 1 pound extra-lean stew beef, cut into 1-inch cubes
> 1 large onion, sliced
> salt and pepper to taste
> $1/4$ cup water
> 4 small potatoes, cubed
> 1 cup green beans, cut into $1/2$ inch pieces
> 4 small carrots
> 1 cup chopped tomatoes
> 1 tablespoon all-purpose flour

In the bottom of a pressure cooker, heat the oil over high heat. Add the meat and brown on all sides. Add the onion, salt, pepper, and 1 cup of the water to the cooker. Place the potatoes, green beans, carrots, and tomatoes on top of the meat. Secure the lid in place. Bring to high pressure over high heat. Adjust the heat to maintain high pressure and cook for 8 minutes. Reduce the pressure with the quick-release method. In a small bowl, make a paste of the flour and the $1/4$ cup water. Remove the cooker lid, tilting it away from you to allow excess steam to escape. Place the cooker over medium heat and stir in the flour paste to thicken the juices.

Serve the meat and vegetables with the pan juices spooned over them.

Nutritional Analysis

Calories	340.62 Kcal.	Protein	26.29 gm.
Fat	10.09 gm.	Carbohydrate	36.27 gm.
Sodium	122.45 mg.	Cholesterol	73.77 mg.
Saturated Fat	3.34 gm.		

Burgundy-Style Beef

Serves: 8

> 2 pounds round steak
> salt and pepper to taste
> 3 onions, chopped
> 4 cloves garlic, minced
> $1/2$ teaspoon dried thyme, crumbled
> 1 bay leaf
> $1/3$ cup fresh minced parsley
> $1 1/4$ cups dry red wine
> 2 tablespoons all-purpose flour
> 1 cup beef broth
> $3/4$ pound mushrooms, sliced

Cut the meat into 2-inch cubes and place in a dish. Season with salt and pepper. Spread one-third of the onions and all of the garlic over the meat. Add the thyme, bay leaf, and parsley. Pour in the wine. Cover and marinate for at least 2 hours at room temperature or longer in the refrigerator, turning occasionally.

In a large skillet, heat the oil over medium heat. Add the rest of the onions and sauté until soft, about 5 minutes. Drain the meat, reserving the marinade, and dredge in the flour. Add to the skillet and sauté for several minutes with the

(continued)

onions. Add the marinade, stir well, and add the broth. Bring to a boil, cover, reduce the heat to low, and simmer until the meat is tender, 1½ hours. Add the mushrooms during the last 10 minutes of cooking, then serve.

Nutritional Analysis

Calories	207.22 Kcal.	Protein	27.40 gm.
Fat	5.84 gm.	Carbohydrate	10.52 gm.
Sodium	150.01 mg.	Cholesterol	65.83 mg.
Saturated Fat	1.92 gm.		

Spicy Chinese Beef

Serves: 12

1 tablespoon peanut oil
2 onions, sliced
4 cloves garlic, minced
4 teaspoons peeled and minced fresh ginger
1 pound extra-lean beef, thinly sliced
2 tomatoes, cut into chunks
2 green bell peppers, cut into long, narrow strips
¼ cup oyster sauce
2 tablespoons soy sauce
2 teaspoons chili paste
2 cups bean sprouts
4 cups cold cooked white rice
3 tablespoons peanuts
5 scallions, chopped

In a wok or large, deep skillet, heat the oil over high heat for 30 seconds. Add the onions and stir-fry for 2 minutes. Add the garlic, ginger, and beef

and stir-fry until beef is browned, another 2 minutes. Add the tomatoes, bell peppers, oyster sauce, soy sauce, and chili paste. Stir-fry for another 2 minutes. Add the bean sprouts and stir well. Add the rice and toss with the beef mixture. Sprinkle with the peanuts and scallions and serve.

Nutritional Analysis

Calories	173.86 Kcal.	Protein	12.19 gm.
Fat	4.39 gm.	Carbohydrate	21.42 gm.
Sodium	459.88 mg.	Cholesterol	21.94 mg.
Saturated Fat	1.01 gm.		

Pork Pinwheels with Apricot Stuffing

Serves: 6

1 pork tenderloin, about 1 pound

Stuffing:
⅔ cup reduced-sodium, fat-free chicken broth, heated
⅓ cup snipped dried apricots
2 tablespoons chopped celery
1 small onion, chopped
1 tablespoon buttery light, reduced-fat margarine
⅛ teaspoon ground cinnamon
dash of pepper
2 cups whole-wheat bread cubes

Sauce:
1½ teaspoons cornstarch
dash of ground nutmeg
1 cup apricot nectar

Preheat broiler.

Split the tenderloin lengthwise, but do not cut all the way through. Open the tenderloin out flat, as if it were a book. Pound the tenderloin lightly with meat mallet to a 10-by-6-inch rectangle.

To make the stuffing, place the apricots in a small bowl and pour the broth over them. Let stand for 5 minutes. In a small skillet, melt the margarine over medium heat. Add the celery and onion and sauté until soft but not browned, about 5 minutes. Remove from the heat and stir in the cinnamon and pepper. In a large bowl, mix together the bread cubes, onion mixture, and apricot mixture; toss lightly to moisten.

Spread the stuffing evenly over the tenderloin. Roll up jelly-roll style, starting from the short side. Secure the roll with wooden toothpicks or tie with kitchen string at 1-inch intervals. Cut the meat roll crosswise into six 1-inch-thick slices. Place the meat slices on a broiler pan, cut side down. Slip under the broiler about 4 inches from the heat source and broil for 12 minutes. Turn the slices over and broil until the meat is cooked through, 11 to 12 minutes. Remove the toothpicks or string and transfer the meat slices to a serving platter.

Meanwhile, to make the sauce, combine the cornstarch and nutmeg in a small saucepan. Stir in the apricot nectar and place over medium heat. Cook, stirring, until bubbly, then cook and stir for 2 minutes more. Serve the sauce with meat slices.

Nutritional Analysis

Calories	188.18 Kcal.	Protein	17.05 gm.
Fat	3.69 gm.	Carbohydrate	19.83 gm.
Sodium	179.19 mg.	Cholesterol	46.23 mg.
Saturated Fat	1.53 gm.		

Pork Chops Dijon

Serves: 4

> 1 pound boneless lean pork chops
> 1 onion, chopped
> 3 tablespoons Dijon mustard
> 2 tablespoons low-fat Italian dressing
> 1/4 teaspoon pepper

Spray a large skillet with nonstick cooking spray and place over medium-high heat. Add the chops and brown on both sides, turning once. Transfer the chops to a plate and set aside. Add the onions to the skillet and cook and stir over medium heat until soft, about 3 minutes. Push the onions to the side of the skillet and return the chops to the skillet. In a small bowl, quickly stir together the mustard, dressing, and pepper. Spread the mixture over the chops. Cover and cook over medium-low heat until the meat is tender, about 15 minutes. Serve immediately.

Nutritional Analysis

Calories	211.64 Kcal.	Protein	24.80 gm.
Fat	6.72 gm.	Carbohydrate	4.24 gm.
Sodium	391.28 mg.	Cholesterol	66.90 mg.
Saturated Fat	2.22 gm.		

Pork and Wild Rice Salad with Plums

Serves: 4

1 package (6 ounces) white and wild rice mix
1/4 cup herb vinegar
1 tablespoon Dijon mustard
1 tablespoon minced garlic
1 tablespoon honey
2 teaspoons cornstarch
1 cup water
2 tablespoons diced scallions
2 teaspoons dried parsley flakes
1/4 teaspoon red pepper flakes
8 cups mixed salad greens
2 3/4 cups thinly sliced carrots
1 1/2 cups slivered snow peas
10 ounces roast pork, trimmed and thinly sliced
8 plums, pitted and sliced

Cook white and wild rice mix as directed on the package. Set aside.

In a saucepan over medium heat, combine the vinegar, mustard, garlic, honey, and cornstarch. Stir in the water and cook, stirring, until thickened, about 5 minutes. Remove from the heat and stir in the scallions, parsley, and red pepper flakes. Let cool, cover, and chill.

In a bowl, toss together the greens, carrots, and snow peas. Divide among individual salad plates. Spoon the rice into the center of the plates, and top with the pork and plums. Drizzle with the dressing and serve.

Nutritional Analysis

Calories	504.91 Kcal.	Protein	29.04 gm.
Fat	10.71 gm.	Carbohydrate	73.83 gm.
Sodium	701.54 mg.	Cholesterol	63.75 mg.
Saturated Fat	4.24 gm.		

Pork and Garbanzo Bean Curry

Serves: 4

1 pound pork fillets, cut into 1-inch chunks
1 tablespoon olive oil
2 cloves garlic, minced
1 onion, chopped
2 teaspoons peeled and minced fresh ginger
1 tablespoon all-purpose flour
1 teaspoon curry powder
1/2 teaspoon ground coriander
1/2 teaspoon ground cumin
salt and pepper to taste
2 carrots, grated
2 russet potatoes, peeled and cubed
1/2 cup water
1 can (19 ounces) garbanzo beans, drained and rinsed
1 apple, peeled, cored, and chopped

In a skillet, brown the pork in olive oil over medium heat for 5 minutes. Add the garlic, onion, and ginger and cook for 2 minutes. Stir in the flour, curry powder, coriander, cumin, salt, and pepper. Add the carrots, potato, and water and bring to a boil. Reduce the heat to low, cover, and cook for 10 minutes, adding the 1/2 cup water if the

mixture begins to dry out. Add the garbanzo beans and apple, cover, and cook over medium heat until the vegetables are cooked through, about 10 minutes longer. Serve immediately.

Nutritional Analysis

Calories	400.22 Kcal.	Protein	30.78 gm.
Fat	12.08 gm.	Carbohydrate	41.74 gm.
Sodium	232.05 mg.	Cholesterol	77.18 mg.
Saturated Fat	2.71 gm.		

Veal Scaloppine Dijon

Serves: 4

4 dry-packed unsalted sun-dried tomato halves
1 pound veal cutlets
1/4 teaspoon salt
1/4 teaspoon coarse black pepper
3 medium-size cucumbers
1 medium-size leek
3 tablespoons low-fat milk
1 tablespoon Dijon mustard
3/4 teaspoon cornstarch
3 teaspoons light corn-oil spread
3/4 teaspoon instant low-fat chicken bouillon
3/4 cup water

Place sun-dried tomato halves in small bowl with 1 cup boiling water. Let stand 15 minutes to soften.

Meanwhile, with meat mallet, pound veal cutlets to 1/8-inch thickness. Cut each veal cutlet crosswise in half. Sprinkle with salt and pepper. With vegetable peeler, remove several strips of peel from each cucumber. Cut cucumbers into 1 1/2-inch chunks. Cut off roots and trim leaf ends of leek. Separate leek into leaves and rinse with running cold water to remove sand. Cut leaves crosswise into 3-inch pieces, then cut lengthwise into 1/4-inch-thick strips. Drain and thinly slice sun-dried tomato halves.

In a small bowl, mix milk, mustard, and corn-starch until smooth. Set aside.

Melt 1 teaspoon of the light corn-oil spread in a 12-inch nonstick skillet over medium-high heat. Place cucumbers and 1/2 teaspoon salt in pan, stir frequently, and sauté until golden and tender-crisp. Remove cucumbers to bowl. Keep warm.

In the same skillet over medium-high heat, melt the remaining light corn-oil spread. Place in veal cutlets, half at a time. Cook about 2 minutes, turning once, until veal just loses its pink color. Remove veal cutlets to a plate as they are done.

In the same skillet, bring leek, low-fat chicken bouillon, and water to a boil. Reduce heat to low. Cover and simmer until leek is tender, 3 to 5 minutes. Stir in cornstarch mixture and dried tomatoes. Over medium-high heat, bring to a boil. Boil 1 minute. Add veal with any juices in plate to sauce in skillet. Heat through. Serve veal with sauce and cucumbers.

Nutritional Analysis

Calories	204.61 Kcal.	Protein	26.41 gm.
Fat	2.42 gm.	Carbohydrate	14.45 gm.
Sodium	545.73 mg.	Cholesterol	88.98 mg.
Saturated Fat	1.23 gm.		

THE EVERYTHING
LOW-FAT HIGH-FLAVOR COOKBOOK

Poultry Dishes

CHAPTER TEN

Amount Per Chapter

45 Recipes

	% Daily Value
Easy to Prepare	**100%**
Low Fat / High Flavor	**100%**
Simple to Understand	**100%**

DELICIOUS, EASY, LOW-FAT RECIPES

I can't think of anyone I know who doesn't like chicken. No doubt that's because it's tasty and easy to fix. Plus, it's low in fat and cholesterol if you remove the skin and trim away any visible fat.

Chicken is also versatile, the main reason why I like it so much. You can spread a grilled chicken breast with a bit of pesto, place it between two slices of bread with some lettuce and tomato, and you have a quick lunch. On the other hand, you can go all out and create a dish that will fit right in with a gourmet dinner, and it will still be low in fat.

The following recipes underscore the versatility and wonderful flavor of chicken, so let the cooking begin.

Chicken Marsala

Serves: 4

> 1 tablespoon buttery light, reduced-fat margarine
> 4 skinless, boneless chicken breast halves
> 1/8 teaspoon salt
> 1/8 teaspoon pepper
> 2 tablespoons shallots or scallions, finely chopped
> 1/2 cup Marsala wine
> 1/2 cup reduced-sodium, fat-free chicken broth
> 2 cups tomatoes, peeled, seeded, and chopped
> 1/4 cup finely chopped fresh parsley

In a skillet, melt the margarine over medium heat. Add the chicken and brown on both sides, about 5 minutes. Sprinkle with the salt and pepper and remove from the skillet.

Add the shallots or scallions, wine, broth, and tomatoes to the skillet. Simmer over medium heat until the liquid is partially reduced, about 10 minutes. Return the chicken to the skillet,

spooning sauce over it. Cover and simmer over low heat until the chicken is tender, about 15 to 20 minutes longer. To serve, transfer the chicken to warmed plates and spoon the sauce over the top. Sprinkle with the parsley.

Nutritional Analysis

Calories	195.43 Kcal.	Protein	28.66 gm.
Fat	4.61 gm.	Carbohydrate	8.87 gm.
Sodium	266.41 mg.	Cholesterol	68.44 mg.
Saturated Fat	0.88 gm.		

Chicken Gumbo

Serves: 8

> 1/3 cup all-purpose flour
> 1 tablespoon canola oil
> 1/2 pound boneless, skinless chicken breasts, cut into thin strips
> 3 ounces kielbasa sausage, thinly sliced
> 1 onion, chopped

1 large green bell pepper, seeded and diced
1 stalk celery, finely chopped
4 cloves garlic, minced
3 cups reduced-sodium, fat-free chicken broth
1 can (15 ounces) diced tomatoes, undrained
1 package (10 ounces) frozen okra, slightly
*   thawed and sliced (2 cups)*
4 jalapeño peppers, pierced all over with a
*   fork*
1 bay leaf
¹/₂ teaspoon dried thyme leaves
Louisiana hot sauce, such as Crystal or
*   Tabasco, to taste*
Salt and pepper to taste
3 cups cooked white rice

Heat a heavy cast-iron skillet over medium heat. Add flour and cook, stirring constantly with a wooden spoon, until flour turns deep golden in color, 7 to 10 minutes. (There will be a strong aroma similar to burned toast. Be careful not to let flour burn; reduce heat if flour seems to be browning too quickly. Alternatively, you can toast the flour in a pie pan in a 400°F oven for 20 minutes.) Transfer to a plate to cool.

In a Dutch oven or heavy soup pot, heat ¹/₂ tablespoon of the oil over high heat. Add chicken and sausage; cook, stirring, until browned on all sides, about 3 minutes. Remove from pot and drain on paper towels.

Reduce heat to medium; heat remaining ¹/₂ tablespoon oil. Add onions, bell peppers, celery, and garlic. Cook, stirring, until onions are lightly browned, about 7 minutes. Stir in the toasted

flour. Gradually stir in chicken broth and bring to a simmer.

Add tomatoes and their juice, okra, jalapeños, bay leaf, and thyme. Stir. Reduce heat to low, cover, and simmer for 30 minutes.

Add reserved chicken and sausage and simmer for 5 minutes more. Discard jalapeños and bay leaf. Season with hot sauce, salt, and pepper. Serve with rice, passing additional hot sauce.

Nutritional Analysis

Calories	219.98 Kcal.	Protein	12.89 gm.
Fat	5.41 gm.	Carbohydrate	29.61 gm.
Sodium	437.75 mg.	Cholesterol	23.57 mg.
Saturated Fat	1.34 gm.		

Yogurt Chicken Paprika

Serves: 6

3 chicken thighs, skinned
3 skinless chicken breast halves
¹/₈ teaspoon pepper
¹/₄ cup all-purpose flour
1 tablespoon olive oil
¹/₄ cup diced onion
1 cup hot water
2 teaspoons lemon juice
2 tablespoons cornstarch
2 cups plain low-fat yogurt
2 teaspoons paprika

Season the chicken pieces with the pepper. Roll the chicken in the flour, coating well. In a

(continued)

large skillet, heat the oil over medium heat. Add the chicken and brown on both sides, 10 to 15 minutes. Add the onion, water, and lemon juice. Cover and cook over low heat until tender, about 40 minutes. Remove the chicken from the pan to a warmed platter and keep warm.

In a bowl, stir the cornstarch into 2 tablespoons of the yogurt, then mix in the remaining yogurt. Stir into pan drippings. Simmer over low heat until thickened, about 5 minutes. Add paprika and mix well. Pour the yogurt sauce over the chicken and serve.

Nutritional Analysis

Calories	207.79 Kcal.	Protein	25.06 gm.
Fat	5.64 gm.	Carbohydrate	12.83 gm.
Sodium	122.10 mg.	Cholesterol	67.38 mg.
Saturated Fat	1.59 gm.		

Raspberry Chicken

Serves: 4

4 chicken leg quarters, skinned
$1/2$ teaspoon salt
$1/2$ teaspoon black pepper
$1/2$ cup seedless red raspberry jam
2 tablespoons balsamic vinegar
1 tablespoon reduced-sodium soy sauce
$1/8$ teaspoon crushed red pepper or $1/2$
    teaspoon red pepper flakes

Preheat the oven to 375°F. Spray a 9 x 13-inch baking dish with nonstick cooking spray. Place the chicken leg quarters in the baking dish and

sprinkle with salt and black pepper. Bake for 45 to 50 minutes, or until the chicken is golden and cooked through.

In a small saucepan, combine the remaining ingredients; mix well. Cook over low heat for about 1 minute, until the sauce is smooth, stirring occasionally. Remove the chicken from the baking dish and place on a serving platter. Top with the sauce and serve.

Nutritional Analysis

Calories	259.22 Kcal.	Protein	26.71 gm.
Fat	5.31 gm.	Carbohydrate	26.66 gm.
Sodium	567.86 mg.	Cholesterol	104.00 mg.
Saturated Fat	1.27 gm.		

Curried Chicken

Serves: 6

$1/2$ cup all-purpose flour
$1/8$ teaspoon salt
$1/2$ teaspoon pepper
1 chicken, about $2^1/2$ pounds, skinned and cut
    into serving pieces
2 tablespoons corn oil
1 onion, chopped
1 green bell pepper, chopped
1 clove garlic, minced
1 can (6 ounces) tomato paste
2 cups water
$1^1/2$ teaspoons curry powder
$1/2$ teaspoon dried thyme, crumbled
1 teaspoon raisins

In a shallow bowl, combine the flour, salt, and pepper, mixing well. Coat the chicken pieces with the seasoned flour. In a large skillet, heat the oil over medium heat. Add the chicken pieces and brown on both sides, about 7 minutes a side. Add the onion, bell pepper, and garlic and cook until soft, about 10 minutes.

Drain off the fat. Add the tomato paste, waste, curry powder, and thyme. Simmer, uncovered, over medium heat, until the juices run clear when the chicken is pierced, about 30 minutes. Add the raisins, heat through for another 5 minutes, and serve.

Nutritional Analysis

Calories	218.71 Kcal.	Protein	22.10 gm.
Fat	6.67 gm.	Carbohydrate	17.54 gm.
Sodium	344.53 mg.	Cholesterol	63.56 mg.
Saturated Fat	1.18 gm.		

Grilled Yogurt-Lemon Chicken

Serves: 10

2 cups plain low-fat yogurt
1/3 cup vinegar
2 tablespoons lemon juice
2 cloves garlic, minced
2 teaspoons coriander seeds, crushed
1/4 teaspoon ground cloves
8 drops of Tabasco sauce
1/2 teaspoon pepper
1 teaspoon dry mustard

(continued)

Bulgur

Bulgur is a crunchy, nutty wheat grain that adds texture to dishes. Similar to cracked wheat, it can be substituted for rice or tiny pasta in many menus. It is also easy to prepare, for all you need to do is pour boiling water over it and then let it sit until the liquid is absorbed. You can create your own recipes by adding onion and garlic, vegetables, chicken, or anything else you'd like.

1/2 teaspoon ground ginger
5 pounds chicken parts, skinned

In a large bowl, mix together all the ingredients except the chicken. Add the chicken, turn to coat, cover, and refrigerate overnight.

Preheat oven to 325°F. Transfer the chicken to a baking dish. Bake, basting every 30 minutes with pan juices, until the juices run clear when the chicken pieces are pierced, 2 to 2½ hours. (Alternatively, cook over medium-hot coals, turning and basting every 15 minutes, for 2 to 2½ hours.)

Nutritional Analysis

Calories	163.31 Kcal.	Protein	25.81 gm.
Fat	4.17 gm.	Carbohydrate	4.31 gm.
Sodium	117.21 mg.	Cholesterol	78.99 mg.
Saturated Fat	1.31 gm.		

Poached Chicken

Serves: 4

> 1 tablespoon buttery light, reduced-fat
>   margarine
> 1 onion, sliced
> 3 carrots, julienned
> 3 celery stalks, cut into strips
> 2½ pounds chicken parts, skinned
> 3 to 4 cups reduced-sodium, fat-free chicken
>   broth
> ¼ cup dry vermouth or white wine (optional)
> 1 bay leaf
> 3 parsley sprigs
> ½ teaspoon dried thyme, crumbled

1/8 teaspoon salt
1/8 teaspoon pepper

In a heavy saucepan, melt the margarine over medium heat. Add the onion, carrots, and celery and sauté until soft, about 5 minutes. Add the chicken, cover the pan, and cook for another 5 minutes.

Add the broth, vermouth or wine, bay leaf, parsley, thyme, salt, and pepper. Cook gently until the juices run clear when the chicken is pierced, about 25 minutes. Remove and discard the bay leaf. Serve with poaching liquid in individual bowls.

Nutritional Analysis

Calories	246.51 Kcal.	Protein	33.08 gm.
Fat	7.27 gm.	Carbohydrate	10.63 gm.
Sodium	749.38 mg.	Cholesterol	95.34 mg.
Saturated Fat	1.56 gm.		

Very Lemony Chicken

Serves: 4

> 1½ pounds chicken parts, skinned
> ½ cup lemon juice
> 2 tablespoons distilled white vinegar
> ½ cup slivered lemon zest
> 1 tablespoon chopped fresh oregano or 1
>   teaspoon dried oregano, crumbled
> 1 onion, sliced
> ¼ teaspoon salt
> 1/8 teaspoon pepper
> ½ teaspoon paprika

Place the chicken parts in a 9 x 13 x 2-inch baking dish. In a small bowl, mix together the lemon juice, vinegar, lemon zest, oregano, and onion. Pour over the chicken, cover, and marinate in the refrigerator for several hours or as long as overnight, turning occasionally. Sprinkle with salt, pepper, and paprika.

Preheat oven to 300°F. Cover the baking dish with foil and bake for 30 minutes. Uncover and continue to bake until the juices run clear when a chicken piece is pierced, about 30 minutes longer. Serve immediately.

Nutritional Analysis

Calories	131.21 Kcal.	Protein	18.34 gm.
Fat	2.74 gm.	Carbohydrate	8.34 gm.
Sodium	214.53 mg.	Cholesterol	57.20 mg.
Saturated Fat	0.66 gm.		

Skillet Chicken and Rice

Serves: 6

2 pounds chicken parts, skinned
3 cups sliced mushrooms
4 carrots, cut into 1/2-inch-thick slices
3/4 cup long-grain white rice
1/2 cup chopped onion
1 teaspoon low-fat chicken bouillon granules
1 teaspoon poultry seasoning
1/4 teaspoon salt
2 cups water

Spray a 12-inch skillet with nonstick spray coating and place over medium heat. Brown the

chicken pieces on both sides, about 15 minutes. Remove the chicken from the skillet. Drain off the fat from the pan, if necessary. Add the mushrooms, carrots, rice, onion, bouillon granules, poultry seasoning, salt, and water. Place the chicken on top of the rice mixture. Cover and simmer over low heat until the juices run clear when a chicken piece is pierced and the rice is tender, about 30 minutes. Serve at once.

Nutritional Analysis

Calories	208.77 Kcal.	Protein	18.55 gm.
Fat	2.80 gm.	Carbohydrate	26.41 gm.
Sodium	344.75 mg.	Cholesterol	50.84 mg.
Saturated Fat	0.64 gm.		

Strawberry Chicken Salad

Serves: 4

1/2 cup low-fat mayonnaise
2 tablespoons chutney
1 tablespoon lemon juice
1 teaspoon grated lemon zest
1 teaspoon salt
1 teaspoon curry powder
2 cups diced cooked chicken
1 cup sliced celery
1/4 cup chopped red onion
4 lettuce leaves
1 1/2 pints strawberries, stemmed
fresh mint sprigs

In a large bowl, stir together the mayonnaise, chutney, lemon juice and zest, salt, and curry

(continued)

183

powder, mixing well. Add the chicken, celery, and onion. Toss well, cover, and chill.

Just before serving, slice 1 pint of the strawberries. Add to the chicken mixture and toss gently. Line a platter or individual serving plates with the lettuce leaves. Mound the chicken mixture on the lettuce. Garnish with the whole strawberries and mint. Serve at once.

Nutritional Analysis

Calories	252.74 Kcal.	Protein	21.61 gm.
Fat	7.77 gm.	Carbohydrate	24.56 gm.
Sodium	969.90 mg.	Cholesterol	62.30 mg.
Saturated Fat	1.45 gm.		

Chicken Pizza

Serves: 6

Handling Chicken Safely

Today, with everyone so aware of salmonella and other bacteria that can easily be transmitted through raw chicken, the following standards bear repeating:

- **Always wash your hands before and after handling raw chicken.**
- **Thoroughly wash all cutting boards and utensils you've used to prepare raw chicken.**
- **Make sure chicken is thoroughly cooked (to 180°F) before serving.**
- **If chicken smells funny, throw it out.**

2/3 cup julienned dry-packed sun-dried tomatoes
1/4 cup olive oil
3/4 pound skinless chicken meat, diced
1 teaspoon dried oregano, crumbled
1/2 teaspoon dried basil, crumbled
1/2 teaspoon dried thyme, crumbled
1/2 teaspoon salt
1/2 teaspoon pepper
1 ready-made pizza crust, 12 inches in diameter
2 cups cooked, peeled, and diced shrimp
1 avocado, pitted, peeled, and diced
1 jalapeño pepper, seeded and finely diced
1 cup red currant preserves
1 cup shredded low-fat cheddar or low-fat mozzarella cheese

Soak the tomatoes in hot water for 30 minutes. Drain and set aside.

In a skillet, heat 2 tablespoons of the oil over medium heat. Add the chicken, oregano, basil, thyme, salt, and pepper and cook, stirring often, until the chicken is tender, about 15 minutes. Drain off the oil and set aside.

Preheat oven to 450°F.

Prepare the pizza crust for topping as directed on the package. Brush with the remaining 2 tablespoons oil. Spoon the chicken over the dough. Scatter the tomatoes, shrimp, avocado, and jalapeño over the chicken. Pour the red currant preserves over the top, and sprinkle with the cheese.

Bake until the crust is golden brown, 15 to 20 minutes. Cut into wedges to serve.

Nutritional Analysis

Calories	636.22 Kcal.	Protein	32.91 gm.
Fat	21.89 gm.	Carbohydrate	76.52 gm.
Sodium	652.85 mg.	Cholesterol	133.85 mg.
Saturated Fat	3.93 gm.		

Sweet-and-Sour Chicken

Serves: 8

1 tablespoon vegetable oil
1 chicken, about 3 pounds, cut into serving
   pieces and skinned
1 can (20 ounces) pineapple chunks, drained,
   juice reserved
1/2 cup sliced celery
1 green or red bell pepper, cut into chunks
1/4 cup firmly packed brown sugar

1/2 cup vinegar
2 tablespoon soy sauce
1 tablespoon ketchup
1 1/2 teaspoons Worcestershire sauce
1/4 teaspoon ground ginger
2 tablespoons cornstarch
2 tablespoons cold water

In the bottom of a pressure cooker, heat the oil over medium heat. Add the chicken pieces and brown on both sides, about 5 minutes. Measure out 1 cup of the reserved pineapple juice and combine with the celery, bell pepper, brown sugar, vinegar, soy sauce, ketchup, Worcestershire sauce, and ginger. Mix well and pour over the chicken. Secure the lid in place. Bring to high pressure over high heat. Adjust the heat to maintain high pressure and cook for 8 minutes. Reduce the pressure with the quick-release method.

Remove the chicken and vegetables to a warmed platter. In a small bowl, stir together the cornstarch and water, then stir into the hot liquid. Place over high heat and cook, stirring, until the mixture boils and thickens, about 5 minutes. Add the pineapple chunks and heat through. Pour the sauce over the chicken and serve.

Nutritional Analysis

Calories	199.22 Kcal.	Protein	18.18 gm.
Fat	4.28 gm.	Carbohydrate	22.33 gm.
Sodium	363.05 mg.	Cholesterol	57.20 mg.
Saturated Fat	0.85 gm.		

Fiesta Chicken

Serves: 6

1 can (8 ounces) tomato sauce
½ cup orange juice
½ cup finely chopped onion
2 tablespoons raisins
2 tablespoons chopped pimiento
½ teaspoon dried oregano, crumbled
½ teaspoon chili powder
1 clove garlic, minced
several dashes of Tabasco sauce
6 skinless, boneless chicken breast halves
2 teaspoons cornstarch
1 tablespoon water
¼ cup finely chopped fresh parsley
3 cups hot cooked white rice

In a large skillet, combine the tomato sauce, orange juice, onion, raisins, pimiento, oregano, chili powder, garlic, and Tabasco sauce. Bring to a boil, cover, reduce the heat to low, and simmer for 5 minutes. Add the chicken to the pan and return to a boil. Cover, reduce the heat to low, and simmer until the juices run clear when a chicken breast is pierced, 12 to 15 minutes.

Meanwhile, in a small bowl, combine the cornstarch and water. Stir into the skillet and cook and stir until thickened and bubbly, about 5 minutes. Cook and stir for 2 minutes longer. Toss the parsley into the hot rice and spoon the rice onto a platter or individual plates. Serve the chicken mixture over rice.

Nutritional Analysis

Calories	274.19 Kcal.	Protein	30.39 gm.
Fat	1.83 gm.	Carbohydrate	32.26 gm.
Sodium	311.55 mg.	Cholesterol	68.44 mg.
Saturated Fat	0.44 gm.		

Sesame Chicken Teriyaki

Serves: 2

2 tablespoons teriyaki sauce
1 tablespoon water
2 cloves garlic, minced
¼ teaspoon ground ginger
2 skinless, boneless chicken breast halves, cut into long ¾-inch-wide strips
¼ teaspoon sesame seeds, toasted

In a small bowl, combine the teriyaki sauce, water, garlic, and ginger, mixing well. Stir in the chicken. Let stand for 20 minutes at room temperature, stirring occasionally.

Preheat broiler.

Drain the chicken and thread it onto two 10- to 12-inch skewers or four 6-inch skewers, weaving it accordion style. Place on a broiler pan and slip under the broiler 4 to 5 inches from the heat source. Broil for 3 minutes. Turn the chicken over and continue to broil until the chicken is tender and no longer pink, 2 to 3 minutes longer. Sprinkle with the sesame seeds and serve.

Nutritional Analysis

Calories	152.26 Kcal.	Protein	28.57 gm.
Fat	1.66 gm.	Carbohydrate	4.09 gm.
Sodium	767.26 mg.	Cholesterol	68.44 mg.
Saturated Fat	0.40 gm.		

Chicken Breasts with Curried Stuffing

Serves: 4

1 tablespoon butter
¹/₂ cup shredded carrot
¹/₄ cup sliced scallion
1 teaspoon curry powder
¹/₂ cup fresh bread crumbs
2 tablespoons raisins
1 tablespoon water
4 skinless, boneless chicken breast halves
¹/₈ teaspoon salt
¹/₄ teaspoon paprika
¹/₄ cup plain low-fat yogurt
2 teaspoons orange marmalade

In a small saucepan, melt the butter over medium heat. Add the carrot, scallion, and curry powder, and cook, stirring, until tender, about 5 minutes. Remove from the heat and stir in the bread crumbs, raisins, and water.

Preheat oven to 350°F.

Place 1 chicken breast half, boned side up, between 2 sheets of plastic wrap. Working from the center to the edges, pound lightly with a meat mallet to a ¹/₄-inch thickness. Remove the plastic wrap. Repeat with the remaining chicken. Sprinkle the chicken pieces lightly with salt. Place one-fourth of the stuffing mixture on half of each piece of chicken. Fold the other half of the chicken breast over the filling. Secure with a toothpick. Place chicken in an 8-inch square baking dish with 2-inch sides. Sprinkle with the paprika. Cover with foil.

Bake until the chicken is tender and the juices run clear when a piece is pierced, about 25 minutes.

Meanwhile, in a small bowl, combine the yogurt and marmalade. Serve with about 1 tablespoon of the yogurt mixture atop each piece of chicken.

Nutritional Analysis

Calories	211.42 Kcal.	Protein	28.99 gm.
Fat	4.88 gm.	Carbohydrate	11.81 gm.
Sodium	225.53 mg.	Cholesterol	77.27 mg.
Saturated Fat	2.34 gm.		

Cheesy Chicken Rolls

Serves: 4

¹/₂ cup shredded low-fat mozzarella cheese
1 jar (2¹/₂ ounces) sliced mushrooms, drained
¹/₄ cup plus 1 tablespoon plain low-fat yogurt
1 tablespoon snipped fresh chives
1 tablespoon minced fresh parsley
1 tablespoon chopped pimiento
4 skinless, boneless chicken breast halves
salt and pepper to taste

(continued)

1 teaspoon fine dried bread crumbs
1 tablespoon paprika

Preheat oven to 350°F.

In a small bowl, combine the cheese, mushrooms, the ¼ cup yogurt, chives, parsley, and pimiento. Stir well. Place 1 chicken breast half, boned side up, between 2 pieces of plastic wrap. Working from the center to the edges, pound lightly with a meat mallet to a ⅛-inch thickness. Remove the plastic wrap. Repeat with the remaining chicken. Sprinkle lightly with salt and pepper. Spread an equal amount of the filling on each chicken breast half. Fold in the sides and roll up. Secure with toothpicks. Arrange the rolls, seam side down, in a baking dish with 2-inch sides. In a small bowl, combine the bread crumbs and paprika. Brush the chicken with the 1 tablespoon yogurt, then sprinkle with the crumb mixture.

Bake until the chicken is tender and the juices run clear when a piece is pierced, 20 to 25 minutes. Serve immediately.

Nutritional Analysis

Calories	176.43 Kcal.	Protein	33.40 gm.
Fat	2.06 gm.	Carbohydrate	4.69 gm.
Sodium	251.19 mg.	Cholesterol	71.00 mg.
Saturated Fat	0.60 gm.		

Nutty Chicken Fingers

Serves: 6

⅓ cup cornflake crumbs
¼ cup finely chopped pecans

1 tablespoon dried parsley flakes
⅛ teaspoon garlic powder
⅛ teaspoon salt
*4 skinless, boneless chicken breast halves, cut
    into strips 3 inches long by 1 inch wide*
2 tablespoons nonfat milk

Preheat oven to 400°F.

In a shallow dish, stir together the cornflake crumbs, pecans, parsley, garlic powder, and salt. Dip the chicken in the milk, then roll in the crumb mixture. Place in a 10-by-15-inch baking dish with 1-inch sides.

Bake until the chicken is tender and the juices run clear when a piece is pierced, 7 to 9 minutes. Serve at once.

Nutritional Analysis

Calories	214.65 Kcal.	Protein	28.81 gm.
Fat	6.05 gm.	Carbohydrate	9.79 gm.
Sodium	270.93 mg.	Cholesterol	68.59 mg.
Saturated Fat	0.74 gm.		

Crab-Stuffed Chicken

Serves: 6

*¼ pound cooked crabmeat, picked over for
    shells and flaked*
¼ cup finely chopped water chestnuts
2 tablespoon fine dried bread crumbs
2 tablespoons low-fat mayonnaise
1 tablespoon minced fresh parsley
¼ teaspoon Dijon mustard
6 skinless, boneless chicken breast halves

2 tablespoons white wine Worcestershire sauce
2 scallions, minced

In a bowl, combine the crabmeat, water chestnuts, bread crumbs, mayonnaise, parsley, and mustard. Stir well. Place 1 piece of chicken, boned side up, between 2 pieces of plastic wrap. Working from the center to the edges, pound lightly with a meat mallet to a 1/8-inch thickness. Remove the plastic wrap. Repeat with the remaining chicken. Spoon an equal amount of the filling onto half of each chicken piece. Fold in the sides and roll up. Secure with toothpicks. Arrange the chicken, seam side down, in a 7-by-12-inch baking dish with 2-inch sides. Brush with some of the Worcestershire sauce.

Bake until the chicken is tender and the juices run clear when a piece is pierced, 20 to 25 minutes. Brush with remaining Worcestershire sauce and sprinkle with the scallions, then serve.

Nutritional Analysis

Calories	201.29 Kcal.	Protein	31.56 gm.
Fat	5.54 gm.	Carbohydrate	4.13 gm.
Sodium	223.59 mg.	Cholesterol	90.05 mg.
Saturated Fat	0.98 gm.		

Chicken-and-Vegetable Casseroles

Serves: 2

1 1/2 cups sliced zucchini
1 small onion, chopped
1 small tomato, cut in thin wedges

2 tablespoons sliced pitted black olives
2 tablespoons minced fresh parsley
1 tablespoon minced fresh basil
1/8 teaspoon garlic powder
2 skinless, boneless chicken breast halves
1 teaspoon butter, cut into bits
1/8 teaspoon salt
1/8 teaspoon pepper

Halve any large zucchini slices. In a bowl, stir together the zucchini, onion, tomato, olives, parsley, basil, and garlic powder. Divide evenly between 2 individual baking dishes or gratin dishes. Top each with a chicken breast half. Dot the tops with the butter. Sprinkle with the salt and pepper. Cover with foil.

Bake until the chicken is tender and the juices run clear when a piece is pierced, about 40 minutes. Serve immediately.

Nutritional Analysis

Calories	205.02 Kcal.	Protein	29.70 gm.
Fat	4.67 gm.	Carbohydrate	11.11 gm.
Sodium	327.11 mg.	Cholesterol	73.62 mg.
Saturated Fat	1.73 gm.		

Ginger and Peach Chicken

Serves: 4

4 skinless, boneless chicken breast halves
1 can (8 ounces) peach slices in light syrup
1 teaspoon cornstarch
1/2 teaspoon peeled and grated fresh ginger
1/4 teaspoon salt

(continued)

¹/₂ cup sliced water chestnuts
2 cups hot cooked white rice
*1 package (6 ounces) frozen snow peas,
    cooked and kept hot*

Spray a large skillet with nonstick cooking spray and heat over medium heat. Add the chicken and cook, turning to brown evenly, until tender and the juices run clear when a piece is pierced, 8 to 10 minutes. Remove from the skillet; keep warm.

Meanwhile, drain the peaches, reserving juice. If necessary, add water to the juice to equal ¹/₂ cup. Stir in the cornstarch, ginger, and salt. Add to the skillet and cook and stir over medium heat until thickened and bubbly, about 10 minutes. Cook and stir for 1 minute longer. Gently stir in the peaches and water chestnuts and heat through.

On a serving platter or 4 individual plates, arrange the rice, snow peas, and chicken. Spoon the sauce over the chicken and serve.

Nutritional Analysis

Calories	301.86 Kcal.	Protein	31.01 gm.
Fat	2.07 gm.	Carbohydrate	37.89 gm.
Sodium	227.29 mg.	Cholesterol	68.44 mg.
Saturated Fat	0.46 gm.		

Chicken Medallions

Serves: 4

1¹/₂ cups sliced mushrooms
2 tablespoons shredded carrot
2 tablespoons sliced scallions
2 tablespoons finely chopped celery

2¹/₂ teaspoons lemon juice
¹/₄ teaspoon dried thyme, crumbled
¹/₈ teaspoon pepper, or more to taste
1 tomato, peeled, seeded, and chopped
4 skinless, boneless chicken breast halves
¹/₈ teaspoon salt
¹/₂ teaspoon chicken bouillon granules
¹/₂ cup water
1 tablespoon cornstarch
¹/₄ cup nonfat milk

In a saucepan, combine the mushrooms, carrot, scallions, celery, and add water to cover. Bring to a boil, cover, and cook until tender, about 5 minutes. Drain and place in a bowl. Stir in 1¹/₂ teaspoons of the lemon juice, half of the thyme, and ¹/₈ teaspoon pepper. Stir in the tomato. Place 1 chicken breast half, boned side up, between 2 sheets of plastic wrap. Working from the center to the edges, pound lightly with a meat mallet to a ¹/₈-inch thickness. Remove the plastic wrap. Repeat with the remaining chicken. Sprinkle the chicken breasts with the salt and a dash of pepper. Spoon an equal amount of the filling onto half of each chicken piece. Fold in the sides and roll up. Secure with toothpicks.

Spray a skillet with nonstick cooking spray and heat over medium heat. Add the chicken and brown, turning occasionally, for 3 to 4 minutes. Add the remaining 1 teaspoon lemon juice and remaining thyme, the bouillon granules, and the water. Cover and simmer over low heat until the chicken is tender and the juices run clear when a piece is pierced, about 15 minutes. Remove the chicken.

In a small bowl, stir together the cornstarch and milk. Add to the skillet and cook and stir over medium heat until thickened and bubbly, about 10 minutes. Cook and stir for 2 minutes longer. Remove from the heat. Remove the toothpicks. Cut the chicken into 1/2-inch-thick slices. Spoon the sauce onto individual plates and arrange the chicken slices on top. Serve immediately.

Nutritional Analysis

Calories	162.75 Kcal.	Protein	28.67 gm.
Fat	1.94 gm.	Carbohydrate	6.26 gm.
Sodium	297.04 mg.	Cholesterol	68.74 mg.
Saturated Fat	0.41 gm.		

Marinated Chicken Kabobs

Serves: 4

> 1 tablespoon lemon juice
> 1 tablespoon water
> 1 tablespoon olive oil
> 1/2 teaspoon dried tarragon, crumbled
> 1/4 teaspoon Tabasco sauce
> 1/8 teaspoon salt
> 1 clove garlic, minced
> 4 skinless, boneless chicken breast halves, cut into 1-inch cubes
> 1 red bell pepper, cut into 1-inch squares
> 2 medium zucchini, cut into 1-inch-thick slices

In a small bowl, combine the lemon juice, water, oil, tarragon, Tabasco sauce, salt, and garlic. Place the chicken in a lock-top plastic bag and set in a deep bowl. Pour the lemon juice

mixture into the bag, secure the top closed, and let the chicken stand for 20 minutes at room temperature, turning the bag frequently.

Preheat broiler.

Drain the chicken, reserving the marinade. Thread the chicken, bell pepper, and zucchini alternately onto 4 10- to 12-inch long skewers. Arrange the skewers on a broiler pan. Slip under the broiler 4 to 5 inches from the heat source. Broil, turning once and brushing occasionally with the reserved marinade, until the chicken is tender and cooked through, about 8 minutes. Serve immediately.

Nutritional Analysis

Calories	179.00 Kcal.	Protein	28.47 gm.
Fat	4.99 gm.	Carbohydrate	4.21 gm.
Sodium	155.74 mg.	Cholesterol	68.44 mg.
Saturated Fat	0.85 gm.		

Lime-Sauced Chicken

Serves: 4

> 4 skinless, boneless chicken breast halves
> 1/2 medium lime
> 3/4 cup apple juice or cider
> 2 teaspoons cornstarch
> 1/2 teaspoon chicken bouillon granules

Spray a large skillet with nonstick cooking spray and heat over medium heat. Add the chicken and cook, turning to brown evenly, until tender and the juices run clear when a piece is pierced, 8 to 10 minutes. Remove from the skillet and keep warm.

(continued)

Safe Barbecuing

Studies conducted in the last few years have caused some people to forego barbecued chicken and other foods because some cooking techniques—including grilling over a charcoal fire or on a gas grill—may cause carcinogens to form on the meat.

To enjoy the taste of barbecued chicken safely, follow these steps:

- **Cook the chicken in a saucepan or skillet first, then transfer to the grill for the last few minutes of cooking.**
- **Wrap the chicken in foil before grilling.**

Meanwhile, using a vegetable peeler, remove strips of zest from the lime half. Cut peel into narrow strips; set aside. Squeeze 1 tablespoon juice from the lime half. Combine the lime juice, apple juice, cornstarch, and bouillon granules in a bowl, stirring well. Add to the skillet and cook and stir over medium heat until thickened and bubbly, about 10 minutes. Cook and stir for 2 minutes longer. To serve, cut each chicken breast half on the diagonal into 1-inch pieces. Spoon some of the sauce over each serving. Garnish with the reserved lime zest. Pass the remaining sauce.

Nutritional Analysis

Calories	160.76 Kcal.	Protein	27.27 gm.
Fat	1.76 gm.	Carbohydrate	7.10 gm.
Sodium	207.72 mg.	Cholesterol	68.44 mg.
Saturated Fat	0.38 gm.		

Chicken Jerusalem

Serves: 6

6 skinless, boneless chicken breast halves
1 teaspoon paprika
1/4 cup butter
2 scallions, chopped
3/4 cup dry white wine
3/4 cup water
1 cup sliced fresh mushrooms
2 cans (14 ounces each) artichoke hearts, drained
1 pound egg noodles, cooked, drained
1/2 teaspoon parsley
2 tablespoons grated Parmesan cheese

Dust the chicken with the paprika. In a skillet, melt the butter over medium heat. Add the chicken and brown on both sides, about 10 minutes. Add the scallions, wine, and water and simmer over medium heat for 45 minutes. Add the mushrooms and artichoke hearts and cook slowly until the chicken is tender and the juices run clear when a piece is pierced, about 15 minutes longer.

Serve over noodles sprinkled with parsley. Sprinkle the Parmesan cheese over the chicken.

Nutritional Analysis

Calories	530.37 Kcal.	Protein	41.02 gm.
Fat	12.88 gm.	Carbohydrate	61.27 gm.
Sodium	462.91 mg.	Cholesterol	162.32 mg.
Saturated Fat	6.13 gm.		

Hunter's Chicken

Serves: 8

1 chicken, about 3 pounds, skinned and cut into 8 pieces
1 tablespoon olive oil
1/2 cup plus 2 tablespoons dry white wine
3 scallions, chopped
1/4 cup chopped onion
2 large cloves garlic, minced
1/2 pound mushrooms, sliced
1 tablespoon dried thyme
1 can (16 ounces) tomatoes, drained and chopped
salt and pepper to taste
1 tablespoon chopped fresh parsley
3/4 pound egg noodles, cooked, drained, and kept hot

Preheat broiler.

Place the chicken pieces in a roasting pan. Slip under the broiler 3 inches from the heat source and broil for 7 minutes. Turn the chicken over and broil for another 5 minutes. Remove from the broiler.

In a skillet, heat the oil and 2 tablespoons of wine over medium heat. Add the scallions, onion, and garlic until soft, about 5 minutes. Add the mushrooms and thyme, cover, and cook for 5 minutes. Stir in the rest of the wine and tomatoes. Add the chicken, cover, and cook over low heat until the chicken is tender, about 25 minutes. Season with salt and pepper and garnish with the parsley. Serve over the noodles.

Nutritional Analysis

Calories	318.75 Kcal.	Protein	24.96 gm.
Fat	8.26 gm.	Carbohydrate	35.68 gm.
Sodium	302.82 mg.	Cholesterol	94.65 mg.
Saturated Fat	1.87 gm.		

Spicy Chicken Enchiladas

Serves: 6

5 skinless, boneless chicken breast halves
1 cup reduced-sodium, fat-free chicken broth
2 tablespoons olive oil
1 onion, chopped
2 cloves garlic, minced
2 tablespoons all-purpose flour
1 can (4 ounces) diced green chile peppers, drained

(continued)

1 can (28 ounces) tomatoes, drained and
   chopped
12 corn tortillas
1 cup shredded Parmesan cheese

Preheat oven to 350°F. Spray a medium baking dish with nonstick cooking spray.

In a saucepan, combine the chicken breasts and broth. Place over low heat and simmer gently until the chicken is tender and the juices run clear when a piece is pierced, about 15 minutes. Remove the chicken, reserving the broth, and chop into bite-sized pieces. Set the broth and chicken aside.

In a skillet, heat the oil over medium heat. Add the onion and sauté until soft, about 5 minutes. Add the garlic and flour and cook, stirring, for 1 minute. Stir in 1/2 cup of the reserved broth and cook, stirring occasionally, until the mixture thickens, about 5 to 8 minutes. Add the chiles and tomatoes and simmer for 10 minutes.

Dip a tortilla in the sauce and set in the prepared baking dish. Place a spoonful each of the cheese, chicken, and sauce across the middle of the tortilla and roll it up folding in the sides as you roll. Place seam side down in the dish. Repeat, using all of the tortillas. Spoon the remaining sauce over enchiladas and top with the remaining cheese. Bake until cheese melts completely, about 15 minutes. Serve hot.

Nutritional Analysis

Calories	381.46 Kcal.	Protein	33.63 gm.
Fat	12.05 gm.	Carbohydrate	35.36 gm.
Sodium	818.32 mg.	Cholesterol	67.56 mg.
Saturated Fat	3.84 gm.		

Szechuan-Style Chicken and Vegetables

Serves: 6

2 tablespoons peanut oil
2 cloves garlic, minced
1 teaspoon red pepper flakes
1 teaspoon peeled and grated fresh ginger
3 skinless, boneless chicken breast halves, cut
   into small chunks
2 teaspoons Chinese black bean sauce
2 tablespoons water
4 cups chopped cauliflower
4 cups broccoli florets
2 carrots, sliced
1 green or red bell pepper, chopped
6 scallions, sliced
2 cups reduced-sodium, fat-free chicken broth
2 tablespoons cornstarch
3 cups hot cooked white rice

In a wok or large, deep skillet, heat 1 tablespoon of the oil over high heat. Add the garlic, red pepper flakes and ginger and stir-fry for 3 minutes. Add the chicken and stir-fry until the meat turns white, about 7 minutes. Soften 1 teaspoon of the bean sauce in 1 tablespoon of

the water, add to the pan, and stir to coat the chicken. Remove from the pan.

Add the remaining 1 tablespoon oil to the pan over high heat. Stir in the cauliflower, broccoli, carrots, bell pepper, and scallions. Soften the remaining 1 teaspoon bean sauce in the remaining 1 tablespoon water, add to the pan, and stir to coat the vegetables. Reduce the heat to medium, cover the pan, and cook for 1 minute. Uncover, raise the heat to high, and stir-fry for 2 minutes. Add 1³/₄ cups of the chicken broth, cover, and bring to a boil.

Meanwhile, in a small bowl, stir the cornstarch into the remaining ¹/₄ cup broth and add to the vegetables. Return the chicken to the pan and cook until the sauce thickens slightly, about 5 minutes. Serve over the rice.

Nutritional Analysis

Calories	289.04 Kcal.	Protein	21.79 gm.
Fat	6.28 gm.	Carbohydrate	37.49 gm.
Sodium	425.94 mg.	Cholesterol	34.22 mg.
Saturated Fat	1.09 gm.		

Jamaican-Style Chicken

Serves: 6

1 onion, quartered
1 jalapeño pepper, seeded
2 cloves garlic, cut up
1 large onion, coarsely chopped
¹/₃ cup orange juice
¹/₄ cup soy sauce
1 tablespoon peanut oil
2 tablespoons red wine vinegar
1 teaspoon dried thyme, crumbled
1 teaspoon ground allspice
¹/₂ teaspoon ground cinnamon
¹/₂ teaspoon curry powder
salt and pepper to taste
2 pounds boneless, skinless chicken parts

In a food processor, process the onion, jalapeño, garlic, and onion until puréed. Add the orange juice, soy sauce, oil, vinegar, thyme, allspice, cinnamon, curry powder, salt, and pepper. Process until smooth. Place the chicken pieces in a shallow dish and pour the puréed ingredients over them. Cover and refrigerate for 2 hours, turning occasionally.

Prepare a fire in a charcoal grill.

Remove the chicken from the marinade. Place on the grill rack over hot coals and grill, turning once, until the chicken is tender and the juices run clear when a piece is pierced, 8 to 10 minutes on each side. (Alternatively, bake in a 325°F oven until it tests done, about 40 minutes.) Serve hot.

Nutritional Analysis

Calories	211.88 Kcal.	Protein	33.18 gm.
Fat	5.85 gm.	Carbohydrate	4.78 gm.
Sodium	474.58 mg.	Cholesterol	105.93 mg.
Saturated Fat	1.38 gm.		

Easy Barbecued Chicken

Serves: 8

½ cup buttermilk
1 tablespoon Dijon mustard
1 tablespoon honey
2 cloves garlic, minced
1 teaspoon dried oregano, crumbled
1 teaspoon dried basil, crumbled
1 teaspoon dried thyme, crumbled
1 teaspoon dried rosemary, crumbled
salt and pepper to taste
3 pounds chicken parts, skinned

In a large bowl, combine the buttermilk, mustard, honey, garlic, oregano, basil, thyme, rosemary, salt, and pepper. Add the chicken, turn to coat, cover, and refrigerate for 3 hours.

Prepare a fire in a charcoal grill.

Remove the chicken from the marinade. Place on the grill rack over hot coals and grill, turning once, until the chicken is tender and the juices run clear when a piece is pierced, 8 to 10 minutes on each side. (Alternatively, bake in a 325°F oven until it tests done, about 40 minutes.) Serve hot.

Nutritional Analysis

Calories	188.54 Kcal.	Protein	24.24 gm.
Fat	6.20 gm.	Carbohydrate	7.22 gm.
Sodium	151.82 mg.	Cholesterol	73.10 mg.
Saturated Fat	1.76 gm.		

Chicken and Dumpling Stew

Serves: 8

4 skinless, boneless chicken breasts, cut into
  chunks
4 russet potatoes, peeled and cut into chunks
2 carrots, cut into chunks
2 onions, cut into chunks
3 celery stalks, minced
2 sweet potatoes, peeled and cubed
4 cups reduced-sodium, fat-free chicken broth
1 teaspoon dried thyme, crumbled
1 teaspoon dried sage, crumbled
salt and pepper to taste
1 cup frozen peas

Dumplings:
1 cup unbleached all-purpose flour
3 tablespoons chopped fresh parsley
1 tablespoon butter
2 teaspoons baking powder
½ teaspoon salt
½ cup low-fat milk

In a large soup pot, combine the chicken, potatoes, carrots, onions, celery, sweet potatoes, broth, thyme, sage, salt, and pepper. Place over high heat, bring to a boil, cover, reduce the heat to low, and cook for 20 minutes.

Meanwhile, make the dumplings: In a food processor, combine the flour, parsley, butter, baking powder, and salt. Process with on-off pulses until mixture has the consistency of coarse crumbs. Add the milk and process for a few

seconds. The dough should be stiff. Add the peas to the soup pot. Then drop the dumpling dough by tablespoonfuls into the soup pot. Cover and cook over low heat until the dumplings are tender and cooked through, about 15 minutes. Ladle into shallow bowls to serve.

Nutritional Analysis

Calories	295.11 Kcal.	Protein	21.12 gm.
Fat	2.92 gm.	Carbohydrate	45.34 gm.
Sodium	661.04 mg.	Cholesterol	38.71 mg.
Saturated Fat	1.24 gm.		

Jambalaya

Serves: 8

> 1 tablespoon butter
> 2 large onions, chopped
> 2 cups minced celery
> 1 green bell pepper, chopped
> 3 ounces sausage, diced
> 1½ pounds skinless, boneless chicken breasts, cut into chunks
> 2 cloves garlic, minced
> 2 bay leaves
> 2 teaspoons dried oregano, crumbled
> 1 teaspoon dried thyme, crumbled
> 1 teaspoon salt
> 1 teaspoon cayenne pepper
> 1 teaspoon black pepper
> 1 can (23 ounces) tomatoes, drained
> 1 can (8 ounces) tomato sauce
> 4 cups reduced-sodium, fat-free chicken broth

(continued)

Where's the Fat?

Even though it's a pain to remove the skin from chicken, and you feel like you're missing out by not eating that crunchy, satisfying skin, consider these figures:

- **A ½-pound chicken breast—one serving—without the skin contains 9 grams of fat.**
- **A ½-pound serving from a whole chicken with the skin removed contains 13 grams of fat.**
- **A ½-pound serving from a whole chicken with the skin left on contains 38 grams of fat.**

2¹/₂ cups long-grain white rice
1 pound medium shrimp, peeled and deveined
1 red bell pepper, chopped
1 onion, minced
¹/₂ cup chopped fresh parsley

In a large soup pot, melt the butter over medium heat. Add the chopped onion and celery and sauté until vegetables begin to soften, about 3 minutes. Add the green bell pepper, sausage, chicken, garlic, bay leaves, oregano, thyme, salt, cayenne pepper, and black pepper. Cook, stirring, for 5 minutes. Add the tomatoes, tomato sauce, broth, and rice. Reduce the heat to low, cover, and cook until rice is tender, 20 to 30 minutes.

Add the shrimp, stir, and cook until the shrimp turn pink, another 5 to 10 minutes. Garnish with the minced onion, red bell pepper, and the parsley before serving.

Nutritional Analysis

Calories	488.26 Kcal.	Protein	38.46 gm.
Fat	8.44 gm.	Carbohydrate	62.56 gm.
Sodium	1118.77 mg.	Cholesterol	130.34 mg.
Saturated Fat	3.00 gm.		

Chicken and Snow Peas with Hoisin Sauce

Serves: 4

²/₃ cup reduced-sodium, fat-free chicken broth
2 tablespoons soy sauce
1 tablespoon sherry
1 teaspoon sugar

2 teaspoons cornstarch
1 teaspoon Asian sesame oil
1 tablespoon peanut oil
3 tablespoons hoisin sauce
2 cloves garlic, minced
2 tablespoons peeled and minced fresh ginger
1 teaspoon red pepper flakes
1 pound skinless, boneless chicken breasts, cut into narrow strips
2 cups snow peas / carrots / onion water chestnuts

In a small bowl, stir together the broth, soy sauce, sherry, sugar, cornstarch, and sesame oil; set aside. In a wok or a large, deep skillet, heat the peanut oil over high heat. Add the hoisin sauce, garlic, ginger, and red pepper flakes. Stir-fry for 1 minute. Add the chicken and stir-fry for 5 minutes. Add the snow peas and stir-fry until the chicken is tender and the snow peas are crisp-tender, about 5 minutes. Stir the soy sauce mixture and add to the pan. Stir-fry over medium heat until the sauce thickens slightly, 1 to 2 minutes. Serve immediately.

Nutritional Analysis

Calories	256.55 Kcal.	Protein	29.36 gm.
Fat	6.13 gm.	Carbohydrate	16.83 gm.
Sodium	922.49 mg.	Cholesterol	65.83 mg.
Saturated Fat	1.13 gm.		

Chicken Simmered in Barbecue Sauce

Serves: 6

- 1 tablespoon olive oil
- 1 onion, chopped
- 1/2 cup ketchup
- 1/2 cup water
- 2 tablespoons red wine vinegar
- 2 tablespoons brown sugar
- 1 tablespoon Worcestershire sauce
- 1 teaspoon chili powder
- 1 chicken, about 2 1/2 pounds, skinned and cut into serving pieces

In a large skillet, heat the oil over medium heat. Add the onion and sauté until translucent, about 5 minutes. Add the ketchup, water, vinegar, brown sugar, Worcestershire sauce, and chili powder. Bring to a boil, reduce the heat to low, and add the chicken. Spoon the sauce over the chicken pieces, cover, and cook for 30 minutes. Uncover, turn the chicken over, and cook until the chicken is tender, about 15 minutes longer. Serve immediately.

Nutritional Analysis

Calories	181.21 Kcal.	Protein	20.21 gm.
Fat	5.21 gm.	Carbohydrate	13.22 gm.
Sodium	341.45 mg.	Cholesterol	63.56 mg.
Saturated Fat	1.02 gm.		

Chicken in Buttermilk

Serves: 6

- 1 tablespoon olive oil
- 1 chicken, about 2 1/2 pounds, skinned and cut into serving pieces
- 6 scallions, minced
- 1 can (35 ounces) tomatoes, drained
- 2 cups low-fat buttermilk
- 1 teaspoon dried dill, crumbled
- 1 teaspoon sugar
- salt and pepper to taste
- Tabasco sauce to taste
- 1 cup plain low-fat yogurt
- 1/4 cup grated Parmesan cheese

In a large skillet, heat the oil over medium heat. Add the chicken and brown on both sides, almost 10 minutes. Add half of the scallions to the skillet and cook the chicken for about 2 minutes longer. Remove from the heat.

In a food processor, combine the tomatoes, buttermilk, dill, sugar, salt, pepper, and Tabasco. Process until smooth. Pour the sauce over the chicken and return the skillet to medium heat. Bring to a boil, cover, reduce the heat to low, and cook until the chicken is tender, about 20 minutes. Add the yogurt and the Parmesan and heat the chicken for 10 minutes longer to blend flavors. Garnish with the remaining chopped scallions.

(continued)

Nutritional Analysis

Calories	1487.74 Kcal.	Protein	165.80 gm.
Fat	47.36 gm.	Carbohydrate	98.58 gm.
Sodium	3284.58 mg.	Cholesterol	440.76 mg.
Saturated Fat	15.62 gm.		

Reducing the Fat Even More

Since chicken is naturally low in fat, and even lower once you remove the skin, it's generally necessary to use a little bit of fat when cooking chicken in a skillet. Choose a nonstick skillet, or use a bit of water or chicken broth in place of the usual oil or butter. Or you might find that you can cut the amount of fat in a traditional recipe by half, without reducing the appeal of the dish. Cooking methods such as broiling, baking, poaching, and microwaving also use little fat in cooking.

Chicken Marsala

Serves: 6

1 tablespoons olive oil
4 cloves garlic, minced
2 onions, sliced
2 tablespoons peeled and minced fresh ginger
1 cinnamon stick
2 bay leaves
2 teaspoons ground cloves
2 teaspoons ground cardamom
2 tablespoons curry powder
salt and pepper to taste
1/4 cup water
1 chicken, about 3 pounds, skinned and cut into 6 pieces
1 tomato, chopped

In a large skillet, heat the oil over medium heat. Add the garlic, onion, ginger, cinnamon, bay leaves, cloves, cardamom, and curry powder. Cook until the onion is translucent, about 5 minutes. Stir in the salt, pepper, and water, then add the chicken pieces. Cook over low heat for 30 minutes until the chicken is tender. During the last 5 minutes of cooking, stir the tomato into the skillet.

200

Nutritional Analysis

Calories	191.09 Kcal.	Protein	24.62 gm.
Fat	6.25 gm.	Carbohydrate	8.99 gm.
Sodium	90.86 mg.	Cholesterol	76.27 mg.
Saturated Fat	1.21 gm.		

Garlicky Grilled Chicken

Serves: 8

10 cloves garlic, chopped
3 tablespoons dried oregano, crumbled
1 large red onion, chopped
1/2 cup olive oil
salt and pepper to taste
1 cup reduced-sodium, fat-free chicken broth
8 skinless, boneless chicken breast halves

In a large shallow dish, combine the garlic, oregano, onion, oil, salt, pepper, and broth. Mix well. Add the chicken, turn to coat well, cover, and marinate in the refrigerator overnight.

Prepare a fire in a charcoal grill. Remove the chicken from the marinade and place on the grill rack. Grill, turning once, until tender and the juices run clear when a piece is pierced, about 10 minutes on each side. Serve hot or at room temperature.

Nutritional Analysis

Calories	166.83 Kcal.	Protein	27.53 gm.
Fat	5.01 gm.	Carbohydrate	1.23 gm.
Sodium	95.19 mg.	Cholesterol	68.44 mg.
Saturated Fat	0.86 gm.		

Chicken Chimichanga

Serves: 5

3 tablespoons olive oil
1 skinless, boneless whole chicken breast, diced
1 red onion, chopped
3 cloves garlic, minced
1 large tomato, chopped
2 tablespoons chopped fresh coriander
1 tablespoon chili powder
2 teaspoons ground cumin
1 jalapeño pepper, seeded and chopped
1 cup shredded low-fat cheddar cheese
1/4 cup low-fat sour cream
salt and pepper to taste
5 flour tortillas, each 12 inches in diameter, heated
1/4 cup tomato salsa

Preheat oven to 350°F.

In a large skillet, heat 2 tablespoons of the oil over medium heat. Add the chicken and sauté for 5 minutes. Add the onion, garlic, tomato, coriander, chili powder, cumin, and jalapeño. Continue to cook over medium heat for 10 more minutes. Remove from the heat.

Stir the cheese, sour cream, salt, and pepper into the chicken mixture. Place a couple spoonfuls of the chicken filling in the middle of each warmed tortilla. Roll up and secure with a tooth-pick. Place on a baking sheet. Repeat with the remaining tortillas and filling. Lightly brush the rolled tortillas with the remaining tablespoon of oil.

(continued)

Bake, uncovered, until crispy brown on the outside, about 10 minutes. Serve with the salsa.

Nutritional Analysis

Calories	468.43 Kcal.	Protein	27.56 gm.
Fat	15.66 gm.	Carbohydrate	55.02 gm.
Sodium	739.89 mg.	Cholesterol	33.77 mg.
Saturated Fat	2.72 gm.		

Mexican Chicken Roll-ups

Serves: 4

> 1 tablespoon olive oil
> 1 green bell pepper, chopped
> 1 red bell pepper, chopped
> 1 onion, chopped
> 2 cloves garlic, minced
> 1 skinless, boneless whole chicken breast, diced
> 4 flour tortillas, 12 inches in diameter, heated
> 4 cups shredded lettuce
> 3 cups chopped tomatoes
> 1/4 cup chopped scallions
> 1/4 cup shredded low-fat cheddar cheese
> 1/4 cup salsa

In a large skillet, heat the oil over high heat. Add the bell peppers, onion, and garlic and sauté until soft, about 7 minutes. Add the chicken, cover, reduce the heat to low, and cook until the chicken is tender, about 8 minutes.

Transfer the chicken mixture to a serving bowl. Set out the warmed tortillas. Place the lettuce, tomato, scallions, cheese, and salsa in separate small bowls. Let diners make their own roll-ups.

Nutritional Analysis

Calories	397.24 Kcal.	Protein	23.98 gm.
Fat	9.82 gm.	Carbohydrate	52.21 gm.
Sodium	630.49 mg.	Cholesterol	34.97 mg.
Saturated Fat	1.51 gm.		

Quick Chicken Parmesan

Serves: 2

> 1 skinless, boneless whole chicken breast, split
> 1/4 cup seasoned dried bread crumbs
> 1 tablespoon olive oil
> 2 slices low-fat mozzarella cheese
> 2 thick tomato slices
> 1/2 teaspoon dried basil, crumbled

Place 1 piece of chicken, boned side up, between 2 pieces of plastic wrap. Working from the center to the edges, pound lightly with a meat mallet to a 1/8-inch thickness. Remove the plastic wrap. Repeat with the other piece of chicken. Place the bread crumbs in a shallow dish. Dip the chicken cutlets into the bread crumbs, coating thoroughly. In a skillet, heat the oil over medium heat. Add the chicken and sauté, turning once, until golden and tender, about 8 minutes.

Reduce the heat to low and place the cheese, tomato, and basil on top of the chicken cutlets. Cover for 1 minute, then serve.

Nutritional Analysis

Calories	288.59 Kcal.	Protein	38.54 gm.
Fat	8.65 gm.	Carbohydrate	12.47 gm.
Sodium	685.66 mg.	Cholesterol	71.43 mg.
Saturated Fat	1.39 gm.		

Chicken with Couscous

Serves: 2

 1 box (8 ounces) instant couscous
 1/2 teaspoon ground cinnamon
 1/2 cup diced cooked chicken breast
 1 can (8 ounces) garbanzo beans, drained
   and rinsed
 1/4 cup raisins
 1/3 cup low-fat plain yogurt

Cook the couscous according to package directions, adding the cinnamon at the start of cooking. Remove from heat and place in a serving bowl. Stir in the chicken, garbanzos, raisins, and yogurt. Serve immediately.

Nutritional Analysis

Calories	641.37 Kcal.	Protein	32.03 gm.
Fat	4.41 gm.	Carbohydrate	116.49 gm.
Sodium	191.28 mg.	Cholesterol	32.36 mg.
Saturated Fat	0.95 gm.		

Broiled Chicken with Yogurt and Spices

Serves: 6

 1 teaspoon ground cumin
 1 teaspoon ground coriander
 1 teaspoon cayenne pepper
 1/4 teaspoon ground allspice
 1 cup plain low-fat yogurt
 1 teaspoon grated lemon zest
 2 tablespoons lemon juice
 3 cloves garlic, chopped
 salt to taste
 6 skinless, boneless chicken breast halves

In a shallow dish, combine the cumin, coriander, cayenne, and allspice. Stir well. Add the yogurt, lemon zest and juice, garlic, and salt. Stir well again. Add the chicken and spoon the sauce over the chicken to coat. Cover and refrigerate overnight.

Preheat a broiler. Remove the chicken from the marinade and drain well. Place the chicken on a broiler pan. Slip under the broiler about 3 inches from the heat source. Broil, turning once, until nicely browned and cooked through, about 5 minutes. Serve immediately.

Nutritional Analysis

Calories	144.71 Kcal.	Protein	28.31 gm.
Fat	1.80 gm.	Carbohydrate	1.94 gm.
Sodium	90.97 mg.	Cholesterol	69.57 mg.
Saturated Fat	0.56 gm.		

Turkey Tetrazzini

Serves: 4

1 tablespoon butter
¹/₂ pound mushrooms, sliced
2 tablespoons all-purpose flour
salt and pepper to taste
2 cups low-fat milk
1 teaspoon Worcestershire sauce
¹/₂ cup shredded low-fat Swiss cheese
1 green bell pepper, sliced
4 scallions, minced
2 cups diced cooked turkey
¹/₂ pound spaghetti, cooked and drained
¹/₃ cup grated Parmesan cheese

Preheat oven to 350°F. Spray a 2-quart baking dish with nonstick cooking spray.

In a skillet, melt the butter over medium heat. Add the mushrooms and sauté, stirring occasionally, until tender, about 5 to 7 minutes. Add the flour, salt, and pepper and stir until well blended. Slowly pour in the milk, stirring constantly. Add the Worcestershire sauce, and simmer, stirring occasionally, until the sauce thickens, about 5 minutes. Add the Swiss cheese, bell pepper, and scallions and mix well. Add the turkey and spaghetti, mixing well. Transfer to the prepared baking dish and sprinkle with the Parmesan cheese.

Bake, uncovered, until flavors have blended, about 20 minutes. Serve immediately.

Nutritional Analysis

Calories	537.07 Kcal.	Protein	40.68 gm.
Fat	15.57 gm.	Carbohydrate	57.06 gm.
Sodium	518.46 mg.	Cholesterol	84.79 mg.
Saturated Fat	7.84 gm.		

Turkey Cutlets, Indian Style

Serves: 6

2 large limes
¹/₃ cup plain low-fat yogurt
1 tablespoon vegetable oil
2 teaspoons minced, peeled ginger
1 teaspoon ground cumin
1 teaspoon ground coriander
1 teaspoon salt
1 garlic clove, crushed
1¹/₂ pounds turkey cutlets
cilantro sprigs for garnish

Prepare a fire in a charcoal grill.

Grate the peel and extract the juice from 1 lime. Place 1 teaspoon of grated peel and 1 tablespoon juice in large bowl. Cut the other lime into wedges and set aside. Add yogurt, vegetable oil, ginger, cumin, coriander, salt, and garlic to the lime peel and juice and mix until blended.

Just before grilling, add turkey cutlets to bowl with yogurt mixture, stirring to coat cutlets. Do not let cutlets marinate in yogurt mixture, as their texture will become mealy.

Place turkey cutlets on grill over medium-hot coals. Cook cutlets 5 to 7 minutes until they just lose their pink color throughout. Serve with lime wedges. Garnish with cilantro sprigs

Nutritional Analysis

Calories	160.77 Kcal.	Protein	28.75 gm.
Fat	3.28 gm.	Carbohydrate	2.74 gm.
Sodium	453.78 mg.	Cholesterol	71.11 mg.
Saturated Fat	0.63 gm.		

Turkey Shish Kabob

Serves: 6

1¼ pounds turkey breast tenderloins
⅓ cup bottled chili sauce
2 tablespoons lemon juice
1 tablespoon sugar
8 mushrooms
8 cherry tomatoes
1 medium zucchini, cut into ½-inch-thick slices
½ green bell pepper, cut into ½-inch squares
2 onions, quartered
2 tablespoons olive oil

Cut the turkey tenderloins into 1½-inch cubes and place in a bowl. In a small bowl, stir together the chili sauce, lemon juice, and sugar. Pour over the turkey cubes. Toss to coat. Cover and refrigerate for at least 4 hours or as long as overnight, stirring occasionally.

(continued)

Turkey Year-Round

Turkey isn't just for Thanksgiving anymore. Its popularity has risen dramatically, and now it is a common sight on dinner tables, tucked into sandwiches, or tossed in stir-fries. Benjamin Franklin's observations of the bird merit mentioning here: "I wish the bald eagle had not been chosen as the representative of our country. The turkey is a much more respectable character and a true original native of America."

Show your patriotism: Eat more turkey.

Prepare a fire in a charcoal grill. Remove the turkey from the marinade. Thread the turkey onto skewers alternately with the mushrooms, cherry tomatoes, zucchini, bell pepper, and onions. Brush lightly with the oil and place on the grill rack about 6 inches above medium-hot coals. Grill, turning as needed, and basting occasionally with the marinade, until the turkey is cooked through and the vegetables are tender, about 10 minutes. (Alternatively, cook in a preheated broiler about 6 inches from the heat source for the same amount of time.) Serve hot.

Nutritional Analysis

Calories	206.49 Kcal.	Protein	25.30 gm.
Fat	5.45 gm.	Carbohydrate	14.18 gm.
Sodium	253.24 mg.	Cholesterol	58.64 mg.
Saturated Fat	0.81 gm.		

Pistachio-Turkey Taco Salad

Serves: 6

1 head iceberg lettuce
8 prepared taco shells
1 pound cooked turkey breast meat, shredded
1 pound tomatoes, chopped
1 large green bell pepper, chopped
1/4 cup low-fat sour cream
1/4 cup pistachios, chopped
1 cup bottled salsa, mild or hot
1 teaspoon grated lime zest
2 tablespoons lime juice

Shred the lettuce and divide among 4 plates. Stand 2 taco shells upright in the center of each bed of lettuce. Fill the shells with the turkey, tomatoes, and bell pepper, dividing evenly. Top with the sour cream and pistachios, again dividing evenly.

In a bowl, stir together the salsa, lime zest, and lime juice. Spoon over the tacos and serve.

Nutritional Analysis

Calories	271.52 Kcal.	Protein	27.01 gm.
Fat	8.79 gm.	Carbohydrate	21.44 gm.
Sodium	550.27 mg.	Cholesterol	66.13 mg.
Saturated Fat	1.72 gm.		

THE EVERYTHING
LOW-FAT HIGH-FLAVOR COOKBOOK

Vegetarian Dishes

CHAPTER ELEVEN

Amount Per Chapter
28 Recipes

	% Daily Value
Easy to Prepare	**100%**
Low Fat / High Flavor	**100%**
Simple to Understand	**100%**

DELICIOUS, EASY, LOW-FAT RECIPES

E ven if you grew up eating hamburgers at least once a day, there are times when all you crave is a lunch or dinner rich in carbohydrates—rice or pasta—and vegetables, with no meat in sight.

The following recipes have many influences—Chinese, Indian, Jewish—and all of them deliver a hearty, satisfying meal. Some families have adopted the practice of eating a vegetarian dinner on the same night every week, focusing on a different culture each time. Everyone takes a turn researching a cuisine and preparing a dish. This is a great way to introduce your family to a variety of cultures and at the same time provide them with low-fat meals.

Italian Vegetable Bake

Serves: 8

*1 can (28 ounces) tomatoes, coarsely chopped,
    juices reserved*
1 onion, sliced
1/2 pound green beans, sliced
1/2 pound okra, cut into 1/2-inch lengths
3/4 cup finely chopped green bell peppers
2 tablespoons lemon juice
1 tablespoon chopped fresh basil
1 1/2 teaspoons fresh oregano leaves, chopped
3 medium zucchini, cut into 1-inch cubes
1 eggplant, peeled and cut into 1-inch chunks
2 tablespoons grated Parmesan cheese

Preheat oven to 325°F.

In a baking dish, combine the tomatoes and their liquid, onion, green beans, okra, bell peppers, lemon juice, basil, and oregano. Cover with foil or a lid.

Bake for 15 minutes. Mix in the zucchini and eggplant, cover, and continue to bake, stirring occasionally, until the vegetables are tender, about 1 hour. Sprinkle the top with Parmesan cheese just before serving.

Nutritional Analysis

Calories	82.48 Kcal.	Protein	4.27 gm.
Fat	0.84 gm.	Carbohydrate	17.05 gm.
Sodium	195.07 mg.	Cholesterol	0.98 mg.
Saturated Fat	0.28 gm.		

Wintertime Chili
Serves: 6

*1 green bell pepper, cut into 1-inch pieces,
    seeds reserved*
*1 red bell pepper, cut into 1-inch pieces, seed
    reserved*
1 cup very coarsely chopped onion
3 cloves garlic, minced

208

1 teaspoon ground cumin
1½ to 3 tablespoons chili powder, to taste
¼ teaspoon finely chopped habañero pepper
(very hot) or jalapeño pepper (medium-hot)
or 2 tablespoons dried chopped ancho
pepper (mild)
½ teaspoon cocoa powder
½ teaspoon brown sugar
1 can (8 ounces) tomato sauce
1 to 2 cans (16 ounces each) dark kidney
beans, drained
1½ cups water or tomato juice
salt and pepper to taste

In a large nonstick saucepan, combine all the ingredients, including the bell pepper seeds. Bring to a boil, cover, reduce the heat to low, and simmer, stirring to loosen the bottom occasionally, until heated through, 35 to 50 minutes. Adjust the seasoning and serve piping hot.

Nutritional Analysis

Calories	122.28 Kcal.	Protein	7.35 gm.
Fat	1.33 gm.	Carbohydrate	21.94 gm.
Sodium	400.28 mg.	Cholesterol	0.00 mg.
Saturated Fat	0.05 gm.		

Welsh Rarebit with Vegetables
Serves: 2

¼ cup finely chopped cabbage
¼ cup finely chopped carrot
2 tablespoons finely chopped green bell pepper
2 tablespoons finely chopped celery

2 tablespoons finely chopped onion
2 tablespoons finely chopped radishes
2 slices whole-wheat bread, toasted
½ cup shredded low-fat cheddar cheese
dash of red pepper flakes
2 tablespoons water
¼ cup alfalfa sprouts

Preheat broiler.

In a bowl, combine the cabbage, carrot, bell pepper, celery, onion, and radishes. Top each slice of toast with an equal amount of the vegetable mixture. Place the slices on a baking sheet. In a small saucepan, combine the cheese, red pepper flakes, and water. Place over low heat and stir until the cheese melts. Spoon over the sandwiches, dividing evenly. Slip the baking sheet under the broiler about 4 inches from the heat source and broil until the cheese is bubbly, about 5 minutes. Transfer to serving plates. Top with the sprouts.

Nutritional Analysis

Calories	132.01 Kcal.	Protein	13.39 gm.
Fat	1.30 gm.	Carbohydrate	18.86 gm.
Sodium	374.76 mg.	Cholesterol	3.00 mg.
Saturated Fat	0.26 gm.		

Stuffed Zucchini
Serves: 4

2 medium zucchini
1 cup frozen corn kernels
½ cup low-fat small-curd cottage cheese
⅛ teaspoon salt

(continued)

¹⁄₈ teaspoon pepper
2 tablespoons chopped scallions
¹⁄₄ cup grated Parmesan cheese

Preheat oven to 400°F. Spray an 8-inch square baking dish with nonstick cooking spray. Cut each zucchini in half lengthwise. Using a teaspoon, scoop out the seeds from each half.

In a bowl, mix together the corn, cottage cheese, salt, pepper, and scallions. Spoon the mixture into the squash halves, mounding it slightly. Top with the Parmesan cheese. Place the squash in the prepared baking dish.

Bake, uncovered, until the squash is tender and the cheese topping has melted, about 15 minutes. Serve immediately.

Nutritional Analysis

Calories	100.77 Kcal.	Protein	7.84 gm.
Fat	3.15 gm.	Carbohydrate	12.18 gm.
Sodium	295.11 mg.	Cholesterol	7.67 mg.
Saturated Fat	1.78 gm.		

Pizza Crust

Yield: Two 9-inch crusts

1 teaspoon active dry yeast
¹⁄₂ cup plus 1 tablespoon lukewarm water (105 to 110°F)
1¹⁄₂ cups bread flour or all-purpose flour
2 teaspoons sugar
1 teaspoon salt
1 tablespoon extra-virgin olive oil
1 teaspoon olive oil for coating

In a small bowl, sprinkle the yeast over the lukewarm water and set aside until bubbles appear on the surface, 5 to 10 minutes. Place the flour, sugar, and salt in a large bowl. Make a well in the center and pour the yeast mixture and extra-virgin olive oil into it. Using a wooden spoon, gradually combine the wet and dry ingredients. When a dough has formed, lightly oil your hands and knead the dough for 5 minutes. It should be slightly tacky. Lightly oil the dough ball.

Rub the surface of a 1-quart bowl with the oil and place the dough ball in it. Cover the bowl with plastic wrap, sealing it airtight. Set aside at room temperature to rise until doubled in size, 1¹⁄₂ to 2 hours.

To obtain a wonderfully chewy, flavorful dough, punch it down, reform a nice round ball, and return it to the same bowl. Cover again airtight with plastic wrap, and place in the refrigerator overnight.

About 2 hours before you are ready to assemble the pizza, remove the dough from the refrigerator and, using a sharp knife, divide it into 2 equal portions. Roll each portion into a round, smooth ball; seal any holes by pinching them closed. Place the dough balls in a glass dish, spaced far enough apart to allow room for rising, and let rise at room temperature until doubled in size, about 2 hours. The balls should be smooth and puffy.

Place a pizza stone in an oven and preheat to 500°F.

To stretch the dough to shape the pizza, sprinkle flour on a work surface. Using a spatula,

carefully transfer 1 dough ball to the surface. Be very careful to preserve its round shape. Flour the dough liberally. Using your hand or a rolling pin, press down the dough to form a flat round about 1/2 inch thick. Pinch the dough between your fingers around edge, forming a 1/4-inch high rim. Continue this outward stretching until you have formed a dough round 9 inches in diameter.

Top the pizza rounds as directed in individual recipes, then bake until cheese is bubbly, 8 to 10 minutes.

Nutritional Analysis

Calories	473.00 Kcal.	Protein	13.07 gm.
Fat	11.04 gm.	Carbohydrate	79.47 gm.
Sodium	1168.19 mg.	Cholesterol	0.00 mg.
Saturated Fat	1.55 gm.		

California French Bread Pizza

Serves: 8

> 1 loaf sourdough French bread, 1 1/2 pounds
> 1 onion, thinly sliced into rings
> 1 green bell pepper, thinly sliced into rings
> 1 cup sliced mushrooms
> 1 clove garlic, minced
> 1 1/2 cups tomato sauce
> 1/2 cup shredded low-fat mozzarella cheese
> 2 tablespoons grated sharp romano cheese
> salt and pepper to taste
> dried oregano and basil, crumbled, to taste
> red pepper flakes to taste

Preheat oven to 425°F. Spray a baking sheet with nonstick cooking spray.

Cut bread loaf in half lengthwise. Pull out doughy center from each half, leaving only the crust. Layer the onion, bell pepper, and mushrooms inside the hollowed-out loaf halves. Sprinkle with the garlic and spoon on tomato sauce. Sprinkle with the mozzarella and romano cheeses and seasonings. Place both bread halves on the prepared baking sheet.

Bake, uncovered, until cheese is slightly browned and bubbly, about 20 minutes. To serve, slice each half into 4 pieces.

Nutritional Analysis

Calories	159.22 Kcal.	Protein	7.50 gm.
Fat	1.86 gm.	Carbohydrate	28.58 gm.
Sodium	604.48 mg.	Cholesterol	2.05 mg.
Saturated Fat	0.48 gm.		

Rosie's Pizza Dough

Yield: 8 individual pizza crusts

> 3/4 cup lukewarm water
> 1 teaspoon honey
> 1 tablespoon active dry yeast
> 1 1/2 cups semolina flour
> 1/2 teaspoon salt
> 1 teaspoon olive oil
> 1/2 cup cornmeal

In a medium bowl, combine the water and honey. Sprinkle the yeast on top and set aside

(continued)

until bubbles form on the surface, about 5 to 10 minutes.

In a food processor, combine the flour and salt. Turn the machine on and slowly add the yeast mixture through the feed tube. Process for about 1 minute, or until the dough forms a ball, drizzling a little additional water into the feed tube if necessary. Continue to process for another 2 minutes.

Rub the surface of a large bowl with the olive oil. Transfer the dough ball to the bowl and turn to coat the surface with oil. Cover the bowl with a towel and let stand in a warm place until the dough doubles in size, about 1 hour.

Preheat oven to 400°F.

Dust a work surface with the cornmeal. Place the dough on the work surface and roll out 1/4-inch thick. Using a sharp knife and a saucer as a template, cut out eight 5 1/2-inch rounds.

Spray a baking sheet 3 times with nonstick cooking spray. Transfer the pizza rounds to the prepared sheet. Bake until golden, 3 to 5 minutes. Remove from the oven and top as desired.

Nutritional Analysis

Calories	159.01 Kcal.	Protein	5.27 gm.
Fat	1.45 gm.	Carbohydrate	30.79 gm.
Sodium	146.13 mg.	Cholesterol	0.00 mg.
Saturated Fat	0.12 gm.		

Rosie's Pizza Sauce

Yield: 1 1/2 cup sauce

1 tablespoon tomato paste
1 cup tomato purée
1/4 teaspoon red pepper flakes
2 teaspoons dried oregano, crumbled
2 teaspoons dried basil, crumbled
2 teaspoons dried thyme, crumbled

In a small saucepan, combine all the ingredients and cook over low heat until the sauce thickens, about 15 minutes.

Nutritional Analysis

Calories	24.17 Kcal.	Protein	0.97 gm.
Fat	0.19 gm.	Carbohydrate	5.72 gm.
Sodium	188.37 mg.	Cholesterol	0.00 mg.
Saturated Fat	0.02 gm.		

California Vegetable Pizza Topping

Yield: One 12-inch pizza (serves: 8)

1 recipe Rosie's Pizza Dough
1/2 cup Rosie's Pizza Sauce
1/2 cup lightly steamed tiny broccoli florets
1/2 cup chopped artichoke hearts
1/4 cup sliced black olives
1 tomato, sliced
6 green bell pepper rings

Prepare the dough as directed.

Preheat oven to 500°F. Oil a 12-inch pizza pan.

Place the dough on a lightly floured work surface and press to flatten. Lightly roll out the dough into a 12-inch round, transfer to the prepared pizza pan, and pinch the edge to form a rim.

Spread the sauce on the dough to within 1 inch of the rim. Arrange all the vegetables in layers on the sauce, ending with the tomatoes and peppers.

Bake until the crust is brown and crisp, about 15 minutes. Remove from the oven and let cool for 5 minutes, then cut into wedges to serve.

Nutritional Analysis

Calories	1511.69 Kcal.	Protein	51.33 gm.
Fat	23.69 gm.	Carbohydrate	275.53 gm.
Sodium	2057.89 mg.	Cholesterol	0.00 mg.
Saturated Fat	2.21 gm.		

Top-Hat Pizza

Yield: One 12-inch pizza (serves: 8)

1 recipe Rosie's Pizza Dough
2 cups shredded low-fat mozzarella cheese
¼ cup julienned red bell peppers
¼ cup julienned green bell peppers
1 can (4 ounces) diced mild green chile
*   peppers, drained*

(continued)

Olives

Olives are a great way to add a bit of texture and saltiness to a dish. But be careful, they are also high in fat and sodium. As a rule of thumb, black olives contain less fat and sodium than green olives. To cut down further on the fat content, select olives that have been packed in brine, not oil, and be sure to rinse them thoroughly before cooking with them.

2 tablespoons pitted black olives, sliced
2 scallions, sliced
2 avocados
1 tablespoon lemon juice
1 teaspoon garlic salt
1/2 teaspoon seasoned salt
5 drops of Tabasco sauce
1/4 cup finely crushed tortilla chips
12 plum tomatoes, sliced

Prepare the dough as directed.

Preheat oven to 400°F. Oil a 12-inch pizza pan.

Place the dough on a lightly floured work surface and press to flatten. Lightly roll out the dough into a 12-inch round and transfer to the prepared pan. Sprinkle with the mozzarella cheese, red and green bell peppers, chiles, olives, and scallions.

Bake until cheese is melted, 10 to 12 minutes.

Meanwhile, pit and peel the avocados. Cut up, place in a bowl, and mash with a fork. Add the lemon juice, garlic salt, seasoned salt, Tabasco sauce, and crushed chips. Mix well to form a guacamole.

Remove the pizza from the oven. Arrange the tomato slices on top. Place a generous mound of the guacamole in the center of each tomato slice. Serve at once. Pass the remaining guacamole at the table.

Nutritional Analysis

Calories	315.06 Kcal.	Protein	16.18 gm.
Fat	10.25 gm.	Carbohydrate	41.73 gm.
Sodium	745.92 mg.	Cholesterol	3.00 mg.
Saturated Fat	1.52 gm.		

Sweet Potato Tart

Serves: 12

Crust:
1/2 cup graham cracker crumbs
1 teaspoon ground cinnamon
1 egg white

Filling:
4 medium sweet potatoes, baked until tender
    and peeled
6 egg whites
1/4 teaspoon ground nutmeg
1/4 teaspoon ground cloves
1/4 teaspoon ground allspice
1/4 teaspoon ground ginger
2 teaspoons pure vanilla extract
5 tablespoons pure maple syrup
1 tablespoons honey
6 ounces light cream cheese
1/4 cup orange juice

Preheat oven to 350°F.

Spray a 12-inch tart pan 3 times with nonstick cooking spray. To make the crust, combine the cracker crumbs, cinnamon, and egg white in a food processor. Pulse 5 times. Transfer the

mixture to the prepared tart pan and pat to cover the bottom evenly.

To make the filling, put the baked sweet potatoes in a large bowl and mash with a fork. Add the egg whites, nutmeg, cloves, allspice, and ginger. Whisk to blend. Add all the remaining filling ingredients and continue to whisk until smooth. Pour the filing into the crust.

Bake until the center of the tart is firm and not sticky to the touch, 30 to 45 minutes. Transfer to a rack and let cool for 30 minutes, then refrigerate for 1 hour before serving.

Nutritional Analysis

Calories	146.79 Kcal.	Protein	4.71 gm.
Fat	3.48 gm.	Carbohydrate	23.24 gm.
Sodium	127.83 mg.	Cholesterol	10.00 mg.
Saturated Fat	2.01 gm.		

Caribbean Rice and Beans

Serves: 6

1 tablespoon olive oil
2 teaspoons minced garlic
1 cup coarsely chopped onions
1 hot red chile pepper, seeded and chopped, or 1 generous pinch of red pepper flakes
1 cup diced red bell pepper
1 cup coarsely chopped plum tomatoes
2 to 2¼ cups boiling water
1½ cups long-grain brown rice
½ cup unsweetened grated dried coconut
½ teaspoon dried thyme or oregano, crumbled
1 teaspoon salt, or to taste
1 cup cooked pigeon or black-eyed peas
¼ cup finely minced fresh coriander
2 very ripe plantains, peeled, cut on the diagonal into thin slices

Heat the oil in a pressure cooker over medium-high heat. Add the garlic, onions, and chile pepper or pepper flakes, and cook, stirring frequently, for 1 minute. Add the bell pepper, tomatoes, boiling water (add the larger amount if you have a jiggle-top cooker), rice, coconut, oregano or thyme, and salt.

Secure the lid in place. If using a jiggle-top cooker, set on a flame tamer and bring to high pressure over high heat. Adjust the heat to maintain high pressure and cook for 25 minutes. Allow the pressure to reduce naturally, which will take 10 minutes. (If after 10 minutes the pressure is not released, use the quick-release method.)

Remove the lid, tilting away from you to allow excess pressure to escape. Add the cooked peas and coriander. Stir well to distribute all the ingredients. Serve topped with the plantains.

Nutritional Analysis

Calories	358.95 Kcal.	Protein	7.62 gm.
Fat	7.53 gm.	Carbohydrate	68.42 gm.
Sodium	402.10 mg.	Cholesterol	0.00 mg.
Saturated Fat	3.64 gm.		

Legumes

Legumes—dried beans, peas, and lentils—were largely regarded as peasant food for many years in this country. Now, they have caught on in many circles as an efficient and delicious way to add fiber and nutrients to a low-fat diet. Legumes are high in protein, as well as being rich in iron and calcium.

My favorite quick meal is to cook some spaghetti and top it with some spaghetti sauce, garbanzo beans, scallions, and Parmesan cheese. Even my cats like legumes—garbanzo beans in particular.

St. Tropez Vegetables

Serves: 6

2 pounds summer squash, cut into 1/4-inch-thick slices
2 pounds tomatoes, cut into wedges
1 onion, very thinly sliced
2 teaspoons dried basil
1/4 teaspoon pepper
4 teaspoons minced garlic
3 tablespoons pistachio nuts, chopped

Preheat oven to 400°F.

Cut six 15-inch squares of parchment paper or foil. Place on a work surface. Divide the squash, tomatoes, and onion evenly among the squares, stacking the ingredients. Sprinkle with the basil, pepper, and garlic. Bring together the opposite sides of the square and fold down tightly. Next, fold the ends under to seal in any juices. Place in a shallow baking pan. Bake until the vegetables are tender, about 40 minutes. To test for doneness, open 1 packet and check for firmness and temperature. (Be careful of steam.) Sprinkle the vegetables with the pistachios just before serving.

Nutritional Analysis

Calories	100.67 Kcal.	Protein	4.41 gm.
Fat	2.79 gm.	Carbohydrate	18.11 gm.
Sodium	18.30 mg.	Cholesterol	0.00 mg.
Saturated Fat	0.37 gm.		

Summer Vegetable Paella

Serves: 6

1 teaspoon olive oil
3 cups broccoli florets
2 zucchini, sliced on the diagonal
1 tomato, diced
2 nectarines, pitted and sliced

In a large nonstick skillet, heat the oil over high heat. Add the broccoli and zucchini and cook, stirring often, for 5 minutes. Add the tomato and nectarines, cover, lower heat to medium, and cook until the vegetables are crisp-tender, 2 to 3 minutes longer.

Nutritional Analysis

Calories	61.04 Kcal.	Protein	3.43 gm.
Fat	1.43 gm.	Carbohydrate	11.19 gm.
Sodium	31.18 mg.	Cholesterol	0.00 mg.
Saturated Fat	0.16 gm.		

Vegetable Egg Scramble

Serves: 6

1 teaspoon olive oil
3 scallions, minced
2 cloves garlic, minced
1/2 pound mushrooms, sliced
1 green bell pepper, chopped
1 can (8 ounces) corn kernels, drained
2 whole eggs
6 egg whites
salt and pepper to taste

In a large skillet, heat the oil over medium heat. Add the scallions, garlic, mushrooms, bell pepper, and corn and sauté, stirring occasionally, until vegetables are tender, about 5 minutes.

Meanwhile, beat the whole eggs and egg whites in a medium bowl. Add the eggs to the vegetables, season with salt and pepper, and scramble until thoroughly cooked. Serve at once.

Nutritional Analysis

Calories	85.66 Kcal.	Protein	7.34 gm.
Fat	2.85 gm.	Carbohydrate	8.73 gm.
Sodium	133.89 mg.	Cholesterol	70.83 mg.
Saturated Fat	0.66 gm.		

Vegetable Casserole with Mozzarella

Serves: 6

2 cups sliced carrots
1 onion, sliced
1 package (10 ounces) chopped frozen spinach
1 1/2 cups water
1 tablespoon butter
3 tablespoons all-purpose flour
1 1/2 cups nonfat milk
1 cup shredded low-fat mozzarella cheese
1/4 teaspoon salt
pepper to taste

Place carrots, onion, and spinach on a rack in a pressure cooker. Add 1/2 cup of the water. Secure the lid in place. Place over high heat and

(continued)

as soon as the pressure regulator begins to rock, reduce the pressure with the quick-release method.

In a small saucepan, melt the butter over low heat. Add the flour and cook, stirring, until well blended, 1 to 2 minutes. Gradually add the milk, stirring constantly. Continue to cook, stirring, until the sauce thickens, about 4 minutes. Remove from the heat and stir in the cheese, salt, and pepper. Stir until the cheese is melted.

Place half of the spinach in a 6-cup metal bowl that will fit loosely in the pressure cooker. Top with half of the carrots and onions. Cover with half of the cheese sauce. Repeat the layers, ending with the sauce. Cover the bowl tightly with foil. Pour the remaining 1 cup water into the cooker, place the cooking rack in place, and place the bowl on the rack. Secure the lid in place. Bring to high pressure over high heat. Adjust the heat to maintain high pressure and cook for 7 minutes. Allow the pressure to reduce naturally, which takes 10 minutes.

Remove the lid, tilting it away from you to allow excess steam to escape. Serve directly from the bowl.

Nutritional Analysis

Calories	121.68 Kcal.	Protein	10.67 gm.
Fat	2.31 gm.	Carbohydrate	15.73 gm.
Sodium	339.15 mg.	Cholesterol	8.39 mg.
Saturated Fat	1.29 gm.		

Vegetable Tamale Pie

Serves: 8

Vegetable Filling:
1 can (14 ounces) pinto beans, drained
1 white onion, chopped
1/2 green bell pepper, diced
2 jalapeño peppers, seeded and chopped
2 cups drained, chopped, canned tomatoes
1/2 red bell pepper, diced
1 1/2 cups shredded low-fat sharp cheddar cheese
8 pitted black olives, sliced
3/4 teaspoon minced garlic
3/4 teaspoon ground cumin
3/4 teaspoon chili powder

Tamale Topping:
1/2 cup plus 1 tablespoon all-purpose flour
1 cup yellow cornmeal
1 1/2 teaspoons baking powder
1/2 teaspoon baking soda
1/8 teaspoon salt
1/2 cup plain low-fat yogurt
1 egg, at room temperature
2 teaspoons butter, melted and cooled
1 tablespoon snipped fresh chives (optional)

Preheat oven to 375°F.
Spray an 8-inch square baking pan with nonstick cooking spray. Combine all of the filling ingredients in the prepared pan. Toss until well mixed; set aside.

To make the topping, in a medium bowl, combine the flour, cornmeal, baking powder, baking soda, and salt; stir until evenly mixed. In a small bowl, beat together the yogurt, egg, and butter. Add to the flour mixture and stir just until the dry ingredients are moistened. Spoon the mixture evenly on top of the vegetable filling. If desired, sprinkle evenly with the chives.

Bake until the filling is hot and bubbly, the topping is lightly browned, and a toothpick inserted into the center of the topping comes clean, 35 to 40 minutes. Let stand for 5 minutes before cutting into slices.

Nutritional Analysis

Calories	214.69 Kcal.	Protein	14.31 gm.
Fat	3.11 gm.	Carbohydrate	33.28 gm.
Sodium	608.45 mg.	Cholesterol	32.25 mg.
Saturated Fat	1.05 gm.		

Stuffed Onions

Serves: 6

6 large onions
2 stalks celery
1 sprig fresh rosemary
5 sprigs fresh parsley
1 sprig fresh thyme
2 garlic cloves
2 tablespoons vegetable oil
2 1/4 cups long-grain rice
2 ounces pine nuts

1 tablespoon olive oil
2 tablespoons balsamic vinegar
Salt and pepper to taste

Peel the onions. Slice off both ends of the onions, so they are able to stand upright. Place the onions in a saucepan with enough water to cover them. Bring to a boil, then reduce the heat, cover, and let simmer for 10–15 minutes depending on the size and type of onion, until they are tender.

Using a slotted spoon, gently remove the onions and drain.

When cool, gently push out the cores of the onions with your fingers, leaving the onion shell intact. Reserve the shells and cores.

To prepare the filling, trim and finely chop the celery, onion cores and herbs. Peel and chop the garlic. Heat the vegetable oil in a saucepan. Add the chopped onion, celery, garlic, and herbs. Cook until the vegetables are soft but not brown. Stir frequently. Add the rice and fry it with the vegetables for 3 to 4 minutes. Pour in 4 1/2 cups boiling water, cover, and simmer for 15 to 20 minutes, until the rice is soft and the water has been absorbed. Add the pine nuts and salt and pepper to taste.

To prepare the vinaigrette, combine the olive oil and balsamic vinegar with some salt and pepper in a bowl. Beat with a whisk.

Preheat the oven to 325°F. Pour the vinaigrette into the baking dish. Using a teaspoon, stuff the onions with the rice filling. Arrange the onions

(continued)

upright in the baking dish and cover with aluminum foil. Place in the oven and bake for 30 minutes.

Nutritional Analysis

Calories	453.10 Kcal.	Protein	10.00 gm.
Fat	12.40 gm.	Carbohydrate	77.48 gm.
Sodium	23.04 mg.	Cholesterol	0.00 mg.
Saturated Fat	1.78 gm.		

Stuffed Tomatoes

Serves: 2

2 large tomatoes
2 tablespoons chopped fresh parsley
2 tablespoons chopped onion
2 cloves garlic, minced
1/4 teaspoon dried thyme, crumbled
1 tablespoon dried basil
1/4 cup seasoned dried bread crumbs
salt and pepper to taste
1 teaspoon olive oil

Preheat oven to 350°F. Slice the top off each tomato, reserving the "lids." Scoop out the pulp and reserve in a bowl. To the tomato pulp, add the parsley, onion, garlic, thyme, and basil and blend. Add the bread crumbs, salt, pepper, and oil and mix well. Fill the tomato shells with this mixture. Replace the lids.

Bake until mixture is heated through. Serve immediately.

Nutritional Analysis

Calories	138.21 Kcal.	Protein	4.76 gm.
Fat	3.50 gm.	Carbohydrate	24.66 gm.
Sodium	421.03 mg.	Cholesterol	0.00 mg.
Saturated Fat	0.51 gm.		

Dal

Serves: 4

1 cup dried lentils
2 cups water
1 teaspoon salt
1/2 teaspoon ground turmeric
1/4 teaspoon cayenne pepper
2 tablespoons Asian sesame oil
1 medium onion, thinly sliced
1 teaspoon ground cumin
1 teaspoon ground coriander

In a saucepan, combine the lentils, water, salt, turmeric, and cayenne pepper. Bring to a boil. Meanwhile, in a large saucepan, heat the sesame oil over medium heat. Add the onion and sauté until soft, about 5 minutes. Add the cumin and coriander, and cook for 5 minutes longer. Add the onion mixture to the lentils, cover, and cook over medium heat until the lentils are tender, about 30 minutes.

Nutritional Analysis

Calories	242.04 Kcal.	Protein	14.07 gm.
Fat	7.47 gm.	Carbohydrate	31.56 gm.
Sodium	589.74 mg.	Cholesterol	0.00 mg.
Saturated Fat	1.03 gm.		

Potato Pancakes

Serves: 8

2 pounds potatoes, peeled and coarsely grated

1 large onion, coarsely grated

1 egg white

1 whole egg

1/4 cup 1% milk

1 carrot, grated

1/4 cup matzoh meal or 1/2 cup unbleached all-
*   purpose flour*

1 teaspoon salt

pepper to taste

1 to 2 tablespoons vegetable oil

Put the potatoes and onion in a colander and press against the vegetables to extract the extra water. Let the mixture stand for a few minutes, then press them again. Transfer to a bowl. In a small bowl, beat together the egg white and whole egg until blended. Add to the potato mixture along with the milk, carrot, matzo meal or flour, salt, and pepper. Stir to combine thoroughly.

In a large skillet, heat 1 to 2 tablespoons of the oil—just enough to cover the bottom of the pan—over medium heat. Measure out 1/4 cup batter for each pancake, and add to the skillet.

(continued)

Perfect Potato Pancakes

Since potato pancakes are traditionally fried in oil, they can be very greasy if not cooked properly. First, start out by using just a thin layer of oil, only enough to coat the pan with a film. Next, make sure that the oil is hot before you spoon the batter into the pan. After the pancakes have finished cooking, place them on paper towels and blot as much of the oil out of them as you can.

Do not crowd the pan. Fry, turning once, until golden brown on both sides, about 4 minutes on each side. Using a slotted spatula, transfer to paper towels to drain. Keep warm while you cook the remaining pancakes. Serves hot.

Nutritional Analysis

Calories	135.24 Kcal.	Protein	4.03 gm.
Fat	3.42 gm.	Carbohydrate	22.54 gm.
Sodium	318.96 mg.	Cholesterol	26.86 mg.
Saturated Fat	0.58 gm.		

Vegetable Lo Mein

Serves: 6

3 tablespoons soy sauce
2 tablespoons oyster sauce
1 tablespoon Asian sesame oil
1/2 teaspoon sugar
4 quarts water
1/2 pound fresh Chinese wheat noodles
1 tablespoon peanut oil
8 cloves garlic, chopped
1 cup chopped celery
1 can (6 ounces) bamboo shoots, drained
1 cup shredded napa cabbage
1 cup chopped bok choy
1 cup bean sprouts
4 cups loosely packed, coarsely chopped spinach

In a small bowl, combine the soy sauce, oyster sauce, sesame oil, and sugar; stir well. Set aside. In a large saucepan, bring the water to a boil. Add

Lo Mein Noodles

Although you can use the packaged dried lo mein noodles found in most supermarkets, you'll come much closer to creating the lo mein you're familiar with in Chinese restaurants if you purchase the fresh Chinese wheat noodles now available in many supermarkets, usually in the produce section. The noodles, sold in half- or one-pound bags, can be kept in the refrigerator for a week or in the freezer for a month. Whenever I find them, I stock up.

the noodles, boil for 3 minutes, and drain. Rinse under cold water and drain again. Set aside. In a wok or large, deep skillet, heat the peanut oil over high heat. Add the garlic, celery, bamboo shoots, napa cabbage, bok choy, and bean sprouts. Stir-fry for 1 minute. Add the cooked noodles, mix well, and then add the spinach. Stir-fry to mix. Add the sauce and stir and toss to mix well and heat through. Serve immediately.

Nutritional Analysis

Calories	194.75 Kcal.	Protein	8.43 gm.
Fat	5.75 gm.	Carbohydrate	28.99 gm.
Sodium	835.41 mg.	Cholesterol	27.61 mg.
Saturated Fat	0.86 gm.		

Rice with Black Beans and Ginger

Serves: 4

1 tablespoon olive oil
2 cloves garlic, minced
2 tablespoons chopped onion
1 tablespoon peeled and minced fresh ginger
1 cup white rice
2 cups reduced-sodium, fat-free chicken broth
1 cup cooked black beans
salt and pepper to taste

In a skillet, heat the oil over medium heat. Add the garlic, onion, and ginger and cook, stirring, for 1 minute. Add the rice and chicken broth. Lower heat, cover, and cook until the rice is tender and the liquid has been absorbed, about 20 minutes.

Add the black beans and salt and pepper and stir to heat through, then serve.

Nutritional Analysis

Calories	268.09 Kcal.	Protein	8.75 gm.
Fat	3.91 gm.	Carbohydrate	48.31 gm.
Sodium	283.96 mg.	Cholesterol	0.00 mg.
Saturated Fat	0.59 gm.		

John Barleycorn Casserole

Serves: 4

1 tablespoon olive oil
1 onion, chopped
2 cloves garlic, minced
1 cup grated carrots
1 cup pearl barley
3 cups reduced-sodium, fat-free chicken broth
2 cups corn kernels (fresh or canned)
¹/₄ cup chopped fresh parsley
salt and pepper to taste

Preheat oven to 350°F.

In a flameproof baking dish, heat the oil over medium-high heat. Add the onion, garlic, and carrots and sauté until the onion is translucent, 5 to 7 minutes. Add the barley and broth and cover with foil or a lid.

Bake until the barley is tender, about 1 hour. Uncover and add the corn, parsley, salt, and pepper, mixing well. Cover and continue to bake until heated through, about 5 minutes, then serve.

(continued)

Nutritional Analysis

Calories	314.73 Kcal.	Protein	10.61 gm.
Fat	4.97 gm.	Carbohydrate	60.68 gm.
Sodium	449.75 mg.	Cholesterol	0.00 mg.
Saturated Fat	0.71 gm.		

Potato and Garbanzo Stew

Serves: 4

1 tablespoon olive oil
1 onion, chopped
2 cloves garlic, minced
1 teaspoon paprika
3 tomatoes, coarsely chopped
1 teaspoon dried oregano, crumbled
2 large russet potatoes, peeled and diced
1 cup reduced-sodium, fat-free chicken broth
1 can (19 ounces) garbanzo beans, drained
    and rinsed
1/3 cup chopped fresh basil
salt and pepper to taste
1/2 cup chopped fresh parsley

In a large, heavy saucepan, heat the oil over medium heat. Add the onion and sauté until translucent, about 5 minutes. Add the garlic, paprika, 2/3 of the tomatoes, and oregano. Reduce the heat to low and cook, stirring occasionally, for 5 minutes. Add the potatoes and broth, cover, and bring to a boil. Boil for 5 minutes, stirring occasionally. Add the garbanzo beans, reduce the heat to low, and cook until the potatoes are tender, about 5 minutes.

Add the remaining tomato, the basil, salt, and pepper; heat for 3 minutes to heat through. Garnish with the parsley just before serving.

Nutritional Analysis

Calories	252.49 Kcal.	Protein	9.29 gm.
Fat	6.17 gm.	Carbohydrate	41.51 gm.
Sodium	310.11 mg.	Cholesterol	0.00 mg.
Saturated Fat	0.61 gm.		

Stuffed Baked Potatoes
Serves: 4

4 large potatoes
1/2 cup low-fat milk
1 cup part-skim ricotta cheese
3 cloves garlic, chopped
salt and pepper to taste
2 cups chopped cooked broccoli
1/4 cup grated Parmesan cheese

Preheat oven to 400°F. Scrub potatoes, and pierce skins with a fork. Bake 1 hour. Remove from oven and reduce oven temperature to 375°F.

Cut a lengthwise slice off the top of each potato. Scoop out the potato flesh into a bowl, being careful not to tear the skins. Set both aside.

Add the milk to the potato flesh and mash thoroughly with a fork. Add the ricotta cheese, garlic, salt, pepper, broccoli, and Parmesan cheese. Mix well. Spoon the potato mixture into the potato skins and replace the tops. Place the potatoes on a baking sheet.

Bake until heated through, about 30 minutes.

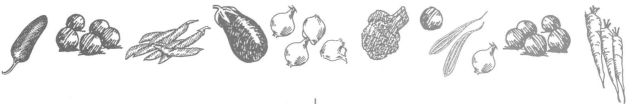

Nutritional Analysis

Calories	311.44 Kcal.	Protein	16.02 gm.
Fat	7.11 gm.	Carbohydrate	47.84 gm.
Sodium	218.04 mg.	Cholesterol	24.23 mg.
Saturated Fat	4.25 gm.		

Cheese-Egg Casserole

Serves: 4

> 5 slices stale French bread
> 2 whole eggs
> 8 egg whites
> 1 cup low-fat milk
> dash of dry mustard
> 1/3 pound sausage meat
> 1 cup shredded low-fat cheddar cheese
> salt and pepper to taste

Arrange the bread slices in a single layer in the bottom of a baking dish. In a bowl, stir together the whole eggs, egg whites, milk, and mustard. Pour over the bread.

In a skillet, cook the sausage, breaking it up, until browned, about 5 minutes. Pour into a sieve to drain well. Sprinkle sausage, cheddar cheese, salt, and pepper on top of the bread. Cover and refrigerate overnight.

The next day, bake in an oven preheated to 350°F until a knife inserted in the center comes out clean, about 30 minutes.

Cut into squares and serve immediately.

Nutritional Analysis

Calories	294.04 Kcal.	Protein	28.45 gm.
Fat	9.72 gm.	Carbohydrate	22.27 gm.
Sodium	806.92 mg.	Cholesterol	126.76 mg.
Saturated Fat	3.33 gm.		

Spicy Chili

Serves: 4

> 1 tablespoon olive oil
> 2 large onions, chopped
> 5 cloves garlic, minced
> 1 green bell pepper, chopped
> 2 jalapeño peppers, seeded and finely chopped
> 1 can (35 ounces) tomatoes in purée, drained and chopped
> 1 teaspoon ground coriander
> pinch of ground cloves
> pinch of ground allspice
> 2 teaspoons dried oregano, crumbled
> 1 tablespoon brown sugar
> 2 tablespoons chili powder
> 2 tablespoons ground cumin
> 2 cups cooked kidney beans
> 2 cups water
> 1 cup white rice

In a large skillet, heat the oil over medium heat. Add the onions, garlic, bell pepper, and jalapeño pepper and sauté until vegetables are tender, about 10 minutes. Add the tomatoes,

(continued)

Combining Proteins for Best Results

Most of us get our protein needs met from eating animal meat that also has lots of saturated fat. But you can get plenty of protein from vegetable sources without saturated fat if you know how to combine foods such as grains, legumes, nuts, and seeds. Combining foods from complementary protein groups provides you with all the protein you need. An example of complementary combinations is rice and kidney beans.

To prepare the kidney beans, soak them overnight in water in the refrigerator. Drain the water and add fresh water to cover. Simmer for about 2¹/₂ hours.

coriander, cloves, allspice, oregano, brown sugar, chili powder, cumin, and beans. Bring to a boil, cover, reduce the heat to low, and cook until the flavors are blended, about 30 minutes.

Meanwhile, in a saucepan, bring the water to a boil. Add the rice, reduce the heat to low, cover, and cook until the rice is tender and the liquid is absorbed, 20 to 30 minutes. To serve, spoon the rice onto individual plates. Serve the chili over the rice.

Nutritional Analysis

Calories	471.99 Kcal.	Protein	16.06 gm.
Fat	5.69 gm.	Carbohydrate	92.63 gm.
Sodium	447.28 mg.	Cholesterol	0.00 mg.
Saturated Fat	0.63 gm.		

THE EVERYTHING LOW-FAT HIGH-FLAVOR COOKBOOK

Desserts

CHAPTER TWELVE

Amount Per Chapter
42 Recipes

	% Daily Value
Easy to Prepare	**100%**
Low Fat / High Flavor	**100%**
Simple to Understand	**100%**

DELICIOUS, EASY, LOW-FAT RECIPES

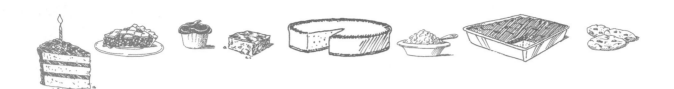

When I was growing up in the 1960s and 1970s, I would regularly have a piece of chocolate cake and a glass of milk for breakfast. Nobody was alarmed, and I made it all the way through to lunch. Perhaps the fact that we have created a systematic categorization of "good" foods and "bad" foods (including dessert) has made us obsess even more about the sweet things we do and don't allow ourselves to eat.

Today, in many circles, dessert gets a bad rap. To true dessert lovers, this is an unfortunate maligning of what often turns out to be the best part of a meal. All too often, we connect being virtuous with eating foods that require too much chewing and that have a taste that makes all that jaw action not worth much. If you forego having dessert too often, the world indeed does seem like a harsher place, no matter what your circumstances are or where you live.

Indeed, dessert is a way you can feel better about your life, as well as being an easy way to make other people happy, too. Have you ever noticed how people brighten whenever someone walks into a room carrying a box tied with bakery string? And how can your best friend stay mad at you after an argument when you knock on her door bearing a freshly baked low-fat lemon meringue pie?

Buttermilk Pops

Yield: 10 pops

*1 can (6 ounces) frozen orange juice
    concentrate, thawed and undiluted*
1 cup nonfat buttermilk
1 cup evaporated skim milk

In a large bowl, combine all the ingredients. Using an electric mixer, beat until blended. Pour into 4-ounce paper cups or popsicle molds and freeze until hardened. If you are using cups, freeze for about 15 minutes until thick and then insert the stick and continue to freeze until solid. Then, when ready to serve, just tear off the paper cup.

Nutritional Analysis

Calories	63.56 Kcal.	Protein	3.23 gm.
Fat	0.30 gm.	Carbohydrate	12.19 gm.
Sodium	55.69 mg.	Cholesterol	2.00 mg.
Saturated Fat	0.16 gm.		

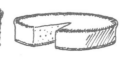

Light Lemon Pudding

Serves: 6

> 1 envelope (1 tablespoon) unflavored gelatin
> ¹/₂ cup plus 1 tablespoon cold water
> 1 cup boiling water
> ¹/₂ cup sugar
> ¹/₄ cup plus ¹/₄ teaspoon lemon juice
> 1 teaspoon grated lemon zest
> ¹/₂ cup regular nonfat dry milk powder
> ¹/₂ cup ice water

In a small bowl, soften the gelatin in the 1 tablespoon of cold water. Add the boiling water to dissolve. Add the sugar, the ¹/₂ cup cold water, the ¹/₄ cup lemon juice, and the lemon zest. Chill until very thick, about 90 minutes.

Chill a deep mixing bowl and beaters. Add the dry milk, ice water, and the ¹/₄ teaspoon lemon juice to the chilled bowl. Beat until fluffy, then cover and chill.

Break up the lemon mixture with a fork. Add to the whipped milk mixture. Using an electric mixer, beat until fluffy but not too soft. Cover and chill until firm before serving, about ¹/₂ hour.

Nutritional Analysis

Calories	91.17 Kcal.	Protein	3.03 gm.
Fat	0.07 gm.	Carbohydrate	20.33 gm.
Sodium	35.81 mg.	Cholesterol	1.02 mg.
Saturated Fat	0.02 gm.		

Strawberry Sorbet

Serves: 8

> 1 pint (2 cups) strawberries, stemmed
> ³/₄ cup orange juice
> ¹/₂ cup 1% milk
> ¹/₄ cup plus 1 tablespoon honey
> 2 egg whites

In a blender, combine the berries, orange juice, milk, and the ¹/₄ cup honey. Blend until smooth, about 1 minute. Pour into a 9-inch square baking pan. Cover and freeze until almost firm, 2 to 3 hours.

In an electric mixer bowl, beat the egg whites at medium speed until soft peaks form. Increase the speed to high and gradually add the 1 tablespoon honey, beating until stiff peaks form.

Beak the frozen mixture into chunks. Transfer the pieces to a chilled large bowl. Beat with an electric mixer until smooth. Fold in the egg whites with a rubber spatula. Return the mixer to the baking pan. Cover tightly and freeze until firm, 6 to 8 hours. To serve, scrape across the surface of the frozen mixture with a spoon, and mound in dessert dishes.

Nutritional Analysis

Calories	73.32 Kcal.	Protein	1.79 gm.
Fat	0.31 gm.	Carbohydrate	17.02 gm.
Sodium	22.46 mg.	Cholesterol	0.61 mg.
Saturated Fat	0.10 gm.		

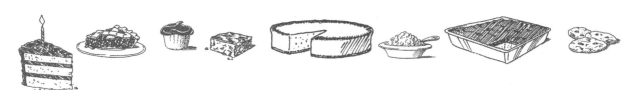

A Low-Fat Crust

The Tangy Lime Pie (page 233) has a crumb crust that is deliberately crumbly. If you prefer a firmer baked crust, bake the unfilled crust at 350°F for 10 to 12 minutes, then let it cool completely before filling it. You can, of course, substitute a regular baked pie crust, but keep in mind that the fat content will be considerably higher.

Applesauce Pound Cake

Yield: 1 loaf cake (serves: 8)

1 cup nonfat milk
1 cup raisins
1 cup applesauce
1/3 cup firmly packed brown sugar
1/4 cup canola oil
1/2 teaspoon ground cinnamon
1/2 teaspoon ground allspice
salt (optional)
1/8 teaspoon ground nutmeg
2 cups cake flour
1 teaspoon baking powder
1 teaspoon baking soda
1 cup chopped peeled apples or pitted dates
1/2 cup chopped walnuts (optional)

Preheat oven to 325°F. Spray a 9-by-4-inch loaf pan with nonstick cooking spray.

In a large bowl, combine the milk, raisins, applesauce, sugar, oil, and spices. Beat until thoroughly mixed. In another bowl, stir together the flour, baking powder, and baking soda. Add the flour mixture to the milk mixture, stirring until just combined. Fold in the apples or dates and the walnuts, if using.

Bake until cake tester comes out clean, about 1 1/4 hours. Cool completely on a rack, then slice and serve.

Nutritional Analysis

Calories	292.22 Kcal.	Protein	3.92 gm.
Fat	7.40 gm.	Carbohydrate	54.64 gm.
Sodium	241.91 mg.	Cholesterol	0.61 mg.
Saturated Fat	0.56 gm.		

Pear Pudding Cake

Serves: 8

3/4 cup whole-wheat pastry flour
3/4 cup all-purpose flour
1 teaspoon baking soda
1 1/2 teaspoons ground ginger
1/4 teaspoon ground cardamom
1/8 teaspoon salt
1/3 cup dried currants or raisins
1/3 cup slivered blanched almonds, toasted
2 cups peeled and diced pears (about 2 large)
2/3 cup pear nectar or other noncitrus fruit juice
1/3 cup pure maple syrup
3 cups boiling water

Spray a 4-cup baking pan or heatproof baking dish with nonstick cooking spray.

In a large bowl, combine the flours, baking soda, ginger, cardamom, salt, currants or raisins, and almonds. Stir in the pears. In a measuring cup, combine the juice and syrup. Stir the juice mixture into the flour mixture just until combined. Pour the batter into the prepared baking pan. Cover tightly with a sheet of aluminum foil large enough to tuck the ends under the bottom of the pan.

Place rack in the bottom of a pressure cooker. Pour in the boiling water. Lower the filled baking pan into the cooker, resting it on the rack. (Be sure there's a 1/2-inch space between the sides of the pressure cooker and the edges of the baking pan.) Secure the lid in place. Bring to high pressure over high heat. Adjust the heat to maintain high pressure and cook for 25 minutes (30 minutes if you're using a baking dish instead of a baking pan.) Allow pressure to come down naturally for 15 minutes. (If after 15 minutes pressure is not released, use a quick-release method. Remove the lid, tilting it away from you to allow any steam to escape.

Lift the baking pan out of the cooker. Remove the foil and set the pan on a rack to cool. Unmold the cake or serve directly from the pan. Serve warm or at room temperature.

Helpful Hint: To lift the baking pan or dish in and out of the cooker, cut a piece of foil 2 feet long by 1 foot wide. Fold it twice lengthwise. Center the pan on the strip, and use the ends of the strip to lower the pan into the cooker. Fold the ends of the foil strip over the top of the pan. Use the ends of the strip to lift the pan out of the cooker.

Nutritional Analysis

Calories	211.10 Kcal.	Protein	4.44 gm.
Fat	4.01 gm.	Carbohydrate	41.80 gm.
Sodium	198.17 mg.	Cholesterol	0.00 mg.
Saturated Fat	0.45 gm.		

Buttermilk Fruit Sherbet

Serves: 4

2 cups frozen unsweetened blueberries
1/2 cup nonfat buttermilk
2 or 3 drops of honey (optional)

In a food processor, combine the frozen berries with 1/4 cup of the buttermilk. Process until the berries are coarsely chopped. Cover and

(continued)

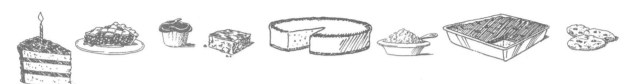

process, adding the remaining ¹/₄ cup buttermilk a little at a time through the cover opening. Uncover and redistribute the berries. Cover and process again until the mixture is smooth and has the texture of frozen custard or soft-serve ice cream. Don't overprocess. If desired, sweeten to taste with a few drops of honey.

Serve immediately.

Nutritional Analysis

Calories	50.78 Kcal.	Protein	1.44 gm.
Fat	0.49 gm.	Carbohydrate	11.05 gm.
Sodium	37.01 mg.	Cholesterol	0.62 mg.
Saturated Fat	0.00 gm.		

Minted Middle Eastern Buttermilk Shake

Serves: 1

a handful of ice cubes
1 cup nonfat buttermilk
pinch of salt
a small handful of fresh mint leaves

Combine all of the ingredients in a blender. Cover and blend until the ice becomes blended. Pour into a tall mug and garnish with more mint leaves.

Nutritional Analysis

Calories	100.51 Kcal.	Protein	8.29 gm.
Fat	2.19 gm.	Carbohydrate	12.20 gm.
Sodium	398.52 mg.	Cholesterol	9.80 mg.
Saturated Fat	1.35 gm.		

Margarita Pie

Serves: 8

1 envelope unflavored gelatin
²/₃ cup sugar
¹/₄ teaspoon salt
¹/₂ cup egg substitute
¹/₂ cup lime juice
1 teaspoon grated lime zest
¹/₄ cup tequila
1¹/₂ cups nonfat whipped topping
9-inch prebaked pie shell
4 lime slices

In a small saucepan, combine the gelatin, sugar, and salt. In a bowl, beat together the egg substitute and lime juice until blended.

Add to the gelatin mixture. Cook over medium heat, stirring, until the gelatin dissolves, 5 to 7 minutes. Remove from the heat.

Stir in the lime zest and tequila. Cover and chill until the mixture thickens to a pudding consistency. Fold the whipped topping into the tequila mixture. Spoon into the pie shell and chill well. Garnish with lime slices just before serving.

Nutritional Analysis

Calories	239.51 Kcal.	Protein	3.74 gm.
Fat	7.81 gm.	Carbohydrate	33.66 gm.
Sodium	230.44 mg.	Cholesterol	0.00 mg.
Saturated Fat	1.93 gm.		

Tangy Lime Pie

Serves: 8

Crust:

15 graham crackers, crushed
2 tablespoons butter, melted

Filling:

1/3 cup frozen apple juice concentrate, thawed
1 envelope unflavored gelatin
1/2 cup sugar
1 tablespoon grated lime zest
1/3 cup lime juice
1 teaspoon pure vanilla extract
1 1/2 cups plain low-fat yogurt

To make the crust, mix together the crumbs and butter in a bowl. Grease a 9-inch pie pan. Transfer the crumb mixture to the prepared pan and pat onto the bottom and sides, forming an even layer. Place in the freezer.

To make the filling, pour the apple juice concentrate into a saucepan, add the gelatin, and let the mixture stand for a few minutes to allow the gelatin to soften. Stir in the sugar and heat the mixture over low heat until the gelatin and sugar dissolve. Pour into a bowl and add 2 teaspoons of the lime zest, the lime juice, and the vanilla. Place the mixture in the refrigerator until partially set (the consistency of unbeaten egg whites), about 30 minutes.

Using a rotary beater, whip the lime mixture until fluffy. Add the yogurt and whip again. Remove the crust from the freezer and pour the lime mixture into it. Sprinkle the remaining 1

(continued)

Quick Fruit Leather

If you're impatient to eat your fruit leather, or want to make this treat in bad weather, you can dry it indoors. Let the prepared fruit sit under a lamp or in the sun for 2 hours, then place the baking sheets in an oven set at 140°F. Leave the door ajar a few inches. The leather will be completely dried in 4 to 5 hours.

teaspoon lime zest over the top. Chill the pie until firm before serving.

Nutritional Analysis

Calories	182.50 Kcal.	Protein	3.99 gm.
Fat	4.90 gm.	Carbohydrate	31.15 gm.
Sodium	144.88 mg.	Cholesterol	10.31 mg.
Saturated Fat	2.53 gm.		

Balancing Your Menu

If you're leafing through this book in order to find the perfect dessert to balance a particular menu, keep in mind that opposites attract. In other words, if your entrée is rich, go for a light fruit-based dessert. Or if you are serving a light salad or sandwiches, choose a calories-be-damned chocolate dessert.

Baked Apple Pancake

Serves: 6

1 tablespoon butter
4 medium apples, peeled, cored, and thinly sliced
3 tablespoons granulated sugar
2 teaspoons pure vanilla extract
1/4 teaspoon ground cinnamon
1 cup all-purpose flour
1 cup 1% milk
2 egg whites
2 whole eggs
3 tablespoons confectioners' sugar

Preheat oven to 425°F.

In an ovenproof skillet, melt the butter over medium heat. Add the apple slices to the skillet, and sprinkle 2 tablespoons of the granulated sugar over them. Cook over medium heat until the apples have softened, about 15 minutes. Sprinkle the apples with the vanilla and cinnamon. Remove from the heat.

In a bowl, stir together the flour, milk, egg whites, whole eggs, and the remaining 1 table-

spoon granulated sugar until blended. Pour the batter over the apples.

Bake the pancake for 20 minutes. Reduce the heat to 350°F, and continue to bake until the top browns, about 15 minutes longer. Remove from the oven, sprinkle with the confectioners' sugar, and cut into wedges. Serve immediately.

Nutritional Analysis

Calories	232.05 Kcal.	Protein	6.87 gm.
Fat	4.47 gm.	Carbohydrate	41.03 gm.
Sodium	79.74 mg.	Cholesterol	77.62 mg.
Saturated Fat	2.03 gm.		

Lemony Cheesecake

Serves: 8

Crust:
12 graham crackers, crushed
2 tablespoons butter, melted

Filling:
2 cups (1 pound) 1% small curd cottage cheese
2 egg whites
2 whole eggs
1/2 cup evaporated skim milk
1/2 cup sugar
1 tablespoon grated lemon zest
1/3 cup lemon juice
1/4 cup all-purpose flour
lemon slices

To make the crust, mix together the crumbs and butter in a bowl. Grease a 9-inch springform pan. Transfer the crumb mixture to the prepared pan and press the mixture onto the bottom. Place in the freezer.

Preheat oven to 300°F.

To make the filling, in a food processor, combine the cottage cheese, egg whites, whole eggs, evaporated milk, sugar, lemon zest, and lemon juice. Process until smooth. Add the flour and process a few seconds longer. Remove the crust from the freezer and pour the cottage cheese mixture into it.

Bake until the filling has set, about 1 hour. Cool on a rack. Release the pan sides and slide onto a serving plate. Decorate with the lemon slices.

Nutritional Analysis

Calories	215.83 Kcal.	Protein	11.86 gm.
Fat	6.36 gm.	Carbohydrate	27.87 gm.
Sodium	373.30 mg.	Cholesterol	63.78 mg.
Saturated Fat	2.92 gm.		

Spicy Cold Pears
Serves: 4

4 pears, peeled, cored, and halved lengthwise
2 cups cranberry juice
2 tablespoons sugar
1/2 teaspoon ground cinnamon
1/2 teaspoon ground cloves
1 teaspoon grated orange zest
1 teaspoon grated lemon zest

In a saucepan, combine all the ingredients. Bring to a boil, cover, reduce the heat to low, and

(continued)

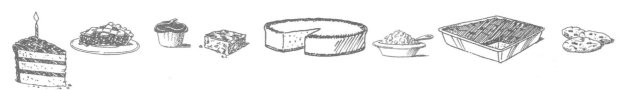

simmer until tender, about 15 minutes. Serve the pears warm or chilled.

Nutritional Analysis

Calories	196.66 Kcal.	Protein	0.66 gm.
Fat	0.83 gm.	Carbohydrate	50.10 gm.
Sodium	3.35 mg.	Cholesterol	0.00 mg.
Saturated Fat	0.04 gm.		

Pineapple Milk Sherbet

Serves: 4

1³/₄ cups milk
¹/₂ cup sugar
1 can (8 ounces) crushed pineapple
2 tablespoons lemon juice
¹/₄ cup orange juice

Combine milk and sugar. Add remaining ingredients and stir until sugar is dissolved. Pour into a loaf pan and freeze. Stir twice during freezing to break up the sugar crystals.

Nutritional Analysis

Calories	204.46 Kcal.	Protein	3.87 gm.
Fat	3.62 gm.	Carbohydrate	41.00 gm.
Sodium	54.85 mg.	Cholesterol	14.94 mg.
Saturated Fat	2.22 gm.		

Cranberry Sherbet

Serves: 4

1¹/₂ teaspoons unflavored gelatin
2 cups cranberry juice
¹/₂ cup sugar
pinch of salt
2 tablespoons regular nonfat dry milk powder
¹/₂ cup corn syrup
3 tablespoons lemon juice

In a small saucepan, sprinkle the gelatin over ¹/₂ cup of the juice. Let stand for a few minutes to allow the gelatin to soften. Place over low heat and heat, stirring, until dissolved. Stir in the sugar and salt until dissolved. Pour the remaining 1¹/₂ cups juice in a bowl. Sprinkle the milk powder over the top and beat with a fork to dissolve. Add the gelatin mixture to the milk-juice mixture, then mix with all the remaining ingredients. Stir until well mixed. Pour into a metal ice cube tray (if you have one—I found one at a garage sale, the old-fashioned kind where you remove the insert that divides the tray into cubes) or load pan and freeze until almost firm. Beat until fluffy. Refreeze until firm, then serve.

Nutritional Analysis

Calories	297.33 Kcal.	Protein	1.52 gm.
Fat	0.16 gm.	Carbohydrate	76.40 gm.
Sodium	103.02 mg.	Cholesterol	0.38 mg.
Saturated Fat	0.00 gm.		

Lo-Cal Orange Sherbet

Serves: 2

*1 cup regular nonfat dry milk powder not
   diluted*
1/2 cup water
3 tablespoons frozen orange juice concentrate

In a blender, combine all the ingredients.
Process until blended. Pour into an ice cube tray.
Freeze. When almost solid, turn out of the tray
into a bowl and beat with a fork. Return to the
tray. Refreeze until firm, then serve.

Nutritional Analysis

Calories	164.05 Kcal.	Protein	12.56 gm.
Fat	0.29 gm.	Carbohydrate	27.90 gm.
Sodium	187.45 mg.	Cholesterol	6.12 mg.
Saturated Fat	0.15 gm.		

Peach or Apricot Leather

Serves: 6

10 peaches or apricots, 2 1/2 to 3 pounds
1 cup sugar

Bring a saucepan of water to a boil. Slip the
peaches or apricots into the water for 30 seconds.
Using a slotted spoon, transfer to cold water and
slip off the skins. Slice the fruit, discarding the
pits. You should have 10 cups. Transfer to a large
saucepan. Add the sugar and bring to a boil, stirring until the sugar is dissolved. Boil for 3
minutes. Pour into a blender and process until
smooth. Cool to lukewarm.

Egg Whites and Yolks

Frequently, a recipe will call for a number of egg whites—or yolks—and you are left with the unused other halves. If you're stuck with extra egg whites, they can be whipped up with a bit of sugar for some meringue cookies, or, used unwhipped for a great face mask. With extra yolks, stir them lightly and then freeze in ice cube trays to be defrosted later to brush on bread as a glaze for baking. Or you can always mix them into the dog's food for a shiny coat.

(continued)

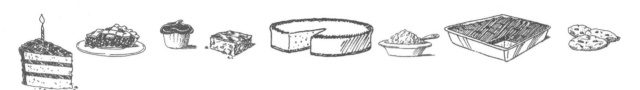

Meanwhile, prepare a smooth, level drying surface in full sunlight. Cover baking sheets or baking pans with plastic wrap. Spread the purée 1/4-inch thick on the prepared surfaces. You can make 4 sheets (12 by 15 inches each). Let dry outdoors in the sunlight. (Drying may take up to 3 days, depending on temperature and humidity.) Bring the pans inside at the end of the day, and then return them to the outdoors the next day. The fruit is fully dried when the purée can easily be peeled off the plastic wrap.

To store, roll up the "leather" in plastic wrap. Wrap in more plastic wrap and seal tightly. The leather will keep at room temperature for 1 month, in the refrigerator for 4 months, or in the freezer for 1 month.

Nutritional Analysis

Calories	197.00 Kcal.	Protein	1.10 gm.
Fat	0.14 gm.	Carbohydrate	50.85 gm.
Sodium	0.33 mg.	Cholesterol	0.00 mg.
Saturated Fat	0.01 gm.		

Spice Cake

Serves: 6

1 tablespoon butter
1 cup sugar
2 eggs, well beaten
1 teaspoon baking soda
1 cup nonfat buttermilk
2 cups all-purpose flour
pinch of salt

1 teaspoon ground nutmeg
1 teaspoon ground cinnamon
1 teaspoon ground allspice
1 teaspoon ground cloves
1 cup raisins

Preheat oven to 350°F.

In a bowl, cream together the butter and sugar. Add the eggs and mix thoroughly. Dissolve the baking soda in the buttermilk, and stir into the sugar-egg mixture. In a bowl, sift together the flour, salt, and spices. Beat the flour mixture into the sugar mixture. Fold in the raisins. Pour the batter into an 8-inch square or round pan. Bake until a knife comes out clean, about 1 hour. Cool on rack.

Nutritional Analysis

Calories	415.06 Kcal.	Protein	8.74 gm.
Fat	4.33 gm.	Carbohydrate	87.53 gm.
Sodium	327.61 mg.	Cholesterol	76.83 mg.
Saturated Fat	1.90 gm.		

Angel Food Cake

Serves: 8

12 egg whites
1/2 teaspoon cream of tartar
3/4 cup granulated sugar
1 1/2 teaspoons pure vanilla extract
1/2 teaspoon pure almond extract
1 cup sifted cake flour
1 1/4 cups confectioners' sugar
1/4 teaspoon salt

Preheat oven to 350°F.

In a large bowl, using an electric mixer set on high speed, beat the egg whites and cream of tartar until foamy. Add the granulated sugar, 1 tablespoon at a time, beating constantly until the sugar is dissolved and whites are glossy and stand in soft peaks. Beat in the vanilla and almond extracts.

In a bowl, sift together the flour, confectioners' sugar, and salt. Sift again. Sift about 1/2 cup of the flour mixture over the egg whites and, using a rubber spatula, fold in gently just until the flour disappears. Repeat, folding in the remaining flour mixture 1/2 cup at a time. Turn into an ungreased 10-inch tube pan.

Bake until the top springs back when touched lightly with a finger, 30 to 40 minutes. Invert the cake in the pan onto a funnel or bottle neck to cool, then remove from the pan.

Nutritional Analysis

Calories	217.64 Kcal.	Protein	6.25 gm.
Fat	0.11 gm.	Carbohydrate	47.46 gm.
Sodium	154.42 mg.	Cholesterol	0.00 mg.
Saturated Fat	0.01 gm.		

Angel Food Cake Secrets

Angel food cakes are leavened with just air: no baking soda and no baking powder in sight. Whether or not you get a light, tender cake will depend on how much you beat the egg whites, the lightness with which you fold in the sugar-and-flour mixture, and the temperature at which you bake the cake. You should beat the egg whites until they are stiff enough to hold up in soft peaks but remain moist and glossy.

Orange-Peach Angel Cake

Serves: 8

1 angel food cake—use recipe on page 239
1 can (8 ounces) sliced peaches
1 package (4 ounces) orange-flavored Jell-O
1/3 cup ice water

(continued)

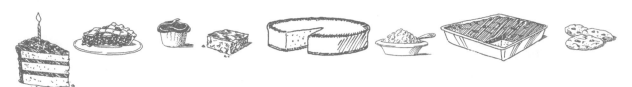

½ cup regular dry nonfat milk powder
2 tablespoons lemon juice
1 can (8 ounces) mandarin oranges, drained

Cut a ½-inch-thick slice off the top of the cake and set aside. With the point of the knife, cut a ring ½ inch in from the edge of the base and ½ inch in from the center hole. Pull out soft cake to form a trough 1½ inches deep.

Drain the peaches, capturing the juice in a measuring cup. Add water to measure ½ cup. Pour into a saucepan and heat to boiling. Place the Jell-O in a bowl and pour in the boiling liquid, stirring to dissolve the Jell-O. Chill until slightly thickened. Mix the ice water and milk powder in a small mixing bowl and beat until thick. Add the lemon juice. Beat until stiff.

Beat the thickened Jell-O until smooth and fold in the whipped milk. Divide the mixture in half. Add the peaches to one-half of the mixture and transfer to the cake shell, spreading evenly. Replace the top of the cake. Chill the remaining Jell-O mixture until it is of a spreading consistency, about 1 hour. Frost the top and sides of the cake. Decorate with the mandarin orange sections.

Nutritional Analysis

Calories	320.23 Kcal.	Protein	9.09 gm.
Fat	0.17 gm.	Carbohydrate	71.43 gm.
Sodium	217.65 mg.	Cholesterol	0.76 mg.
Saturated Fat	0.02 gm.		

Rhubarb Muffins

Yield: 12 muffins

2 cups finely chopped rhubarb
¾ cup sugar
1 teaspoon grated orange zest
2½ cups all-purpose flour
½ teaspoon baking powder
1 teaspoon baking soda
1 teaspoon salt
2 eggs, beaten
¾ cup nonfat buttermilk
3 tablespoons butter or buttery light, reduced-fat margarine, melted

Preheat oven to 375°F. Grease a 12-cup muffin tin.

In a bowl, combine the rhubarb, ¼ cup of the sugar, and the orange zest. Stir well and let stand for 5 minutes.

Meanwhile, in another bowl, stir together the flour, the remaining ½ cup sugar, the baking powder, baking soda, and salt. Make a well in the center. In yet another bowl, stir together the eggs, buttermilk, and butter or margarine. Add all at once to the flour mixture, stirring just until moistened. The batter should be lumpy. Gently fold in the rhubarb mixture. Spoon into the prepared muffin tin, filling each cup two-thirds full.

Bake until a knife comes out clean, 20 to 25 minutes. Remove from the oven and cool on a rack for 15 minutes before serving.

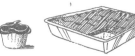

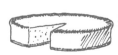

Nutritional Analysis

Calories	197.47 Kcal.	Protein	4.50 gm.
Fat	4.70 gm.	Carbohydrate	34.27 gm.
Sodium	378.81 mg.	Cholesterol	43.48 mg.
Saturated Fat	2.24 gm.		

Apple Date Bread

Serves: 8

Topping:

3/4 cup firmly packed light brown sugar
3/4 cup nuts, chopped
2 tablespoons butter, softened
1/4 cup all-purpose flour
1/4 teaspoon ground cinnamon
1/4 teaspoon salt

1 1/2 cups all-purpose flour
1 1/2 cups whole-wheat flour
1 cup sugar
1 tablespoon baking powder
1 1/2 teaspoons salt
1 cup flaked dried coconut
1 1/2 cups 1% milk
1 egg, lightly beaten
1 cup dates, pitted and diced
*1 cup apples, peeled, cored, and finely
   chopped*

Preheat oven to 350°F. Spray a 9 x 3-inch loaf pan with nonstick cooking spray.

To make the topping, combine all the ingredients in a bowl, mixing well. Set aside.

In a bowl, stir together the flours, sugar, baking powder, and salt. Stir in the coconut. In another bowl, stir together the milk and egg. Add the milk mixture to the flour mixture, blending well. Stir in the apples and dates, mixing well. Turn into the prepared loaf pan. Sprinkle with the topping. Bake until a knife comes out clean, about 1 1/4 hours. Cool on a rack, then turn out of the pan and slice to serve.

Nutritional Analysis

Calories	598.47 Kcal.	Protein	10.66 gm.
Fat	15.24 gm.	Carbohydrate	110.58 gm.
Sodium	785.80 mg.	Cholesterol	36.15 mg.
Saturated Fat	5.75 gm.		

Pear Tea Bread with Lemon Glaze

Serves: 8

1 can (16 ounces) pear halves
2 1/2 cups all-purpose flour
1/2 cup granulated sugar
1 tablespoon baking powder
1 teaspoon salt
1/8 teaspoon ground cardamom
1/4 cup corn oil
1 egg, lightly beaten
2 teaspoons grated lemon zest

Lemon Glaze:
1 tablespoon lemon juice
1/2 cup confectioners' sugar

(continued)

Reducing Fat in Cakes

Fruit purées, such as pear or applesauce, add sweetness and moistness to baked goods without adding fat. For a tasty, moist cake, use only one-fourth of the oil called for in a recipe, and substitute a fruit purée for the rest.

Preheat oven to 350ºF. Spray a 9 x 4-inch loaf pan with nonstick cooking spray.

Drain the pears, reserving the syrup. Set aside 1 pear half for garnish.

In a blender or food processor, purée remaining pear halves. Add enough of the reserved pear syrup to the puréed pears to measure 1 cup.

In a bowl, stir together the flour, granulated sugar, baking powder, salt, and cardamom. In another bowl, combine the puréed pear mixture with the oil, egg, and lemon zest. Stir the pear mixture into the flour mixture just until combined. Pour into the prepared loaf pan. Slice the reserved pear half into sixths. Arrange the slices on top of the batter. Bake until the bread tests done, when a knife inserted comes out clean, 50 to 55 minutes.

While the bread is baking, make the glaze: In a bowl, stir together the lemon juice and confectioners' sugar to form a thin glaze.

When the bread is done, remove from the oven and let cool in the pan for 5 minutes. Turn onto a rack and spoon the lemon glaze over the top. Let cool completely. Wrap in foil and let stand overnight at room temperature before serving.

Nutritional Analysis

Calories	427.02 Kcal.	Protein	6.69 gm.
Fat	10.64 gm.	Carbohydrate	77.14 gm.
Sodium	647.54 mg.	Cholesterol	35.41 mg.
Saturated Fat	1.48 gm.		

Sherried Egg-White Custard with Spiced Cherry Sauce

Serves: 4

2 tablespoons sugar
1/8 teaspoon salt
1 1/3 cups milk
1/4 teaspoon pure vanilla extract
2 to 3 teaspoons sherry or rum flavoring
3 egg whites, lightly beaten

Spiced Cherry Sauce:

1 can (8 ounces) cherries, unsweetened
3 drops of red food coloring
1 teaspoon cornstarch
2 teaspoons water or lemon juice
pinch of ground cloves
pinch of ground cinnamon
pinch of ground ginger

Preheat oven to 325°F.

In a saucepan, combine the sugar, salt, and milk. Place over medium heat and stir until the sugar dissolves. Cool. Add the vanilla, flavoring, and egg whites. Stir well and pour through a sieve into a 2-cup baking dish. Place in a baking pan, and pour hot water into the pan to reach halfway up the sides of the dish.

Bake until a knife comes out clean, about 1 hour.

Meanwhile, make the sauce: In a saucepan, combine the cherries and food coloring. Place over medium heat and bring to a simmer. In a small bowl, stir together the cornstarch and water or lemon juice. Add to the pan and cook, stirring, until the sauce is clear, about 5 minutes. Stir in the spices.

Remove the custard from the oven. Serve warm with the warm cherry sauce drizzled over the top.

Nutritional Analysis

Calories	121.10 Kcal.	Protein	5.72 gm.
Fat	2.75 gm.	Carbohydrate	16.01 gm.
Sodium	158.26 mg.	Cholesterol	11.35 mg.
Saturated Fat	1.69 gm.		

Sweet Potato Pudding

Serves: 8

1 2/3 cups all-purpose flour
1 1/3 cups sugar
1 teaspoon baking soda
1/4 teaspoon baking powder
1/2 teaspoon salt
1/2 teaspoon ground cinnamon
1/2 teaspoon ground allspice
1/4 teaspoon ground cloves
1 cup mashed cooked sweet potato
1/4 cup butter, at room temperature
1/3 cup water
1 egg

Preheat oven to 350°F. Grease an 8-inch square cake pan.

In a bowl, sift together the flour, sugar, baking soda, baking powder, salt, cinnamon, allspice, and cloves. Add the sweet potato, butter, and water to the flour mixture. Using an electric mixer, beat the

(continued)

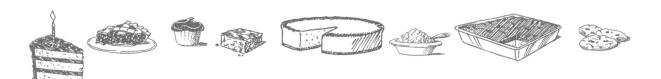

mixture for 2 minutes. Add the egg and beat for another 2 minutes. Pour the batter into the prepared cake pan.

Bake about 40 minutes. Serve warm.

Nutritional Analysis

Calories	332.53 Kcal.	Protein	4.20 gm.
Fat	7.28 gm.	Carbohydrate	63.40 gm.
Sodium	390.23 mg.	Cholesterol	42.08 mg.
Saturated Fat	3.95 gm.		

Fresh Peach Pie

Serves: 8

pastry dough for double-crust 9-inch pie
2/3 cup firmly packed light brown sugar
1 3/4 cups all-purpose flour
1/2 teaspoon ground cinnamon
1/4 teaspoon ground ginger
1/2 teaspoon ground nutmeg
8 peaches, peeled, pitted, and quartered

Preheat oven to 400°F.

Roll out half of the pastry dough on a floured work surface into a 10-inch round. Transfer the round to a 9-inch pie plate.

In a medium bowl, combine the brown sugar, flour, and spices, mixing well. Add the peaches to the sugar-flour mixture, tossing gently. Pour the peach mixture into the pie shell. Roll out the remaining dough into a 10-inch round and drape over the peach filling. Trim and flute the edges of the pastry. Prick the top crust with a fork.

Bake for 10 minutes, reduce the heat to 375°F and continue to bake until the crust is golden brown, 50 to 55 minutes. Cool on a rack. Serve warm or at room temperature.

Nutritional Analysis

Calories	461.04 Kcal.	Protein	6.69 gm.
Fat	15.36 gm.	Carbohydrate	75.54 gm.
Sodium	241.58 mg.	Cholesterol	0.00 mg.
Saturated Fat	3.79 gm.		

Lemon Meringue Pie

Serves: 6

1 1/2 cups plus 6 tablespoons sugar
3 tablespoons cornstarch
3 tablespoons all-purpose flour
pinch of salt
1/2 cup hot water
3 eggs, separated
1/2 teaspoon grated lemon zest
2 tablespoons butter or buttery light, reduced-fat margarine
1/3 cup plus 1 teaspoon lemon juice
9-inch prebaked pie shell

In a saucepan, combine the 1 1/2 cups sugar, cornstarch, flour, and salt. Stir in hot water until smooth. Bring to a boil over high heat, stirring constantly. Reduce the heat to medium. Cook, stirring, until slightly thickened, about 8 minutes. Remove from the heat. In a bowl, lightly beat the egg yolks. Stir a small amount of the hot mixture into the egg yolks and return to the hot mixture.

Bring to a boil over high heat, stirring constantly. Reduce the heat to low and cook, stirring, 4 minutes longer. Remove from the heat. Add the lemon zest and butter or margarine. Stir in the ⅓ cup lemon juice. Cover with plastic wrap, pressing it directly onto the surface, and cool for 10 minutes. Pour into prebaked pie shell. Cool completely.

Preheat oven to 350°F.

In a bowl, using an electric mixer set on high speed, beat the egg whites with the 1 teaspoon lemon juice until soft peaks form. Gradually add the 6 tablespoons sugar, beating until stiff peaks form and the sugar is dissolved. Spread over the cooled filling, sealing to the edges of the pastry.

Bake until egg whites brown, about 12 to 15 minutes. Cool completely on a rack before serving.

Nutritional Analysis

Calories	3027.04 Kcal.	Protein	33.47 gm.
Fat	101.11 gm.	Carbohydrate	507.56 gm.
Sodium	1559.53 mg.	Cholesterol	700.01 mg.
Saturated Fat	34.63 gm.		

Strawberry Whip

Serves: 2

> *1 egg white*
> *1¼ cups strawberries, sliced*
> *¼ cup sugar*
> *a few drops of lemon juice*

In a bowl, using an electric mixer, whip together the egg white and strawberries. When the mixture begins to thicken, gradually add the

Happy Meringue

When I was growing up and watched my mother make lemon meringue pie, I always thought that the meringue part of the process—beating the egg whites and then spooning it onto the lemon part—was fascinating. I was especially intrigued when the peaks of meringue began to lean gently to one side, under their own weight. After the pie was baked and cooled, I always ate the meringue but not the lemon custard, which was never sweet enough for me.

For your own happy meringue, use a copper bowl if you have one to beat the whites, and don't even bother when the humidity is above 80 percent.

(continued)

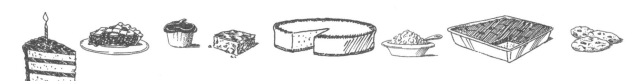

sugar. Continue to beat until the mixture holds soft peaks. Stir in a few drops of lemon juice. Chill before serving.

Nutritional Analysis

Calories	133.66 Kcal.	Protein	2.32 gm.
Fat	0.35 gm.	Carbohydrate	31.82 gm.
Sodium	28.64 mg.	Cholesterol	0.00 mg.
Saturated Fat	0.01 gm.		

Baked Pears

Serves: 6

2 tablespoons lemon juice
6 pears, peeled and cored
2 to 4 tablespoons sugar
1/2 cup low-fat whipped topping

Preheat oven to 375°F.

Put the lemon juice in a 2-quart baking dish and add just enough water to cover the bottom. Add the pears, cover, and bake until tender when pierced with a knife, 20 to 25 minutes.

Remove from the oven. Sprinkle each pear with 1 to 2 teaspoons sugar. Bake, uncovered, for 10 minutes longer to glaze. Serve warm or chilled. Top with whipped cream, if desired.

Nutritional Analysis

Calories	136.51 Kcal.	Protein	0.66 gm.
Fat	1.33 gm.	Carbohydrate	32.97 gm.
Sodium	1.12 mg.	Cholesterol	0.00 mg.
Saturated Fat	0.69 gm.		

Low-Fat Pumpkin Pie

Serves: 8

2/3 cup sugar
1/8 teaspoon salt
1/2 teaspoon ground cinnamon
1/2 teaspoon ground ginger
1/2 teaspoon ground nutmeg
pinch of ground cloves
1 1/2 cups unsweetened canned pumpkin
1 teaspoon pure vanilla extract
1 1/2 cups evaporated skim milk
1/2 teaspoon grated orange zest
3 egg whites, lightly beaten
9-inch unbaked pie shell

Preheat oven to 450°F.

In a bowl, stir together the sugar, salt, cinnamon, ginger, nutmeg, and cloves. Stir in the pumpkin. Add the vanilla, evaporated milk, orange zest, and egg whites. Beat with an electric mixer until smooth. Pour into the unbaked pie shell. Bake for 10 minutes. Reduce the heat to 325°F and continue to bake until a knife inserted in the filling comes out clean, about 45 minutes. Cool on a rack.

Nutritional Analysis

Calories	240.92 Kcal.	Protein	6.81 gm.
Fat	7.72 gm.	Carbohydrate	36.57 gm.
Sodium	231.66 mg.	Cholesterol	1.91 mg.
Saturated Fat	1.99 gm.		

Couscous with Yogurt and Fruit

Serves: 4

1 cup milk
1 tablespoon butter
¹/₄ teaspoon salt
²/₃ cup instant couscous
¹/₂ cup low-fat vanilla yogurt
2 tablespoons sugar
¹/₂ cup berries or diced fresh fruit in season

In a medium saucepan, combine the milk, butter, and salt and bring to a boil. Stir in the couscous, cover, remove from the heat, and let stand for 5 minutes.

Fluff the couscous with a fork to separate the grains. Stir in the yogurt and sugar and fold in the fruit.

Nutritional Analysis

Calories	232.49 Kcal.	Protein	7.46 gm.
Fat	5.51 gm.	Carbohydrate	38.18 gm.
Sodium	224.23 mg.	Cholesterol	17.71 mg.
Saturated Fat	3.29 gm.		

Coffee Almond Float

Serves: 1

1 teaspoon brown sugar
¹/₄ cup brewed cold coffee
splash of orgeat (almond) syrup
ice cubes
¹/₂ cup 1% milk
¹/₂ cup coffee or chocolate low-fat, frozen yogurt

In a parfait glass, dissolve the sugar in the coffee. Add the syrup, stirring to mix well. Add the ice and milk and stir well. Top with the ice cream.

Nutritional Analysis

Calories	171.34 Kcal.	Protein	7.05 gm.
Fat	2.79 gm.	Carbohydrate	30.52 gm.
Sodium	123.97 mg.	Cholesterol	9.87 mg.
Saturated Fat	1.79 gm.		

Pears in Orange Sauce

Serves: 4

1 cup water
2 Bartlett pears, halved lengthwise and cored
²/₃ cup orange juice
2 tablespoons lemon juice
1 tablespoon cornstarch
3 tablespoons honey
¹/₄ teaspoon finely shredded orange zest
¹/₄ teaspoon salt
fresh mint leaves

In a 10-inch skillet, bring the water to a boil. Add the pear halves, cover, and simmer gently over low heat until tender when pierced with a knife, about 10 minutes. Set aside.

In a small saucepan, mix together the orange juice, lemon juice, and cornstarch. Stir until the cornstarch is dissolved. Add the honey, orange zest, and salt and mix well. Place over medium heat and cook until thickened and bubbly, about 10 minutes. To serve, spoon the sauce over the pears and garnish with mint leaves.

(continued)

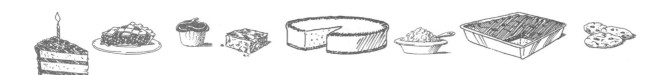

Calories	125.59 Kcal.	Protein	0.68 gm.
Fat	0.37 gm.	Carbohydrate	32.50 gm.
Sodium	145.97 mg.	Cholesterol	0.00 mg.
Saturated Fat	0.01 gm.		

Canned vs. Fresh Fruit

A dessert that combines fruit and cake is one of the few sweets for which canned fruits can be easily substituted for fresh fruits. Such desserts are particularly welcome during the cold weather months. Just be sure to drain the fruit thoroughly—if specified—before using it in the recipe. Otherwise you could end up with a mushy mess. You can even mix two different types of fruit in the same recipe with ease.

Bread Pudding

Serves: 8

4 cups coarsely crumbled stale bread
3 to 4 apples, peeled and grated
1/2 cup raisins
1/2 cup chopped nuts
3 cups 1% milk
3 eggs
2 teaspoons pure vanilla extract
6 tablespoons honey
1 teaspoon ground cinnamon
1/2 teaspoon ground nutmeg
juice of 1/2 lemon

Preheat oven to 350°F.

In an 8-inch square baking pan, stir together the bread crumbs, grated apple, raisins, and nuts. In a blender or food processor, combine all the remaining ingredients. Process until blended. Pour over the bread crumb mixture. Make sure the bread is saturated.

Bake until the bread on top starts to turn slightly brown, about 35 minutes. Serve hot.

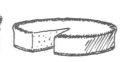

Nutritional Analysis

Calories	273.74 Kcal.	Protein	8.27 gm.
Fat	8.36 gm.	Carbohydrate	43.77 gm.
Sodium	166.17 mg.	Cholesterol	83.51 mg.
Saturated Fat	1.79 gm.		

Pumpkin Pudding

Serves: 4

2 cups 1% low-fat cottage cheese
1/4 teaspoon salt
2 cups unsweetened canned pumpkin
4 eggs
1/4 cup honey
ground nutmeg

Preheat oven to 350°F.

In a blender or food processor, combine all the ingredients. Process until smooth. Pour into individual custard cups. Place the cups in a baking pan. Pour hot water into the pan to reach halfway up the sides of the custard cups. Bake until a knife inserted into the center comes out clean, about 40 minutes. Cool before serving.

Nutritional Analysis

Calories	262.29 Kcal.	Protein	21.70 gm.
Fat	6.51 gm.	Carbohydrate	31.01 gm.
Sodium	673.76 mg.	Cholesterol	217.04 mg.
Saturated Fat	2.45 gm.		

Peach Sorbet

Serves: 4

1 can (16 ounces) sliced peaches in water,
    drained and liquid reserved
1 teaspoon lemon juice
2 tablespoons honey
1 envelope unflavored gelatin
1 teaspoon pure almond extract

Pour the liquid from the peaches into a measuring pitcher. Add water to measure 1 1/2 cups. Pour into a small saucepan. Add the lemon juice, honey, and gelatin. Let stand for about 5 minutes to allow the gelatin to soften. Place the pan over medium heat and heat, stirring constantly, until the gelatin dissolves, just a few minutes. Remove from the heat and add the almond extract. Set aside for 30 minutes.

In a food processor, purée the peaches until smooth. Add the gelatin mixture and process until thoroughly combined. Pour into a 9 x 13-inch metal pan, and place in the freezer for 2 hours.

Transfer to a chilled bowl, and beat with a rotary beater or an electric mixer until the mixture is fluffy. Return to the metal pan, and then return the pan to the freezer for 2 hours. Scoop into individual dishes to serve.

Nutritional Analysis

Calories	69.00 Kcal.	Protein	2.03 gm.
Fat	0.06 gm.	Carbohydrate	15.73 gm.
Sodium	7.55 mg.	Cholesterol	0.00 mg.
Saturated Fat	0.01 gm.		

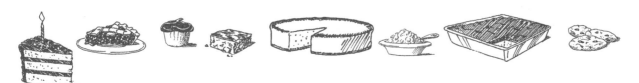

Lemony Blueberry Ice "Cream"

Serves: 4

1 pint (2 cups) blueberries
¹⁄₂ cup sugar
1 tablespoon cornstarch
1 can (12 ounces) evaporated skim milk
2 egg whites
1 teaspoon grated lemon zest
2 tablespoons lemon juice
1 teaspoon pure vanilla extract

In a saucepan, combine the blueberries with ¹⁄₄ cup of the sugar. Place over medium heat and heat, stirring constantly, until the sugar dissolves, about 5 minutes. Remove from the heat. Place a colander over a bowl and pour the blueberry mixture into the colander. Press the berries through the colander with the back of a spoon. Scrape the mashed berries from the outside of the colander into the bowl with the blueberry juice. Place the bowl in the refrigerator.

Add the remaining ¹⁄₄ cup sugar and the cornstarch to the saucepan. Stir in about two-thirds of the evaporated milk. Place over medium heat and bring to a boil, stirring constantly. Cook the mixture until it is as thick as pudding.

Remove from the heat and add the egg whites and the remaining evaporated milk, mixing well. Stir the milk mixture into the blueberry purée. Add the lemon zest, lemon juice, and vanilla. Stir until blended. Chill for 20 minutes.

Pour into an ice cream maker and freeze according to the manufacturer's instructions.

Nutritional Analysis

Calories	233.03 Kcal.	Protein	9.48 gm.
Fat	0.48 gm.	Carbohydrate	48.76 gm.
Sodium	143.92 mg.	Cholesterol	3.82 mg.
Saturated Fat	0.11 gm.		

Chocolaty Ice "Cream"

Serves: 4

1 package (4 ounces) instant chocolate
*   pudding*
¹⁄₄ cup sugar
1 can (12 ounces) evaporated skim milk
1 cup low-fat milk

In a medium bowl, stir together the instant pudding and sugar. Add the evaporated milk and low-fat milk and stir until blended. Pour into an ice cream maker and freeze according to the manufacturer's instructions.

Nutritional Analysis

Calories	180.09 Kcal.	Protein	10.09 gm.
Fat	1.70 gm.	Carbohydrate	31.57 gm.
Sodium	221.18 mg.	Cholesterol	9.37 mg.
Saturated Fat	1.02 gm.		

Frozen Yogurt with Berry Sauce

Serves: 4

1 package (10 ounces) frozen strawberries,
   thawed
1/2 teaspoon pure vanilla extract
1 pint low-fat vanilla frozen yogurt

Place the strawberries and vanilla extract in a food processor. Purée until smooth. Spoon the yogurt into individual dishes and drizzle the strawberry sauce over the top. Serve immediately.

Nutritional Analysis

Calories	159.58 Kcal.	Protein	3.36 gm.
Fat	1.59 gm.	Carbohydrate	35.43 gm.
Sodium	62.16 mg.	Cholesterol	4.99 mg.
Saturated Fat	0.99 gm.		

Sweet Cocoa Sauce

Yield: 1 cup

1/2 cup cocoa powder
1/2 cup sugar
1/4 cup water
1 teaspoon pure vanilla extract

In a saucepan, stir together the cocoa powder and sugar. Stir in the water and place over high heat. Bring to a boil, stirring constantly. Remove from the heat and stir in the vanilla. Refrigerate.

(continued)

The Still-Freeze Method

If you don't have an ice cream maker, you can still make delicious, creamy ice cream in your freezer using the still-freeze method. Follow these steps:

1. Pour the ice cream mixture into a metal loaf pan or an 8-inch square baking pan.
2. Cover with plastic wrap and place in the freezer.
3. Freeze for at least 1 hour until solid.
4. Break up the frozen mixture with a fork and place in a food processor.
5. Process until soft but not melted.
6. Serve.

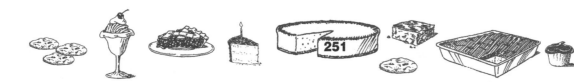

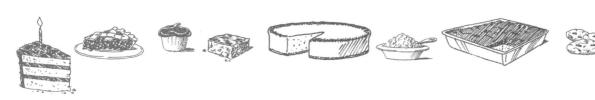

Calories	31.11 Kcal.	Protein	0.52 gm.
Fat	0.36 gm.	Carbohydrate	7.72 gm.
Sodium	0.64 mg.	Cholesterol	0.00 mg.
Saturated Fat	0.21 gm.		

Sweet Vanilla Sauce

Yield: 1¼ cups

¼ cup nonfat buttermilk
2 teaspoons sugar
1 cup vanilla low-fat yogurt

In a small bowl, mix together buttermilk and sugar. Add the yogurt and mix well. Serve over fruit.

Nutritional Analysis

Calories	12.37 Kcal.	Protein	0.66 gm.
Fat	0.14 gm.	Carbohydrate	2.13 gm.
Sodium	11.11 mg.	Cholesterol	0.62 mg.
Saturated Fat	0.09 gm.		

Angelic Strawberry Cake

Serves: 8

1 angel food cake—use recipe on page 239
*2 cups strawberry low-fat frozen yogurt,
    thawed slightly*
1 pint strawberries, stemmed and sliced

Cut the cake in half horizontally. Spread the strawberry yogurt on the bottom half of the cake.

Place half of the strawberry slices on top of the yogurt. Replace the top half of the cake. Place more strawberry slices on top of the cake. Freeze for 15 minutes before serving.

Nutritional Analysis

Calories	274.63 Kcal.	Protein	7.98 gm.
Fat	1.00 gm.	Carbohydrate	58.76 gm.
Sodium	184.82 mg.	Cholesterol	2.49 mg.
Saturated Fat	0.50 gm.		

Salsa Fruit Salad

Serves: 8

2 cups chopped watermelon
1 orange, peeled and diced
*1 pint (2 cups) strawberries, stemmed and
    sliced*
2 tablespoons lemon juice
1 tablespoon honey

In a medium bowl, combine the watermelon, orange, and strawberries. Drizzle with the lemon juice and honey and toss well. Cover and chill for at least 1 hour before serving.

Nutritional Analysis

Calories	42.32 Kcal.	Protein	0.62 gm.
Fat	0.35 gm.	Carbohydrate	10.26 gm.
Sodium	2.09 mg.	Cholesterol	0.00 mg.
Saturated Fat	0.00 gm.		

INDEX